A Rhetoric of the Scene

For my parents

JOAQUÍN MARTÍNEZ PIZARRO

A Rhetoric of the Scene

Dramatic Narrative in the Early Middle Ages

UNIVERSITY OF TORONTO PRESS

Toronto Buffalo London

© University of Toronto Press 1989
Toronto Buffalo London
Printed in Canada

ISBN 0-8020-5754-3

∞

Printed on acid-free paper

Canadian Cataloguing in Publication Data

Pizarro, Joaquín Martínez, 1946–
A rhetoric of the scene : dramatic narrative
in the early Middle Ages

Bibliography: p.
Includes index.
ISBN 0-8020-5754-3

1. Latin prose literature, Medieval and modern –
History and criticism.
2. Byzantine prose literature – History and criticism.
3. Narration (Rhetoric). I. Title.

PA8096.P59 1989   878'.03'0809   C89-093593-9

Contents

Abbreviations

CF   *Chronicarum quae dicuntur Fredegarii scholastici libri iv*
DKR Notker Balbulus. *De Karolo rege*
HE   Bede. *Historia ecclesiastica gentis Anglorum*
HF   Gregory of Tours. *Libri historiarum x*, also known as *Historia Francorum*
HL   Paul the Deacon. *Historia Langobardorum*
LHF *Liber historiae Francorum*
LPR Agnellus of Ravenna. *Liber pontificalis ecclesiae Ravennatis*
RGS Widukind of Corvey. *Rerum gestarum Saxonicarum libri tres*
VSPE *Vitas sanctorum patrum Emeretensium*

Preface

This book is written primarily for students of literature, especially those interested in the history of narrative forms. It is meant to introduce a body of writing often unfamiliar even to practising medievalists, and rarely, if ever, discussed as literature: the Latin narratives of the early middle ages. The neglect of such authors as Gregory of Tours, Gregory the Great, and Paul the Deacon by literary scholars has had at least two easily comprehensible reasons. In the first place, as Latin writers of the so-called dark ages they have suffered the lasting contempt of classicists for all forms of post-classical Latin, and also the lack of interest of most medievalists in literature not written in the vernacular languages. In the second place, their narrative works are histories and saints' lives, and literary scholarship has long treated these genres as if they belonged only marginally to literature. Here, too, the almost exclusive predilection for fictional narrative has limited the interest of informed readers to the productions of the high and late middle ages. Nonetheless, early medieval works deserve to become better known and understood, for, aside from their great intrinsic interest, they document clearly and abundantly the specific features and patterns of narrative in the first medieval centuries.

Historians may object to a reading of historiographic texts that does not take their extra-literary, historical aim into account. The focus of my discussion, however, is on very minimal units, individual scenes, and not at all on macronarrative, which is more directly shaped by the historical purpose. The analysis of single scenes here is intended to bring out the technique of their composition, as well as a practice of narrative representation that underlies it. These issues seem to me to come up in exactly the same way for historical narrative as for fiction:

as long as we are dealing with single scenes, the terms of the analysis can remain unchanged.

It will be obvious to all readers familiar with Erich Auerbach's *Mimesis* and his *Literary Language and the Public* that my study is meant to be a continuation of his pioneering work on late antique and early medieval literature in those two books. I disagree with Auerbach on two fundamental issues: the impact of Judeochristianity on literary form, which in my opinion he overrates, and his tendency to identify syntax and narrative style. The most important difference between his analysis and mine, however, is in the concept of representation, which I use in a limited, exclusively technical sense, such as it has in the German term 'szenische Darstellung' / 'scenic representation,' whereas in Auerbach it denotes a general attitude to reality, a *Weltanschauung* as it expresses itself in literary style.

The text is full of quotations, often quite lengthy ones, and I have made a point of giving them all in the original as well as in translation; the important exceptions are the Greek passages, which would have brought up considerably the cost of printing. My reason for providing the original in almost all other cases is that I quote from many different authors and works, and standard editions of all of them are not readily available to most scholars and students. They certainly were not to me, even as I was writing the book.

The translations are all mine except for passages from the Vulgate, for which I use the Douay version, Serbo-Croatian heroic poetry, which is quoted in the translation of Albert B. Lord, and a passage by Mohammed Mrabet, which I quote as translated from the Moghrebi by Paul Bowles.

I wish to acknowledge the generous help of three friends and colleagues, T.M. Andersson, Carol Clover, and Ralph Hexter, who read this study in draft and offered numerous suggestions for its improvement, most of which I have adopted. One of the anonymous readers for the University of Toronto Press wrote five pages of extraordinarily useful queries, corrections, and addenda. The book and I are in his debt. The American Council of Learned Societies granted me a fellowship in 1985 which made it possible to complete the first draft. My parents, by their affection and constant encouragement, gave me the support I needed to keep on working over the years, and the book is dedicated to them.

Brooklyn, 1 December 1988

A Rhetoric of the Scene

Introduction

FROM LATE ANTIQUE TO EARLY MEDIEVAL

The *Iohannis* of Corippus, an epic poem of the sixth century AD, describes the quelling of a Berber rebellion in Libya by Byzantine troops under the command of the *magister militiae* Johannes Troglita. The first book of the poem gives a stylized account of the departure of the fleet from Constantinople, its journey across the Mediterranean, and its arrival in Northern Africa. Sailing between Sestos and Abydos, past the site of ancient Troy, the soldiers recognize in the landscape of those shores the setting of Homer's *Illiad*, and are able to place within it the spots where the most famous episodes of the poem took place:

> classis Threicias angusto litore fauces,
> Seston Abydenis dirimit qua pontus ab aruis,
> Sigeasque uolat uentis secura per undas
> et legit antiquae litus lacrimabile Troiae.
> inclita tunc referunt Smyrnaei carmina uatis
> significantque locos alta de puppe priorum.
> haec Priami sedes, domus haec Aeneia, longe
> arboribus quae saepta iacet. hic saeuus Achilles
> traxerat Hectoreum curru rapiente cadauer.   (1.171–9)

The fleet [sails past] the narrow shores of the Thracian strait, where the sea separates Sestos from the fields of Abydos; it flies in the wind, safe over the Sigean waves, and coasts along the mournful shore of ancient Troy. Then the men retell the glorious songs of the poet of Smyrna, and from the high deck point out the dwellings of heroes of old. There is the palace of Priam, and there the house of Aeneas,

lying further off surrounded by trees. And here fierce Achilles dragged
the corpse of Hector from his swift chariot.

The evocation of Homer by the Byzantine troops is not without some
admixture of imagery from the second book of Vergil's *Aeneid*. Petrus,
the young son of Johannes, who is sailing with his father, listens to
the older men exchange these literary reminiscences. He is himself
animated by two passions: the desire to learn the deeds of the Trojan
war, and the need to identify his own experience with that of Iulus /
Ascanius, the adolescent son of Aeneas in the Latin epic:

> audiit egregius narrantes proelia Petrus.
> audiit ut pueri praeclarum nomen Iuli,
> arsit amore nouo pectus puerile legendi,
> noscere bella uolens. magna pietate mouetur:
> se putat Ascanium, matrem putat esse Creusam.
> filia regis erat: mater quoque filia regis.
> tunc pater Aeneas, et nunc pater ipse Iohannes.   (1.197–203)

> The noble Petrus listens to the men tell of the wars. And when he
> hears the famous name of the boy Iulus, his boyish heart burns with
> a new desire to read the songs, wishing to learn about the wars.
> Moved by deep emotion, he believes himself Ascanius, believes his
> mother to be Creusa. She indeed was a king's daughter; his own mother
> too is daughter of a king. Ascanius' father had been Aeneas; his is
> Iohannes.

However unlikely as history, the scene is extraordinarily suggestive.
It represents more than an act of faith by the author in the permanent
validity of the Vergilian formula; by conjuring up Aeneas and his son
as heroic models for the Libyan campaign it reveals an incapacity to
visualize a very different historical reality in any other terms.[1] Here it
is perhaps important to recall that this Latin poem was composed in
Byzantine Africa, the furthermost Western bastion of what was already
a Greek empire.[2] In its very language and literary models, the *Iohannis*
is an expression of the Byzantine claim, upheld with vehemence by
Justinian, that Constantinople had succeeded Rome and that the Eastern empire was the heir of the Roman orb: a gesture of fidelity to the
past, a declaration of continuity, a useful and ambitious profession of
faith.[3]

The text of the *Iohannis*, however, betrays the contradictions im-

posed by sixth-century reality on the Vergilian parallel: if the fleet is
headed, like the ships of Aeneas, for the coast of Northern Africa, the
new Romans will not find there the peaceful and prosperous Carthage
of Dido, but a scene of devastation and violence all too familiar to the
contemporaries of Corippus:

> prospexit tandem succensae litora terrae
> ductor et indomitas Martis cognouit habenas
> nec dubium (nam uera ferunt incendia) monstrum:
> uoluebant uenti crispantes uertice flammas
> et fumo commista uolans super astra fauilla
> scintillas tenues summam spargebat in aethram.
> surgit et in medium feruet iam flamma profundum,
> omnia conuoluens succensae robora terrae.
> uritur alma seges cultos matura per agros,
> omnis et augescit crescentem frondibus ignem
> arbor et in cineres sese consumpta resoluit.
> uertuntur miserae caesis cum ciuibus urbes
> cunctaque direptis conflagrant moenia tectis.   (1.323–35)

At last the leader descries the shores of burning lands, and recognizes
the untamed reins of Mars. Nor are the portents doubtful, for the
fire declares them true. The winds tossed about flames that curled as
they rose. Ashes, flying mixed with smoke over the stars, scattered
light sparks high in the sky. Soon a flame springs soaring high above,
embracing all the trees of the burning land. The ripe, nourishing crops
are burnt in the cultivated fields. Every tree feeds the fire that grows
in its branches, and once consumed crumbles into ashes. The
wretched cities are destroyed, their inhabitants slain; their roofs
overturned, all buildings are set ablaze.

The ruin of Roman Africa and its late antique urban and agricultural
civilization is one of the events that have made the imaginary world
of the poet obsolete and inaccessible. Corippus records the destruction
of one of the last areas on the Mediterranean where his literary con-
servatism could have been understood. In describing the agents of this
destruction, he is forced to look away from the past and pay some
attention to the new protagonists of history. At the end of book four
the exotic names of the Berber rebels threaten to shatter the rythm of
the hexameter, to clash with the nostalgic and imitative mood of the
poem:

> Camalus quos deinde secutus
> ardet in aduersos multis cum milibus hostes,
> Hisdreasen Ialdasque ferox et Sinzera feruens,
> quosque referre parans comprendere nomina nullus
> mente potest, saeuasque uolens tot dicere gentes.   (iv.632–6)

Having followed them, Camalus rushes against the approaching enemies with his many warriors. With him came Hisdreasen, fierce Ialdas, seething Sinzera, and all those whose names no one who tries to record them can keep in mind, though he may wish to catalogue so many barbarous nations.

The ship of the *magister militiae*, afloat between the *litus lacrimabile* of antiquity and the burning shores of Roman Africa, is an eloquent image of Western literature at the beginning of the middle ages. The sixth-century soldiers discussing classical epics on the way to this partial holocaust of Mediterranean culture enact the claims of repetition in the face of chaos. The literary vehicle, to be sure, is entirely late antique, but the medieval world is present as a marginal awareness, as an anxiety.

Medievalists today are more aware than ever before that late antiquity brought about fundamental innovations, that it was not all cultural conservation and repetition.[4] This awareness is particularly sharp in the study of religion, and also in art history.[5] The literary originality of late antiquity and the early middle ages, however, is still largely unrecognized. Scholars have long emphasized the activity of preservation in the centuries before and after the breakup of the Western empire.[6] This essay, which is an attempt to examine early medieval narrative form as a new departure, requires particular clarity from the beginning as to the relation between innovation and repetition at the watershed of the two ages. About innovation, the following general points need to be kept in mind.

A   Late antiquity, from the second to the fifth century, developed a new literary language, appropriate for the communication of Christian doctrine, history, and fiction. The emergence of this new language is most clear in Latin, particularly in such texts as the sermons of Augustine and Caesarius of Arles. Christian Latin is already identifiable in its vocabulary and idioms, but it is often more easily recognizable by the general decorum of its style, a *sermo humilis* addressed to a larger and more varied audience than that of the classical period.[7]

B   On the subject of imitation, we must remember that even the most servile repetition, when performed and recognized as such, means something very different from the original. And late antiquity makes the gesture of repetition, the gesture that establishes its claim to continuity, in a great variety of ways. Books such as the *Consolation* of Boethius, or the letters of Sidonius Apollinaris, are a genuine, organic development of classical culture, however changed the circumstances may seem in which they were produced. Readers may spot dozens of echoes and allusions, find themselves unable to identify an original idea in the entire composition, but it is clear that Boethius and Sidonius did not write as antiquarians or in a deliberately archaic manner. Their work is the accurate reflection of the education that had been available to them; they knew of no literary alternative.[8] Turning, however, to the writings of Isidore of Seville, only one century after Boethius, we perceive a very different activity. Isidore's work, though fed by an abundance of classical and late antique sources, is characterized in form and spirit by the mentality of the compiler; it is already part of that labour of collection and abridgment that we associate with the early medieval period. Isidore breaks down the information in his sources and presents it in fragments, torn from its original context and arranged according to new taxonomic, grammatical, and etymological principles wholly alien to it. For him the classics are no longer models, but authorities and legitimizing precedents.[9]

c   Early medieval classicism is complex in that early medieval writers adopted a classical canon larger and broader than ours. For them Christian antiquity – the writings of the church fathers, the works of the first Christian poets of Gaul, Italy, and Spain – was as much a part of the classical corpus as the eclogues of Vergil and the orations of Cicero. In descriptions of the early monastic libraries of Europe, the works of Juvencus, Prudentius, and Arator are mentioned with as much veneration as those of the great Augustan poets.[10] If anything, the Christian classics were more approachable, and not open to charges of futility and immorality such as season the anti-pagan offensive of an Augustine. Within this broader range of classical models, the early medieval authors tend to show clear preferences. We need only compare the literature of the Carolingian renaissance, with its constant Vergilian and Horatian echoes, to the more homespun and limited revival of learning under Alfred the Great in ninth-century England, and its exclusively Christian program of translations: Orosius, Augustine, Boethius, Gregory the Great. Late antiquity, in so far as it can be reduced to Christian antiquity, is not only the culture that stretches to the beginning of the medieval period, but an active ferment, a strand of

early medieval culture itself, and simultaneously part of the remembered, revised, glossed, and edited world, the already legendary shore
of the past.

D   There are too many possible reasons for repetition; the diversity of
motives for bringing up again a form or an idea of the past is too great
for a psychological explanation of medieval classicism to be worth
attempting. Its material conditions of existence are a simpler matter:
in order to make Vergilian allusions or to imitate the periodic sentences
of Cicero or Jerome, the medieval writer needed an education, the
training in grammar and rhetoric that had once been available throughout the Roman world. Educational institutions survived the fall of the
Western empire in Christianized, simplified, often degraded forms, primarily as cathedral or court schools and as monastic schools. With the
political and economic breakdown caused by the Germanic migrations
and the various waves of invasion and settlement that followed them
over Western Europe for the next five centuries, the standards of literary
education became particularly low in the countries hardest hit by the
crisis, while they remained noticeably higher in more marginal areas.
Spain before the Arab conquest and Anglo-Saxon England before the
Danish raids of the ninth century are distinguished in their literature
by a classicizing Latinity and a pervasive awareness of ancient models.[11]

However, if the availability of such models could determine the
character of a national or regional literature, their absence could be
equally influential. We find the stylistic departures, the innovations
that characterize European literature for the next five hundred years
primarily in Italy and Merovingian Gaul. This is particularly true of
the new developments in narrative form which are the subject of this
book.

THE NEW FORMS OF NARRATIVE MIMESIS

Early medieval narrative must be studied in the historiography of the
period, a term that covers not only histories and chronicles but also
biographies, saints' lives, accounts of miracles and relics, and other
ecclesiastical genres, for the classical distinction between historical
and biographic-anecdotal literature had already begun to break down
in the late empire.[12] The few heroic epics that have survived from the
period before 1000 AD, poems such as *Beowulf* and the *Waltharius*, are
so exceptional as remains of a poorly documented Germanic tradition,
but also as early products of a vernacular art of narrative, that they
allow us to draw no general conclusions. The various historical genres,

on the other hand, are fairly well represented throughout Western Europe and in the Greek East. Historiography as a whole shows the familiar tension between repetition and innovation, as well as the objective dependence on formal education to which all literary genres are subject. Bede's *Historia ecclesiastica* and the few extant Visigothic narratives represent, at different levels of achievement, the successful recreation of a late antique narrative manner.[13] As a narrator, Bede is closer to Eusebius and Orosius than to any of his contemporaries, a direct testimony of the high quality of monastic schooling in eighth-century Northumbria. Here our interest is restricted, however, to the new developments, and we must seek them in the more chaotic areas of the West, in Frankish Gaul, in Langobardic and Byzantine Italy, where the weight of a canonized historiographic tradition was less, and the act of setting down history for the record, or for future readers, calls forth a characteristic spontaneity and inventiveness. The new style shared by these narrators contrasts clearly with the classical models, and its features, presumably present in the other narrative genres of the period, continue to characterize narrative literature long after 1000, when writers in Latin and the vernaculars become increasingly productive. To the twentieth-century reader, the form that I am about to illustrate has become second nature and seems almost inevitable in narrative; it began to be used systematically in literature in the sixth century AD.

Let us examine two very different texts. The first is taken from the early eighth-century *Liber historiae Francorum*, the work of an anonymous Neustrian historian. It gives the following account of the intrigue that led to the murder of King Chilperic I:

> Erat autem Fredegundis regina pulchra et ingeniosa nimis atque
> adultera. Landericus quoque tunc erat maiorum domus palacii, vir
> ingeniosus ac utilis, quem memorata regina diligebat multum, quia
> in luxoria commiscebatur cum ea. Quadam die maturius mane cum rex
> ad venationem exercendam de villa Calense in Parisiaco dirigeret,
> cum amaret eam nimis, reversus in camara palacii de stapplo equitum,
> illa caput suum abluens aqua in ipsa camara, rex vero retro veniens,
> eam in natibus suis de fuste percussit. At illa cogitans, quod Landericus
> esset, ait: 'Quae sic facis, Landerice?' Respiciens sursum viditque,
> quod rex esset; expavit vehementer. Rex vero nimis tristis effectus, in
> ipsa venatione perrexit. Fredegundis itaque vocavit ad se Landericum
> et enarravit haec omnia, quae rex fecerat, dicens: 'Cogita, quid agere
> debeas, quia crastina die ad tormenta valida exibimur'. Et ait Lander-

icus, contritu spiritu, commotus lacrimis, dicens: 'Tam mala hora te
viderunt oculi mei! Ignoro enim, quid agere debeam, quia conpre-
munt me undique angustiae'. Et illa dixit ei: 'Noli timere, audi consilium meum, et faciamus hanc rem, et non moriemur. Cum autem rex
de venatione, clauso iam die, ad noctem advenerit, mittamus qui
eum interficiat, et proclament, quod Childebertus rex Auster insidiatus
ei fuisset. Illoque mortuo, nos cum filio meo Chlothario regnemus.'

(LHF chapter 35)

Queen Fredegund was beautiful, extremely cunning, and given to
infidelity. The mayor of the palace was then Landeric, a clever and
resourceful man of whom the queen was very fond, for he was her
partner in adultery. One day, early in the morning, the king was
preparing to ride with a hunting party from his estate at Chelles, near
Paris, but since he loved his wife very much he returned from the
stables to her chamber in the palace. She was in the room, washing
her hair with water. The king, coming from behind, struck her on
the buttocks with a stick. She, thinking that it was Landeric, said:
"What are you doing, Landeric?' Looking back, she saw that it was
the king, and became very frightened. The king, extremely unhappy,
left and went hunting. The queen then called Landeric and told him
everything that had happened with the king, adding: 'Think, therefore,
of what you should do, for tomorrow we shall be subjected to dreadful tortures.' Landeric, feeling wretched and moved to tears, said: 'On
an evil hour did my eyes see you! I do not know what I should do,
for terrors beset me on every side.' And she replied: 'Do not fear. Listen
to my advice. Let us do as I say and we shall not die. When day is
over and in the evening the king comes back from hunting, let us send
someone out to kill him, and let it be proclaimed that Childebert,
the Austrasian king, has plotted this against him. Once the king is
dead, we shall reign together with my son Chlothar.'

The second text, from Agnellus of Ravenna's *Liber pontificalis ecclesiae Ravennatis*, a work of the first half of the ninth century, describes
the confrontation between Charles the Bald and the corrupt and scheming George, archbishop of Ravenna. Their meeting takes place after the
battle of Fontenoy (841) which George has deserted his see to attend,
hoping to acquire influence with the victorious party. The prelate is
arrested on the battlefield.

Tunc iussit eum Carolus ante se venire. Prostratus humo, eius pedibus
se advolvens; stans autem rex indutus iuvenilibus armis, indutus

purpurea, succinctusque aureas fibula, veste, ex sinistro latere obriziaca
pendentia bulla, connixa smaragdus et iacintinis fulgens gemmis,
clipeo tectus humero, lorica indutus, hastam tenens manibus et iuncta
lancea ferro, stans acer in armis, cristatus in agmine caput, emissam
palam omnibus erumpens de pectore vocem: 'O tu pastor, si in te istud
permanet nomen, cur reliquisti ecclesia tibi commissa et plebem,
quam afflixisti, non recuperasti, sed per longinquo itinere, ut videres
praelium, venisti? Quid tibi necesse fuit tuam depopulare ecclesiam,
et quod a christianis principibus vel imperatoribus illatum fuit et a
tuis praedecessoribus adquisitas una amisisti hora? Sciam, si centum
vivas annos, non recuperabis.' Tunc Georgius vates gemens, audiens
improperium talem, deflexit transversa lumina terram et statim ob-
mutuit amens et stabat aporiatus prae cunfusione nec valebat
respondere purpurato regi. Submissoque in terra vultu, aiebat cum
largissimis fletibus: 'Nos pacem postulare venimus, non contra vos
arma parare.'   (*LPR* chapter 174)

Then Charles commanded George to appear before him. George
cowered on the ground, grovelling at Charles' feet. The king, however,
stood, clad in the arms of a young warrior. He was wrapped in
a purple cloak clasped with a golden brooch. A ball of fine gold
hung on his left side, adorned with emeralds and resplendent with
hyacinth-coloured gems. His shoulder was protected by a shield; he
wore a breastplate and held in his hands a spear tipped with iron. He
towered, fierce in his armour, his head covered for battle with a
plumed helmet. In the presence of all who were there he spoke, making
his voice ring out from his chest: 'Oh shepherd, if you can still be
given that name, why did you leave the church that had been committed to you, without bringing back the people you had first abused?
Instead, you travelled a long way so that you might come here and
see the battle. What need did you have to depopulate the church, and
to lose in an hour what had been given by Christian princes and
emperors to your predecessors? I know that even if you should live
one hundred years, you will not get it back.' Bishop George sobbed on
hearing such harsh words. He averted his eyes and turned them to
the ground. Frantic, he could not speak and remained there at a loss,
unable to reply to the purple-clad king. His face downcast, he kept
repeating with interminable sobs: 'We came to ask for peace, not to
plot war against you.'

The episode of Fredegund and Landeric has kept the simple anecdotal
form that we would expect if the event had just taken place and the

story were still circulating at court by word of mouth. Large explanatory factors are brought in awkwardly at the last moment to account for this particular event: 'quia in luxoria commiscebatur cum ea,' 'cum amaret eam nimis' 'for he was her partner in adultery,' 'since he loved his wife very much'; sometimes without need: 'cogitans, quod Landericus esset' 'thinking that it was Landeric.' The narrative seems to have undergone no stylization as yet; Fredegund's fatal words are disarmingly natural and credible, only her lover's expressions of regret in the second part of the episode give the impression of being touched with rhetoric. We have here the narrative of a society still close to the vernacular epic tradition, and to the processes by which history is reduced to legend. The death of Chilperic, who had been characterized by Gregory of Tours as 'the Nero and Herod of our time,' and who was probably murdered by his political rivals, must be explained away in legend as the consequence of a private feud or intrigue. The thinking behind this anecdote is strictly causal: the incident is there to trigger the episode of the king's murder, which follows immediately.[14]

Agnellus, on the other hand, is Oriental, baroque, remarkably stylized by any standards. Nothing is spontaneous or lifelike in this scene, in which Charles and George talk as much or more through their hieratic attitudes and through their garments and insignia (the bishop by his lack of them: his *pluviale* had been taken from him when he was arrested) as through their actual words. The wretched archbishop's speech is fittingly brief and urgent, but the king speaks throughout in a public manner, 'palam omnibus' / 'in the presence of all who were there'; his language is studied and rhetorical. The scene documents the East Roman awareness of court ceremonial as significant form, an awareness that must have been particularly keen in Ravenna, which had been a Byzantine capital less than one century before Agnellus wrote, and where in the sixth-century mosaics of San Vitale the rites of the *aula* and the Great Church of Constantinople had achieved their most memorable expression.[15] Interest in hieratic ceremonial postures and in the vestments and badges of power gives Agnellus' narrative an ideological dimension that is entirely lacking in the Frankish anecdote of the first selection. Charles is more than a historical character here, more also than an angry, punitive figure. His attitude and garb, especially when juxtaposed to the grovelling George, make him the representative of monarchy, and in particular of royal power in its relation to the church, fulfilling its obligation to guide and correct ecclesiastics in the performance of their duties. He is, to quote Gustavo Vinay, 'la regalità paludata e rampognante.'[16] In this context, George must inevitably personify the Errant Clergy.[17] The function of the scene is in no way causal or explanatory; it is not there to account for anything that will follow, for it is fully significant in itself. Its meaning, however, unlike that of the scene from *Liber historiae Francorum*, is not exclusively historical, but also a matter of moral and political abstractions.

Poles apart as the two scenes are, they have fundamental methods in common, though these, as I have pointed out already, are of the sort that the contemporary reader tends to take for granted in a narrative. I am talking fundamentally about the decision on the part of the narrator to let the story speak for itself, that is, to efface himself as much as possible and create the illusion that we are witnessing the events he describes. There is in this decision a more or less implicit narrative gesture inviting us to see for ourselves and form our own reactions and judgments, which is why the voice of the narrating historian is heard seldom, or not at all.

The illusion is created in the first place by marking out the occasion of the scene: a point in time, perhaps also a given place. In any case, specific space is assumed: the space needed by the characters to carry out their motions or strike certain attitudes. Equally important is the fact that we hear the actors speak: their words are quoted; direct speech is used systematically. Dramatic elements such as gesture and posture play a major role. They no doubt contribute by giving the illusion some kind of visual correlative. However, both our stories appear to hinge so much on matters of movement, gesture, and position that these factors would seem to have been primary considerations in the very conception of the two episodes rather than secondary touches intended to make the narrative more vivid. The logic of the first scene in the story from the *Liber historiae Francorum* is dictated entirely by the characters' relative positions: as Fredegund stands washing her hair, and therefore unable to look behind her, the king, coming from behind, hits her on the buttocks. It is only on turning around, after having uttered the fateful words, that she recognizes her husband. In Agnellus, the king's upright stance ('stans autem rex'), matched by the archbishop's ritual prostration before him ('prostratus humo, eius pedibus se advolvens'), conveys the sense of the scene as clearly as any authorial statement. George's self-abasement is emphasized and elaborated in a variety of gestures ('deflexit transversa lumina terram'; 'submissoque in terra vultu' / 'he averted his eyes and turned them to the ground'; 'his face downcast').

Perhaps less central, but remarkably consistent in the scenic conception of both episodes, is the presence of significant objects. Chilperic, coming from the stables, strikes his wife from behind with a stick or switch: he is using his whip hand, and the stick becomes the sign of the master, but also that of the husband assuming a role familiar in traditional storytelling (the man goes out hunting; his wife remains at home). It may even be a pledge of future punishment for infidelity. The gesture itself, in its vulgar familiarity, serves to remind us that this is also in part a cuckold story, not unrelated to the later *fabliau* in its tone and themes. The effect of Agnellus' story depends to a very great extent on the inventory of regalia that constitutes his description of the king. Charles' equipment includes not only robes of state ('purpurea veste,' 'aureas fibula,' 'obriziaca bulla' / 'a purple cloak,' 'a golden brooch,' 'a ball of fine gold') but also the outfit of a warrior ('hasta,' 'clipeus,' 'lorica' / 'spear,' 'shield,' 'breastplate'), for he has just won a battle and comes in directly from the battlefield. In the ceremonial of late antique and medieval courts, royal insignia carried complex theological and political meanings which must have been manifest to the officials and dignitaries and which the scholar can decipher today, at least in part.[18] The general significance of these insignia cannot have been in doubt, and here it is brought out by the fact that the person of the king disappears entirely under his vestments. It is not before an angry warrior but at the feet of the 'rex purpuratus' / the 'purple-clad king' that George cowers. Charles causes his voice to 'ring out from his chest' / 'erumpens de pectore,' and there is a sense that, just as the voice is coming from the physical man, invisible behind the insignia, the words come from a power greater than the man, which expresses itself through him.

The elements of dramatic narrative characteristic of the early middle ages, this particular use of time and space, of speech, gestures, and things, can be found in texts as different as these two, products of cultures as diverse as those of Merovingian Neustria and ninth-century Ravenna. Two conclusions can be drawn from this surprising diffusion of the style: in the first place, it is not a function of the individual manner of the author, but constitutes a basic narrative approach, a fundamental technique adopted by a great variety of narrators. In the second place, being such a deep structure, it is not susceptible of pronounced evolution. Thus, for example, Gregory of Tours and Agnellus often use it in very similar ways in spite of more than two centuries that separate them.

Another important lesson these selections can teach us is brought home with special clarity by the language of the Frankish *Liber*: it is clumsy, childish prose, in no way worthy of literary consideration as such. Its use in narrative can be studied independently of its quality as prose, however, and proves to be most interesting in itself. What little study there has been of early medieval narrative has suffered from an exaggerated estimate of the relevance to narrative form of such factors as parataxis, subordination or the lack of it, and the evolution of prepositional functions in late Latin. Storytelling is never wholly independent of syntax, or unaffected by linguistic change, but its development is not dictated chiefly by these matters.[19]

From what I have said so far it should be clear that the new narrative manner that comes in with the middle ages is identifiable only in historical perspective, that is, in contrast with what came before and perhaps also with the styles of later medieval narrators. The reader may be wondering in what other ways than those I have described one could possibly tell a story. That will become clearer in chapter one, where the various possible sources of the new style are examined.

THESIS AND SCOPE OF THIS STUDY

This book has two separate but related aims: to outline a literary-historical hypothesis and to give analytic descriptions of a number of texts. The texts will provide evidence to back up the theory; the theory, in turn, should make it possible to see the recurring elements that characterize these texts as aspects of a style.

The theory is that the features of the new narrative manner described above were taken over from traditional oral storytelling. Stylistic assimilation of oral form had presumably begun in late antiquity, but the traits studied here appear with regularity from the sixth century on. The adoption of oral style by writers of history, that is to say by men of letters, is encouraged and made possible by the fact that the high culture of the period displays new interests of its own that match those of popular narrative – in particular the hardening of public life into patterns of ritual and ceremony, and the development of an elaborate inventory of significant and symbolic objects – tendencies that coincide in large measure with the oral-traditional emphasis on gestures and objects. This convergence of high and popular culture leaves its unmistakable stamp upon the new style, which turns out to be something far more complex than a naturalized folktale manner. Analytic description, the second aim of the study, is attempted in chapters two, three, and four, where I illustrate what seem to me the three main features of the style and try to give an idea of their broad range of formal realizations and narrative purposes.

This statement indicates already the limits I have set myself. In the first place, this is to be no survey of early medieval narrative styles, but a study of certain new stylistic developments. What we might call medieval classicism and the deliberate imitation of antiquity are not considered at all, fundamental though they are. This explains why Bede's *Historia ecclesiastica*, one of the finest productions of the age, is given so little attention. Secondly, the narrative devices discussed and illustrated here are not considered from the perspective of their evolution in the course of five centuries, but understood to identify a single, though highly adaptable, style that reaches from the end of antiquity to the high middle ages. The risks of defining such a large reality as a single 'style' have been brought out cogently by George Kubler in his reflections on the methodology of art history:

> Everything varies both with time and place, and we cannot fix any-where upon an invariant quality such as the idea of style supposes, even when we separate things from their settings. But when duration and setting are retained in view, we have shifting relations, passing moments, and changing places in historic life. Any imaginary dimen-sions or continuities like style fade from view as we look at them.[20]

Granting that styles are largely abstractions, the creations of art historians and literary scholars, I would argue nevertheless that they seem to be very necessary and useful constructs. Though it is true that the neat outline of any such style will tend to dissolve into a haze of particulars as we get closer to individual authors and works, any study of the evolution of forms over a long period of time is made possible only by such general categories. My attempt to sketch out a style in this broad, generalizing way, and to take my sketch to represent an unvarying factor in European narrative from 500 to 1000 AD, can be justified in part also by the oral-traditional origin of the new narrative devices: traditional forms change very slowly, if at all.

Throughout the book, whenever the origins and manifestations of the new style are considered, I envisage the early middle ages as a de-velopment and transformation of late antiquity, that is, of interests and formal preferences that were already active between 300 and 500 AD. To avoid any suggestion of teleology or progress in the history of narrative forms, I have reserved all discussion of stylistic continuities and developments in the later middle ages for a brief final chapter. Since the dividing line between antiquity and the medieval period remains controversial, I have not attempted to work out a periodization of my own, but have used instead the most widely accepted labels for the individual writers discussed here. Thus Eusebius and Sulpicius Severus are late antique, and Gregory of Tours is medieval. A sixth-century anchronism such as Corippus remains impossible to place, or proves that late antiquity ended later in outlying areas such as Northern Africa and Visigothic Spain.

I work from a limited corpus; most frequently quoted are the Merovingian historians: Gregory of Tours and his continuators, the writer known as Fredegar and the anonymous author of the *Liber historiae Francorum*. Paul the Deacon's *Historia Langobardorum* provides numerous examples, as does Agnellus of Ravenna's *Liber pontificalis*, a history of the archbishops of Ravenna. Notker Balbulus' book of anecdotes about Charlemagne, *De Karolo rege*, and Widukind of Corvey's *Rerum gestarum Saxonicarum libri tres* complete the list of core authors and texts, in which it is clear that national and tribal histories play a central role. Other works, such as the *Dialogues* of Gregory the Great, the Visigothic *Vitas sanctorum patrum Emeretensium*, a seventh-century book on the saints and bishops of Mérida, and Bede's *Historia ecclesiastica*, are used here and there, when they offer uncommon and valuable examples.[21]

Even though the focus of this study is the narrative literature of the Latin West, I have used a considerable number of Greek texts taken from Byzantine hagiography and chronicles. Their inclusion does not represent an attempt on my part to extend my historical hypothesis to Byzantine literature as a whole, or to provide a general account, however summary, of its narrative techniques. Byzantium cannot be left out of the picture in a study of the early medieval period. At that time, Western Europe was still acutely conscious of Constantinople as a centre of learning and political power; military and diplomatic contacts between Greek East and Latin West were frequent and important.[22] Though the abandonment of Greek in the West and growing unfamiliarity with Latin in the Eastern empire soon created a major barrier to cultural influence, the two halves of the former Roman empire present at this time remarkable parallelisms in the form and subject matter of their narrative literature, particularly at the more popular level. Accordingly, most of my illustrations of Byzantine narrative are taken from works written in the low or popular style.[23] My main purpose in discussing them here is to document the significant affinities in formal development that still appear in Latin and Greek throughout the period.

There are, of course, very considerable differences between the West and Byzantium. The stratification of styles in medieval Greek literature has no equivalent in the West. In the highest style, there is the production of a classicizing literary historiography such as Western Europe had given up quite early; contact with the models of antiquity is not intermittent and scanty, as in the Latin West, though the Byzantines turned, of course, to Greek antiquity. Nevertheless, East and West show at this time an important similarity in their cultural predicament: in both areas the culture of the state and the ruling classes, based on an imperial language and its highly developed literature, coexists with the tongues and cultures of many colonized nations. Here and there the subject populations become latinized and hellenized to a considerable degree, but influence travels in both directions, and the high cultures also borrow significantly from the barbarians. Just as the Latin literature of the West assimilated elements of Germanic and Celtic oral tradition, Byzantine hagiography and religious poetry show the marked influence of Semitic traditions encountered by the Greeks in Syria, Palestine, and Egypt. It is not surprising that these influences should be particularly active at the most humble level of literary endeavour, where rather than a deliberate borrowing they represent a process of half-conscious assimilation of vernacular traditions into the least pretentious forms available in the languages of power, the result of cultural contact and stylistic habit over a long period of time.

1 Sources and Models

The first body of writing that offers itself to our investigation as a likely source for the new manner is classical historiography. In the early middle ages the most frequently read and quoted of the classical historians is Sallust; Livy and Suetonius have left far weaker traces of their influence.[1] To look in their pages for any passage or episode that might serve as a term of comparison for the dramatic narratives of a Gregory of Tours or an Agnellus is to discover the novelty of the early medieval style. A scene in narrative as I understand it here, that is, the representation of a transaction between particular characters in their own words and actions, without the mediation of authorial commentary, is rarely to be found in their works. The narrative of classical historiography, if we look beyond important differences of individual manner, is authorial, exemplary, and summarizing.[2] The voice of the narrator is heard constantly; it hovers between the reader and the events described. These are evaluated, interpreted, portrayed in greater or lesser detail according to an explicitly authorial criterion of relevance. The particulars that might serve to make a given moment imaginable are passed over, probably as unimportant or even trifling within the larger schemes of the narrative. In other words, we are offered an interpretation of history, an analysis of certain events, rather than a direct record of what happened. This may be the reason why so much seems to be explained and explicable in Livy and Sallust: theirs is a rationalized reconstruction of events, and any uncertainty, any lack of clarity inherent in the data, however confusing these may seem at times, has been polished away.

Here and there, nevertheless, there is a scene. The quick narrative pace of authorial summary slows down and halts at a specific occasion, 'on the evening of the festival,' or 'the morning after the battle'; the characters' actions are described, their words quoted. Ordinarily, however, dialogue is rendered indirectly, and only through the effects and reactions it brings about, reproducing neither words nor argumentation. There are also long set speeches, unattached to any dramatic action and delivered in the standard contexts of oratory (an address to the people, to the senate, to troops before a battle), speeches which serve to state explicitly and in full the reasoned views of the speaker on the issues of the moment. Comparison with medieval texts reveals above all the rarity of scenic narrative in classical historiography; it shows us that the basic manner of the ancient historian is not dramatic.[3]

Since scenic presentation does occur, however infrequently, it is important to consider it as a possible source for early medieval narrative style; those rare pages from the classical historians may conceivably have served as models for later writers. Even more important, by comparing the two we may learn much about the different functions of dramatic narrative in texts where it is the rule and in those where it is exceptional.

Sallust is the most quoted and imitated of classical historians in the early medieval period, and his works contain dramatic elements of considerable interest. These, however, almost never coalesce into a unit that we might call a scene. Sallust's great popularity requires that his dramatic devices be analysed, but for a satisfactory scene in a classical author we must first look at Livy.

FALL OF SERVIUS TULLIUS

Livy was always conscious of the value of ἐνάργεια or visual quality, and did his best to create it in his writing. He displays it in great *tableaux vivants* of sieges, popular uprisings, and deliberations in the senate, crowd scenes highly choreographed and composed which often culminate in the masterly speech of a hero or ruler.[4] Scenes in my own more limited sense of the word are infrequent in his pages. The one we are about to discuss is well known and has been analysed often: it is the fall from power and death of Servius Tullius in book one of Livy's history.[5] The context of the event may be sketched briefly as follows: Tarquinius, an Etruscan immigrant to Roman territory, is elected king by popular acclaim. A portent that takes place in the royal palace persuades him and his wife Tanaquil to adopt Servius Tullius, a child of their household, as royal successor, sidestepping the claims of their own sons. After their deaths, Servius Tullius reigns with great wisdom and good fortune. He is murdered at the order of Lucius Tarquin, one of the sons of his benefactor, whom he had married to his own daughter Tullia in order to appease his frustrated ambition.

Hic L. Tarquinius – Prisci Tarquini regis filius neposne fuerit parum liquet; pluribus tamen auctoribus filium ediderim – fratrem habuerat Arruntem Tarquinium mitis ingenii iuuenem. His duobus, ut ante dictum est, duae Tulliae regis filiae nupserant, et ipsae longe dispares moribus. Forte ita inciderat ne duo uiolenta ingenia matrimonio iungerentur, fortuna, credo, populi Romani, quo diuturnius Serui regnum esset constituique ciuitatis mores possent. Angebatur ferox Tullia nihil materiae in uiro neque ad cupiditatem neque ad audaciam esse; tota in alterum auersa Tarquinium eum mirari, eum uirum dicere ac regio sanguine ortum: spernere sororem, quod uirum nacta muliebri cessaret audacia. Contrahit celeriter similitudo eos, ut fere fit: malum malo aptissimum; sed initium turbandi omnia a femina ortum est. Ea secretis uiri alieni adsuefacta sermonibus nullis uerborum contumeliis parcere de uiro ad fratrem, de sorore ad uirum; et se rectius uiduam et illum caelibem futurum fuisse contendere, quam cum impari iungi ut elanguescendum aliena ignauia esset; si sibi eum quo digna esset di dedissent uirum, domi se propediem uisuram regnum fuisse quod apud patrem uideat. Celeriter adulescentem suae temeritatis implet; L. Tarquinius et Tullia minor prope continuatis funeribus cum domos uacuas nouo matrimonio fecissent, iunguntur nuptiis, magis non prohibente Seruio quam adprobante.
[47]Tum uero in dies infestior Tulli senectus, infestius coepit regnum esse; iam enim ab scelere ad aliud spectare mulier scelus. Nec nocte nec interdiu uirum conquiescere pati, ne gratuita praeterita parricidia essent: non sibi defuisse cui nupta diceretur, nec cum quo tacita seruiret; defuisse qui se regno dignum putaret, qui meminisset se esse Prisci Tarquini filium, qui habere quam sperare regnum mallet. 'Si tu is es cui nuptam esse me arbitror, et uirum et regem appello; sin minus, eo nunc peius mutata res est quod istic cum ignauia est scelus. Quin accingeris? Non tibi ab Corintho nec ab Tarquiniis, ut patri tuo, peregrina regna moliri necesse est: di te penates patriique et patris imago et domus regia et in domo regale solium et nomen Tarquinium creat uocatque regem. Aut si ad haec parum est animi, quid frustraris ciuitatem? Quid te ut regium iuuenem conspici sinis? Facesse hinc Tarquinios aut Corinthum; deuoluere retro ad stirpem, fratri similior quam patri.' His aliisque increpando iuuenem

instigat, nec conquiescere ipsa potest si, cum Tanaquil, peregrina
mulier, tantum moliri potuisset animo ut duo continua regna uiro ac
deinceps genero dedisset, ipsa regio semine orta nullum momentum
in dando adimendoque regno faceret. His muliebribus instinctus furiis
Tarquinius circumire et prensare minorum maxime gentium patres;
admonere paterni beneficii ac pro eo gratiam repetere; allicere donis
iuuenes; cum de se ingentia pollicendo tum regis criminibus omnibus locis crescere. Postremo ut iam agendae rei tempus uisum est,
stipatus agmine armatorum in forum inrupit. Inde omnibus perculsis
pauore, in regia sede pro curia sedens patres in curiam per praeconem
ad regem Tarquinium citari iussit. Conuenere extemplo, alii iam ante
ad hoc praeparati, alii metu ne non uenisse fraudi esset, nouitate
ac miraculo attoniti et iam de Seruio actum rati. Ibi Tarquinius maledicta ab stirpe ultima orsus: seruum seruaque natum post mortem
indignam parentis sui, non interregno, ut antea, inito, non comitiis
habitis, non per suffragium populi, non auctoribus patribus, muliebri
dono regnum occupasse. Ita natum, ita creatum regem, fautorem
infimi generis hominum ex quo ipse sit, odio alienae honestatis erep-
tum primoribus agrum sordidissimo cuique diuisisse; omnia onera
quae communia quondam fuerint inclinasse in primores ciuitatis;
instituisse censum ut insignis ad inuidiam locupletiorum fortuna esset et parata unde, ubi uellet, egentissimis largiretur.
[48]Huic orationi Seruius cum interuenisset trepido nuntio excitatus,
extemplo a uestibulo curiae magna uoce 'Quid hoc,' inquit, 'Tarquini,
rei est? Qua tu audacia me uiuo uocare ausus es patres aut in sede
considere mea?' Cum ille ferociter ad haec – se patris sui tenere sedem;
multo quam seruum potiorem filium regis regni heredem; satis illum
diu per licentiam eludentem insultasse dominis – clamor ab
utriusque fautoribus oritur et concursus populi fiebat in curiam,
apparebatque regnaturum qui uicisset. Tum Tarquinius necessitate iam
ipsa cogente ultima audere, multo et aetate et uiribus ualidior,
medium arripit Seruium elatumque e curia in inferiorem partem per
gradus deiecit; inde ad cogendum senatum in curiam rediit. Fit fuga
regis apparitorum atque comitum; ipse prope exsanguis, cum semi-
animis regio comitatu domum se reciperet, ab iis qui missi ab
Tarquinio fugientem consecuti erant interficitur. Creditur, quia non
abhorret a cetero scelere, admonitu Tulliae id factum. Carpento certe,
id quod satis constat, in forum inuecta nec reuerita coetum uirorum
euocauit uirum e curia regemque prima appellauit. A quo facessere
iussa ex tanto tumultu cum se domum reciperet peruenissetque ad
summum Cyprium uicum, ubi Dianium nuper fuit, flectenti carpen-

tum dextra in Vrbium cliuum ut in collem Esquiliarum eueheretur, restitit pauidus atque inhibuit frenos is qui iumenta agebat iacent-emque dominae Seruium trucidatum ostendit. Foedum inhumanumque inde traditur scelus monumentoque locus est – Sceleratum uicum uocant – quo amens, agitantibus furiis sororis ac uiri, Tullia per patris corpus carpentum egisse fertur, partemque sanguinis ac caedis pater-nae cruento uehiculo, contaminata ipsa respersaque, tulisse ad penates suos uirique sui, quibus iratis malo regni principio similes propediem exitus sequerentur.   (1.46–8)

This Lucius Tarquin – it is not clear whether he was king Tarquinius Priscus' son or grandson, but following the majority of historians I shall call him his son – had a brother named Arruns Tarquin, a young man of mild disposition. They were both, as I said before, married to the daughters of Servius, both named Tullia and, like their husbands, of very different characters. The matter was arranged so that the two violent temperaments were not joined to each other in marriage. This was fortunate, I believe, for the people of Rome, since on account of this the reign of Servius lasted longer, and the institutions of the state had time to become established. The fierce Tullia was devoured by discontent on finding in her husband no tendency to ambition or audacity. Turning her attention wholly to his brother, she admired him openly, calling him a man, and one born of royal blood. She scorned her sister who, having such a husband, was lacking in feminine courage. Their affinity soon brought these two together, as often happens: one evil person is perfectly suited to another. But the first thought of the plot came entirely from her. Having become used to secret interviews with her sister's husband, she spared him no harsh words about her own husband, his brother, and none about her sister, who was his wife. She said that it would be easier for her to live as a widow and for him to remain unmarried than to continue joined to inferior persons and to grow weak in their feebleness. Should the gods give her the husband of whom she was worthy, she would soon know how to take over the royal power that was now in her father's hands. Quickly she imbued the young man with her recklessness. The deaths [of their spouses] followed shortly thereafter, and having thus made room in their houses, Tarquin and the younger Tullia entered a new marriage alliance and were joined by a matrimonial tie that Servius tolerated rather than approved.

[47]From that day on the life and authority of Servius were endangered. After one crime, the woman began to look forward to another. Nei-

ther by day nor by night did she allow the man any rest, lest the
murders already committed should have been in vain. She had not
merely wanted a husband so as to become a married woman, she
said, or to serve with him in silence. She wanted a man who considered
himself worthy of being king, one who remembered that he was the
son of Priscus Tarquinius, and who would rather wield royal power
than wait in the hope of it. 'If you are he whom I made up my mind
to marry, I call you my husband and my king. If you are less than
that, then things are changed for the worse, for in you cowardice is
added to crime. Will you take action? For you there is no need to
come wandering from Corinth or Tarquinii as your father did, and to
take power over an alien land. Your household gods, your ancestors,
the image of your father, the royal palace and the throne, the name of
Tarquin, all these appoint and declare you king. And if you have too
little courage for that, why do you lead on the citizens? Why do you
let yourself be seen as a prince? Go back to Corinth or Tarquinii, return
to your origins, more similar to your brother than to your father!'
By insulting him with these and other words she rouses the youth.
She can find no rest herself, considering how Tanaquil, an alien
woman, had enough spirit to procure two consecutive reigns, one for
her husband and one for her son-in-law, while she, Tullia, born of
royal blood, had played no part in the giving or taking away of power.

Influenced by these feminine passions, Tarquin begins to seek out
the heads of lesser families and put pressure on them, reminding
them of favours received from his father and asking for support in
return. He attracted the young men with gifts. By promising great
things and making false charges against Servius, he increased his
popularity. Finally, when the time seemed ripe for action, supported
by a throng of armed men he burst into the Forum. While everybody
stood paralysed with terror, he sat on the throne before the curia and
ordered a herald to summon the senators to King Tarquin at the
senate house. They congregated immediately, some of them already
prepared for the event, others afraid of incurring guilt by not coming.
All were astonished by the novelty and the wonder of what had
happened, and thought that Servius had already fallen. Then Tarquin
went back to the first origins of the former ruler, and said that
Servius was born of a slave and a slave-woman, and that after the
shameful death of his own father, Tarquinius Priscus, without an in-
terregnum, as had usually been observed before, without a popular
election or the support of the senators, he had taken power by a
woman's gift. Such had been his birth, thus had he become king, and

friend to the most wretched sort of populace, to which he belonged. From hatred of the nobility of others, he had taken away the lands of the ruling class and shared them out among whoever was most miserable. All the duties that had been held in common before, he had brought to bear exclusively on the leading citizens. He had organized a census so that the good fortune of the wealthy should be displayed to public envy, and he, whenever he wished, might hand it out to the poorest.

[48]Arriving in the middle of this oration, Servius, who had been brought there by the alarming news, called out loudly from the vestibule of the senate: 'What is this, Tarquin? How dare you summon the senate while I am alive, or occupy my seat?' Tarquin replied angrily to this that he was taking his own father's seat, that the king's son was a far better heir to the kingdom than a slave, and that Servius had been allowed long enough to get away with insulting his masters. Then a tumult arose between the supporters of either faction; the people rushed to the senate house, and it soon became clear that whoever won there would be king. Forced by necessity to extreme measures, Tarquin, far superior to Servius in youth and in physical strength, took him up by the waist and, dragging him from the senate, threw him down the steps. Then he returned to the senate house to bring the senators together. The allies and supporters of Servius fled. He himself, feeble and half-dead, as he was returning home with his royal escort, was murdered by men sent out by Tarquin in pursuit of him. It is believed, and it does not seem inconsistent with her previous crimes, that he did so on Tullia's advice.

She had herself driven to the Forum and, without fear of the great number of men, called out her husband from the senate and was the first to hail him king. He ordered her to go away from a scene of such disorder. On her way back home, she came to the highest part of the Vicus Cyprius, where the sanctuary of Diana was until recently, and as the driver turned to the right into the Clivus Urbius so that they might get to the Esquiline hill, he stopped terrified and pulled back the reins, pointing out to his mistress the body of the murdered Servius that lay there. A hideous and inhuman crime is reported by tradition, and the place is its monument: they call it the Street of Crime. Tullia, insane and driven by the avenging ghosts of her first husband and sister, is said to have driven the chariot over her father's body. The vehicle was splashed with his blood, and she herself infected and defiled by it. She took it home with her, to her own and her husband's household gods. Their anger at this was the cause that such a foul beginning of the reign was soon followed by a similar conclusion.

Only one moment of this entire sequence can be considered a scene, and that is the confrontation between the old king and his son-in-law before the curia. The highly dramatic incident in the Street of Crime when Tullia drives over her father's corpse does not amount to a scene, because it is broken off at the critical moment by the use of indirect report ('egisse fertur' / 'is said to have driven') to frame her terrible deed in the uncertainty of tradition, and because none of the important actions and words are described or quoted, save for the visual detail of the blood-spattered chariot and the action of the driver when he pulls at the reins and points out Servius' body lying on the street.

What comes before the scene at the Forum is a good illustration of non-dramatic narrative. Livy focuses on the motives and consequences of particular actions. He never leaves us in doubt as to his judgment of the various characters (see, for instance, his observation on the good fortune of the Romans, which retarded the union of the two ambitious characters, and such sententious remarks as 'Contrahit celeriter similitudo eos, ut fere fit: malum malo aptissimum' / 'Their affinity soon brought these two together, as often happens: one evil person is perfectly suited to another'), and pays closest attention to the reasons they give for their behaviour. These reasons are stated in full in various speeches which Livy either quotes (Tullia's second exhortation, 'Si tu is es ...' / 'If you are he ... ') or gives in indirect form, but with full reproduction of the line of reasoning (her first exhortation, ' ... et se rectius uiduam et illum caelibem... ' / ... that it would be easier for her to live as a widow, and for him to remain unmarried ... '). Whether in direct form or not, none of these speeches constitutes a scene because none is tied to a specific occasion. Tullia's rhetoric represents a steady barrage of goading words spoken over a long period of time; quoted as representative tirades, her two speeches are a way of describing customary behaviour. Nothing here can be properly visualized; we are not invited to witness the secret meetings between Tullia and Tarquin before their marriage, but are informed in a variety of ways of the inevitability of their course of action, given their temperaments, and of every rationalization of their behaviour that the characters themselves share with each other. Tarquin must speak at the decisive moment, but because Tullia has been singled out by Livy as the inspirer and originator of the conspiracy, she speaks long before he does, at greater length, and more memorably. The reader's impression is often that the causes of events and the stated rationale of the actors must be one and the same, that eloquent speeches bring about what actually happens, and that history is determined by the use of rhetoric and persuasion.

The narrator is unceasingly present, passing sentence on the events and interpreting them, choosing not to describe certain things (the murders of Arruns and of Tullia's sister, for example).[6] The one full scene comes smack in the middle of the sequence, and it begins un-surprisingly with 'postremo' / 'finally'; its point in time neatly defined, it opens as the armed men walk into the Forum. It is a fixed point in the middle of an indeterminate, fluid time, a time filled with reasons and argumentation, with the causality of clearly conceived motives and consequences, but bare of any other placeable events. In the de-cision to stop here and nowhere else, we are made aware once more of the narrator's absolute control.

The physical stage is the Forum, with its more or less implicit ar-chitecture: the throne before the curia, the *vestibulum* or forecourt from which Servius challenges the usurper, the steps down which the aged king is flung. Space is defined by the dialogue between Servius in the vestibule and Tarquin on the throne, and by the movement of Tarquin as he carries the old man by force to eject him from the Forum. Though speech by Tarquin is plentiful in indirect form, the only words quoted directly are those of Servius' simple challenge, particularly striking here because such short, dramatic speeches are rare in classical nar-rative. The scene revolves on the question 'How dare you summon the senate while I am alive, or occupy my seat?' The whole situation before our eyes is called in question. The gestural content of this moment is small or non-existent, except of course for the fact that Tullia's husband is sitting; the importance of this comes less from his sitting position, however, than from Servius' throne, which is the significant object at the centre of the scene, the subject of Servius' question, and a second focus of the represented moment in its own right, together with the words from the vestibule. This is also the throne which, in Tullia's words, declares and appoints Tarquin king.

Some dramatic elements are used loosely in the action that follows this scene: a conventional gesture of greeting may be implied when Tullia hails her husband as the new king. Her charioteer's violent start, stopping the chariot, and pointing at the corpse of Servius, is effective and easily the most elaborate gestural component in the whole episode. Nevertheless, we feel distinctly that the critical moment is over and that we are hearing of the aftermath. The single scene, placed in the middle of the sequence, works as an element of emphasis: Whatever is told in such detail that we 'see' it happen must contain the gist of the entire episode, its deepest meaning. This realization has important consequences for our reading of the story of Servius. The narrative usually referred to as 'the murder of Servius' is really not about murder at all, but about usurpation and impiety, two different but intimately connected crimes. While the murder of the deposed king takes place in a single sentence, at the hands of anonymous thugs, and is not described, the taking of the throne, the symbol of royal power, gets the narrator's full attention. In the same way, the earlier murders of Tullia's and Tarquin's first spouses had also been dismissed with two words ('continuatis funeribus' / 'the deaths [of their spouses] followed shortly thereafter'), while Tullia's later desecration of her father's corpse, a grisly act of impiety, receives elaborate dramatic treatment even though it does not quite become a scene. The meaning of the event is made as clear as its causes. Authorial interpretation is tied here to the argument of book one as a whole, and to Livy's broadest view of early Roman history. At this point he is describing the rule of the earliest kings of Rome, and preparing to introduce as a great improvement the republic that followed their overthrow. The principle of hereditary kingship has to be criticized and discredited, and the tale of Servius and Tarquin does the job splendidly. Servius is not of royal blood and rules virtuously, while Tarquin, the son of kings, takes power by treason and murder, becomes a cruel tyrant, and will eventually rape the chaste Lucrece. The very act by which Tarquin takes back the throne of his father is presented as a crime. The story is about power and its transmission rather than individual lives, so it is far less important that the rightful occupant of the throne happens to get murdered in the process.[7]

A MEROVINGIAN MURDER

A fitting term of comparison in early medieval historiography is Gregory of Tours' account of the murder of Praetextatus, bishop of Rouen, in chapter thirty-one of the eighth book of his *History*. In book five Gregory has already described King Chilperic's persecution and exile of the bishop, against whom he has brought false charges before a tribunal of his fellow prelates. After Chilperic dies, Praetextatus becomes the victim of his widow, the ferocious Fredegund, already known to us through the story of her intrigue with the mayor of the palace, Landeric, in the *Liber historiae Francorum*.

Dum haec agerentur et Fredegundis apud Rothomagensim urbem commoraretur, verba amaritudinis cum Praetextato pontifice habuit, dicens, venturum esse tempus, quando exilia, in qua detentus fuerat, reviseret. Et ille: 'Ego semper et in exilio et extra exilium episcopus fui, sum et ero; nam tu non semper regalem potentiam perfrueres. Nos ab exilio provehimur, tribuente Deo, in regnum; tu vero ab hoc regno demergeris in abyssum. Rectius enim erat tibi, ut, relecta stultitia adque malitia, iam te ad meliora converteris et ab hac iactantia, qua semper ferves, abstraheris, ut et tu vitam adipisceris aeternam et parvolum, quem genuisti, perducere ad legitimam possis aetatem'. Haec effatus, cum verba illius mulier graviter acciperit, se a conspectu eius felle fervens abstraxit. Advenientem autem dominicae resurrectionis diae, cum sacerdos ad implenda aecclesiastica officia ad aecclesiam maturius properasset, antefanas iuxta consuetudinem incipere per ordinem coepit. Cumque inter psallendum formolae decumberet, crudelis adfuit homicida, qui episcopum super formolam quiescentem, extracto baltei cultro, sub ascella percutit. Ille vero vocem emittens, ut clerici qui aderant adiuvarent, nullius ope de tantis adstantibus est adiutus. At ille plenas sanguine manus super altarium extendens, orationem fundens et Deo gratias agens, in cubiculo suo inter manus fidelium deportatus et in suo lectulo collocatus est. Statimque Fredegundis cum Beppoleno duce et Ansovaldo adfuit, dicens: 'Non oportuerat haec nobis ac reliquae plebi tuae, o sancte sacerdos, ut ista tuo cultui evenirent. Sed utinam indicaretur, qui talia ausus est perpetrare, ut digna pro hoc scelere supplicia susteneret'. Sciens autem ea sacerdos haec dolose proferre, ait: 'Et quis haec fecit nisi his, qui reges interemit, qui saepius sanguinem innocentem effudit, qui diversa in hoc regno mala commisit?' Respondit mulier: 'Sunt aput nos peritissimi medici, qui hunc vulnere medere possint. Permitte, ut accedant ad te'. Et ille: 'Iam', inquid, 'me Deus praecepit de hoc mundum vocare. Nam tu, qui his sceleribus princeps inventa es, eris maledicta in saeculo, et erit Deus ultur sanguinis mei de capite tuo'. Cumque illa discederit, pontifex, ordinata domo sua, spiritum exalavit.

Ad quem sepeliendum Romacharius Constantinae urbis episcopus advenit. Magnus tunc omnes Rothomagensis cives et praesertim seniores loci illius Francos meror obsedit. Ex quibus unus senior ad Fredegundem veniens ait: 'Multa enim mala in hoc saeculo perpetrasti, sed adhuc peius non feceras, quam ut sacerdotem Dei iuberis interfici. Sit Deus ultur sanguinis innocentes velociter. Nam et omnes nos erimus inquisitores mali huius, ut tibi diutius non liceat tam crudelia exercere'. Cum autem haec dicens discederet a conspectu reginae, misit illa qui eum ad convivium provocaret. Quo renuente, rogat, ut, si convivium eius uti non vellit, saltim vel poculum auriat, ne ieiunus a regale domo discedat. Quo expectante, accepto poculo, bibit absentium cum vino et melle mixtum, ut mos barbarorum habet; sed hoc potum venenum inbutum erat. Statim autem ut bibit, sensit pectorem suum dolorem validum inminere, et quasi se incideretur intrinsecus, exclamat suis, dicens: 'Fugite, o miseri, fugite malum hoc, ne mecum pariter periamini'. Illis quoque non bibentibus, sed festinantibus abire, hic protinus excaecatus, ascensoque aequo, in tertio ab hoc loco stadio caecidit et mortuus est.

Post haec Leudovaldus episcopus epistolas per omnes sacerdotes direxit et, accepto consilio, aeclesias Rothomagensis clausit, ut in his populus solemnia divina non expectaret, donec indagatione communi [variant: indignatione commoni] repperiretur huius auctur sceleris. Sed et aliquos adpraehendit, quibus supplicio subditus veritatem extorsit, qualiter per consilium Fredegundis haec acta fuerat; sed et, ea defensante, ulciscere non potuit. Ferebant etiam, ad ipsum percussores venisse, pro eo quod haec inquirere sagaciter distinaret; sed costodia vallatus suorum, nihil ei nocere potuerunt.   (viii.31)

While these things were happening, Queen Fredegund was living in Rouen. She had bitter words with Bishop Praetextatus and told him that the time was near when he would be exiled once again. He answered: 'In exile and out of exile, I was, am, and shall remain a bishop, but you will not always enjoy royal power. God granting, I was brought back from exile to authority; you, however, will be cast from your present power into hell. It would be better for you if, putting aside your foolishness and malice, you were to turn to better things, if you could wrest yourself from the pride with which you are always seething, so that you might obtain eternal life and bring up to manhood the boy to whom you gave birth.' Those were his words. The woman took great offence at them, and went away boiling with rage.

The day of our Lord's resurrection came, and early in the morning the bishop went to church to perform the office. As is customary, he began to say the antiphonal prayers in their order. During the chanting he rested upon a bench. At that point a cruel murderer, taking a dagger from his belt, stabbed the reclining bishop below the armpit. The bishop cried out so that the clerks who were present would come to his aid, but not one of the many who stood around helped him in any way. He stretched over the altar his hands that

dripped with blood, said prayers and gave thanks to God. On the
hands of the faithful he was carried to his cell and placed on his bed.

Fredegund came immediately, with Duke Beppolen and Ansovald,
and said to him: 'It is grievous to me and to the rest of your flock,
saintly priest, that this should have befallen you, and while you were
performing the office! Please let me know who has been guilty of such
a crime, that he may endure a terrible punishment for it.' Knowing
that she spoke deceitfully, the bishop replied: 'Who else would have
done this but the same person who murders kings, who often spills
innocent blood, and has committed all sorts of crimes in this kingdom?'
The woman answered: 'I have very skilled physicians who could cure
your wound. Allow them to come to you.' He replied: 'God has now
summoned me from this world, but you, who first plotted these
crimes, will be accursed forever, and God will avenge my blood upon
your head.' She departed, and the bishop breathed his last after
putting in order his worldly affairs.

Romachar, bishop of Coutances, came to preside over his funeral.
The citizens of Rouen, and particularly the leading Franks of the
place, were in shock. One of them went to see Fredegund and said:
'You have done many terrible things in this world, but nothing worse
than when you had the priest of God assassinated. Let God be prompt
to avenge innocent blood! All of us shall work to investigate this
murder, so that it may not be possible for you to do such cruel things
any more.' After he had spoken and left the presence of the queen,
she sent someone to invite him to stay and eat there. The Frank
refused, and the man insisted that if he did not want to eat there,
at least he must have something to drink, so as not to leave the royal
residence on an empty stomach. He waited and was handed a cup,
from which he drank wormwood mixed with wine and honey, as is
the custom of the barbarians. But this draught was mixed with
poison: as soon as he had drunk he felt a terrible pain in his chest, as
if he were being stabbed from within. He cried out to his men and
told them: 'Flee, unfortunates, escape from this evil, so that you may
not perish with me!' Without drinking, they hurried away. He, already
blind, jumped on his horse, but dropped dead when he had ridden
only three stadia from the palace.

After this, Bishop Leudovald sent letters to all prelates and, in
agreement with them, closed all the churches in Rouen, so that no holy
rites should be celebrated among that people until a general investigation [ms variant: general outrage] should lead to the discovery of
the murderer. He arrested a few persons and forced them by torture

to confess that the crime had been committed by order of Fredegund. She denied everything, however, so it was impossible to punish her. People said, indeed, that murderers had been sent against Leudovald, because he was investigating the case so shrewdly, but he was kept under such close custody by his men that they were unable to hurt him.

The narrative consists almost exclusively of scenes. There are four of them in all, beginning with the words 'Dum haec agerentur' (the initial quarrel), 'Advenientem autem' (the murder), 'Statimque Fredegundis' (the deathbed interview), and 'Ex quibus unus senior' (the second murder). There is very little authorial summary. Only two sentences between the third and fourth scenes, and the entire section at the end, which describes the consequences of the killings and begins with 'Post haec Leudovaldus episcopus,' provide the sort of generalized report that makes up the bulk of classical narrative. Here it has become a useful sort of connecting tissue between the scenic units. Gregory is one of the purest practitioners of the new manner, and though he is perfectly able to give in one paragraph a summary of the events of a whole year, he most often organizes his work as a series of scenes, casting into this form even episodes with very little dramatic content or none. In this sense, the murder of Praetextatus is far more homogeneously told than the fall of Servius. Livy distributes his scantier dramatic material with a calculated parsimony, deliberately grinding to a halt with a single great scene and adding as a bonus the vivid, partially dramatized moment in the Street of Crime, and in so doing displays an unrelaxing narratorial control over the unequal texture of his story. Gregory, on the other hand, seems almost unable to find an alternative to scenic form.

The first scene is a good instance of this apparent stylistic automatism: we are listening to a dispute between bishop and queen, which ends with the angry exit of Fredegund. It is a specific argument that took place on a given day, and in the course of which the bishop is supposed to have spoken the words that Gregory quotes. Nothing else is specific, neither place, gestures, actions, nor things, and there seems to be no good reason why the substance of Praetextatus' speech should not be summarized and communicated in indirect form, without this token evocation of its circumstances. Yet, unlike Tullia's speeches which, taken as a habitual performance, do not create a scene of any kind, the bishop's words, tied to a particular moment, form a minimal scenic unit. This homogeneity of the narrative text, and the fact that it allows Gregory to display little control of the form of the story, contributes to the self-effacing quality of the narrator's voice in the new style: the sense of choice, of strategy, the knowledge that the narrator can decide where to use his single scene, is absent here. An important consequence of this absence is that it becomes impossible to mark the critical point, the focus of an episode, by presenting it as a scene. The lack of any indication of what the narrator considers the central moment (since every moment is a scene here) makes for an opacity of representation that, as we shall see, is kept up in the detail of the story.

On the other hand, there is great variety in the use of speech. If Praetextatus' admonition in scene one is a rather stiff monologue, scene two, which could easily be the most significant segment of the story, proves that this sort of narrative can be eloquent and dramatic without dialogue. The bishop's murder is almost a pantomime, dependent for its overall effect on the early hour, the ritual setting, the reclining posture of the victim, the gesture of the murderer drawing his knife, the carefully located wound, the bishop's vain cries for help, his gesture of prayer, and the powerful image of his bloody hands over the altar. Though the scene is perfectly convincing and imaginable, its setting and the liturgical attitudes of Praetextatus bring in an element of hieratism and abstract significance which we have already met in Agnellus of Ravenna, in the passage where Archbishop George humiliates himself before Charles the Bald.

The next scene, however, in its final confrontation of the dying bishop with his murderess, is carried forward by an almost naturalistic use of dialogue. Praetextatus, as a prelate who must have preached numerous sermons and issued decrees and exhortations, is made to speak with some rhetorical formality. Fredegund's remarks, however, are those of a polite woman of the ruling class, and perfectly believable as spoken language: 'Sunt aput nos peritissimi medici, qui hunc vulnere medere possint. Permitte, ut accedant ad te.' / 'I have very skilled physicians who could cure your wound. Allow them to come to you.' Her silent refusal to take notice of the bishop's accusations, a refusal clearly expressed by the very irrelevance of her words, by the obvious fact that they in no way answer his, reveals that she has come to gloat, and perhaps to make sure he really does die. The drama of the situation is underscored by their implicit relative positions: Praetextatus lying 'in suo lectulo,' Fredegund standing by the side or at the foot of his bed.

The language used by the second victim, the 'senior Francorum' poisoned in the fourth scene, is also simple and unadorned. An unusual and rather puzzling aspect of this last action is the queen's minimal visibility on stage throughout. The spotlight remains fixed on the anonymous Frankish noble. This is the only scene in the episode that is focused on an object, the cup of poisoned mead offered as a token of hospitality, and introduced by Gregory with a curious ethnographic note.

The self-effacing quality of the narrator, which I have already mentioned, is most striking in the total absence of authorial moralizing. This murder is not an event which could have left Gregory unmoved. In book five he had told of his participation in the trial of Praetextatus, as one of the few churchmen there to take up his colleague's defence before King Chilperic. But the narrator is not only silent about the morality of these happenings; he is also unwilling to draw causal connections, to determine motives, to spell out the political implications of the murder and its investigation. Formally, this is at least in part a consequence of the lack of any summarizing, interpretive narrative between the three first scenes. The sequence acquires in this way a characteristic irrationality, the indistinct shape of an event witnessed recently and not yet understood; basic questions about it remain unanswered. For one thing, we might wonder whether the dispute described in scene one is the actual cause of the bishop's murder. Gregory has described in earlier books the enmity borne by Chilperic and his wife against the bishop of Rouen. Perhaps it is only this narrative style, so hostile to narratorial intervention, that keeps him from referring to such precedents, and accounting more convincingly for the final crime. As things stand, Praetextatus, who had been recalled from exile, and appeared to have found some sort of *modus vivendi* with his surviving enemy, would seem to owe his death only to the angry speech reproduced in the first scene of this episode. When modern historians describe the Merovingians as extraordinarily explosive and unrestrained people, and their bloodfeuds as slumbering volcanoes that now and then become unexpectedly active, they could perhaps be making a psychology of what is primarily a style of presentation.[8]

We also want to know why the wounded bishop was not helped, though surrounded by clerks and assistants; and we cannot help wondering whether the assassin was caught, and what happened to him, since it is not clear whether he was among the people arrested and tortured by Leudovald. We may guess that the queen comes to see the dying Praetextatus in order to experience a moment of triumph, for the dialogue between them is ironic and full of ambiguity, and yet Gregory does not add one line to clarify their intentions or their feelings. The second murder is so brutal and simplistic that we are tempted to give up our search for an acceptable motive: triggered exclusively by the reprimand of the 'senior Francorum,' this crime could be used as evidence to show that Praetextatus too was murdered on the impulse of a moment, and only for a few harsh words, and that there may be something to be said for the theory of the slumbering volcano. The crimes of Fredegund become unforgettably vivid, but there is no attempt to explain in general terms the moral character behind her actions as Livy explains the character of Tullia. Fredegund becomes a monster partly because she is not explained. The recklessness of the poisoning here is particularly enigmatic.

In classical narrative, speeches serve to provide both motives and ideology for what is going to happen: Tullia's exhortations show her obsessive comparison of herself to the dead Tanaquil, who had been able to bestow the throne on Servius, as well as the pride of the born Roman who cannot bear to be less than an Etruscan immigrant. Tarquin's speech before the senate lays out the claims of hereditary monarchy and seeks to tie Servius to the interests of the lower classes. There is not a trace of anything comparable in the speeches of Gregory's characters: their words are either limited to the immediate occasion (Fredegund's condolences), or as monolithic and impersonal as Praetextatus' first speech, which, even though it leads to his murder, contains neither reasoning nor disclosure of personal motives. 'In exile and out of exile, I was, am, and shall remain a bishop, but you will not always enjoy royal power': the words are incontrovertible but quite unenlightening. They place the speaker within a large public category but tell us nothing about the private feud between him and Fredegund. Praetextatus talks as a bishop, not an individual; he is assuming a role, a dignity, like Charles the Bald when he towers over George of Ravenna as embodied royalty. In both the initial dispute and the deathbed dialogue we recognize the influence of a scriptural and hagiographic type-scene: the confrontation of secular and spiritual authority, the angry prophet admonishing a ruler. In the second scene, on the other hand, the wounded prelate at the altar appears as both bishop and martyr.[9] These political and ecclesiastical abstractions merge with realistic detail such as the wound 'sub ascella' and the composition of the poisoned draught in a narrative language that conveys a largely uninterpreted reality.

On the basis of this comparison of classical and early medieval scenic technique, I find little reason to believe that the narrative style of Gregory, or of those who wrote like him, could be derived primarily from classical models. Scenes, the basic units of early medieval narrative, are infrequent in ancient historiography; when they occur, it is with a distinctive emphasis and intensity of purpose that sets them apart from the comparable forms of medieval writing.

SALLUST

In examining the possible classical sources of the new style, I have used Livy because, since his history contains some fully dramatized passages, he presents the strongest possible case for classical influence. We know, nevertheless, that Livy was not read or imitated often before the twelfth century. Historians writing before 1000 AD looked primarily to Sallust's mongraphs *The Conspiracy of Catiline* and *The War with Jugurtha* for their inspiration. A recent discussion of the medieval reception of Sallust provides a brief list of the tokens of his influence on later writers.[10] To begin with, we have innumerable verbal echoes, in some cases even entire speeches recycled, barely modified, and ascribed to medieval kings or warriors; then there is the declamation of set rhetorical pieces in public circumstances, the recourse to maxims and proverbs, the presence of moralizing comments unashamedly authorial, and a tendency to attribute the worst possible motives for the characters' behaviour. Any of these traits may suggest the possibility that Sallust has been used as model. Some of them, it will be noticed, are matters of prose style and not of narrative form, certainly the verbal echoes and taste for proverbial expressions; the others, and in particular the use of long set speeches and the ascription of low motives, may be considered aspects of the storyteller's craft. As such, they are often characteristic of Livy as of Sallust.

The main reason why a comparison of Sallust with early medieval narrative is less useful is that, unlike Livy, he has almost no scenes at all in my sense of the term. His entire work contains only one passage that I would identify as a scene. It occurs in chapter eleven of *The War with Jugurtha*; Micipsa, king of Numidia and father of the princes Adherbal and Hiempsal, has adopted his illegitimate nephew Jugurtha and given him a share in the succession.

> Micipsa paucis post diebus moritur. postquam illi more regio iusta magnifice fecerant, reguli in unum convenerunt, ut inter se de cunctis negotiis disceptarent. sed Hiempsal, qui minumus ex illis erat, natura ferox et iam antea ignobilitatem Iugurthae, quia materno genere inpar erat, despiciens, dextra Adherbalem adsedit, ne medius ex

tribus, quod apud Numidas honori ducitur, Iugurtha foret. dein tamen, ut aetati concederet, fatigatus a fratre, vix in partem alteram transductus est. ibi quom multa de administrando imperio dissererent, Iugurtha inter alias res iacit oportere quinquenni consulta et decreta omnia rescindi, nam per ea tempora confectum annis Micipsam parum animo valuisse. tum idem Hiempsal placere sibi respondit, nam ipsum illum tribus proxumis annis adoptatione in regnum pervenisse. quod verbum in pectus Iugurthae altius, quam quisquam ratus erat, descendit.

Micipsa died a few days later. After celebrating his funeral with the splendour due to a king, the princes met to discuss their affairs. Hiempsal, the youngest, was of harsh character and had earlier expressed disdain for Jugurtha, who came from an inferior line on his mother's side. He sat to the right of his brother Adherbal so that Jugurtha should not take the middle seat between them, which is considered a place of honour among the Numidians. Persuaded by his brother to yield his place to the older Jugurtha, he finally moved with bad grace to the other side. As they talked about various points of the administration of the realm, Jugurtha suggested among other things that the royal decrees and resolutions of the past five years should be abrogated, since Micipsa, owing to the weight of years, had not been in full control of his faculties in that period. Hiempsal replied that he agreed, for Jugurtha had been adopted and put in the line of sucession only three years before. These words cut deeper into Jugurtha's feelings than anyone realized at the time.

Here Hiempsal's actions in sitting and standing up become significant against a background of ceremonial positions explained by Sallust in ethnographic terms. Although the young prince's biting words are not given in direct form, they are quoted. Sallust does not summarize their import, but reproduces Hiempsal's actual reply, keeping the impact of his wit undiminished. This suggests that the formal difference between direct and indirect speech can be less important than we usually believe. It is not clear, however, why Sallust, in his highly elliptical, stylized account of the war in Numidia, chose to reproduce this particular scene in dramatic terms. The incident is not the cause of the war, and does not lead to Jugurtha's usurpation, since only two lines before this passage we have been told that in spite of pious promises at Micipsa's deathbed, Jugurtha 'longe aliter animo agitabat' / 'had long had other plans in his mind.' Though finely drawn, the scene is much

too exceptional to be of any use in our search for models. Its meaning
for Sallust, as the only full scene in his work, is insufficiently clear.

There are two other vivid moments which, although they do not add
up to full dramatic units, can be visualized well and explained by an
unusual sort of causal logic. Both occur in the *Bellum Iugurthinum*.
In the first, Nabdalsa, a traitor in the Numidian army, receives a secret
letter from his accomplice Bomilcar. The passage explains how this
message came to Jugurtha's hands:

> sed quom eae litterae adlatae, forte Nabdalsa exercito corpore fessus
> in lecto quiescebat, ubi cognitis Bomilcaris verbis primo cura, deinde,
> uti aegrum animum solet, somnus cepit. erat ei Numida quidam
> negotiorum curator, fidus acceptusque et omnium consiliorum nisi
> novissumi particeps. qui postquam adlatas litteras audivit et ex
> consuetudine ratus opera aut ingenio suo opus esse in tabernaculum
> introiit, dormiente illo epistulam super caput in pulvino temere
> positam sumit ac perlegit, dein propere cognitis insidiis ad regem pergit.
> Nabdalsa paulo post experrectus ubi neque epistulam repperit et rem
> omnem, uti acta erat, [ex perfugis] cognovit, primo indicem persequi
> conatus, postquam id frustra fuit, Iugurtham placandi gratia adcedit;
> dicit, quae ipse paravisset facere, perfidia clientis sui praeventa; lac-
> rumans obtestatur per amicitiam perque sua antea fideliter acta, ne
> super tali scelere suspectum sese haberet. [72] ad ea rex, aliter atque
> animo gerebat, placide respondit.   (71–2)

When the letter was delivered, Nabdalsa was reclining in bed, exhausted by physical exercise. On reading Bomilcar's words he was first
seized with panic; then, as often happens with an anxious mind, he
fell asleep. He had a Numidian secretary whom he trusted and who
was privy to all his secrets except these latest ones. The man heard that
a letter had arrived, and led by habit to imagine that his labour or
his advice were needed, went into the tent. There, while Nabdalsa
slept, he took up and read the letter his master had recklessly left
lying on his pillow, and as soon as he understood the treachery it
contained, he went to see the king. Nabdalsa woke up shortly thereafter, found the letter gone, and soon learned [from some deserters]
what had happened. He first tried to stop the witness, but when that
proved impossible he appeared before Jugurtha to placate him. He
said that the perfidy of his employee had forestalled what he had been
planning to do himself. In tears, he begged for the sake of their
friendship and his own earlier acts of fidelity not to be suspected of

such a crime. [72] The king, hiding his true state of mind, spoke mildly
to him.

The letter on Nabdalsa's pillow is a surprisingly specific detail in this
passage. The second episode takes place during the campaign of Marius
to capture the fortress that houses the Numidian king's treasury. Because of its location on a steep hillside accessible only by a narrow
path, the citadel seems impregnable and Marius begins to despair.

> quae quom multos dies noctisque aestuans agitaret, forte quidam Ligus,
> ex cohortibus auxiliariis miles gregarius, castris aquatum egressus
> haud procul ab latere castelli, quod avorsum proeliantibus erat, animum
> avortit inter saxa repentis cocleas, quarum quom unam atque alteram,
> dein plures peteret, studio legundi paulatim prope ad summum
> montis egressus est. ubi postquam solitudinem intellexit, more ingeni
> humani cupido difficilia faciundi animum ⟨alio⟩ vortit. et forte in
> eo loco grandis ilex coaluerat inter saxa, paulum modo prona, deinde
> inflexa atque aucta in altitudinem, quo cuncta gignentium natura
> fert. quoius ramis modo, modo eminentibus saxis nisus Ligus in castelli
> planitiem pervenit, quod cuncti Numidae intenti proeliantibus ader-
> ant. exploratis omnibus, quae mox usui fore ducebat, eadem regredi-
> tur, non temere, uti ascenderat, sed temptans omnia et circumspiciens.
> itaque Marium propere adit, acta edocet, hortatur, ab ea parte qua
> ipse ascenderat castellum temptet, pollicetur sese itineris periculique
> ducem.   (93)

When Marius had spent many days and nights in doubt about the
enterprise, it happened that a certain Ligurian, a private in the auxiliary
troops, left the camp to get some water. Not far from the camp, on
the side of the hill that looked away from the battle, he saw some
snails crawling among the rocks. He started picking them up one
by one, and, engaged in the task of collecting them, made his way
almost to the top of the hill. When he saw himself alone and unob-
served, the common human tendency to attempt something difficult
turned his mind to a new enterprise. A huge oak had grown there
among the rocks, leaning forward at first, then curving upward and
rising vertically to a great height, according to the nature of all
growing plants. Holding on to its branches and to the salient rocks on
the hillside, the Ligurian made his way up to the platform on which
the fortress stood, while all the Numidians were intent on the battle.
Having observed and taken note of everything that could be of use later

on, he went back as he had come, yet not heedlessly as before, but looking around him and checking every step of the way. He then went immediately to see Marius, explained what he had done, encouraged him to invade the castle using the approach he had discovered, and offered to guide him on the way and share its dangers with him.

Familiar as we are with the tendency of classical historians to suppress insignificant data, however colourful, we may ask ourselves what the point is of the letter removed while Nabdalsa sleeps, or of the Ligurian soldier's snail-hunt. Could these circumstances not be dismissed in a short phrase, or omitted entirely? Why does Sallust decide to show us Nabdalsa taking his nap, and the entire progress of the Ligurian up the side of the citadel? The answer would seem to be that both incidents had important consequences (the discovery of the letter made Jugurtha permanently suspicious and uneasy; the Ligurian's ascent of the wall led to the taking of the fortress), and that in both cases we are dealing with an unlikely conjunction of small circumstances and large effects: a soldier hunting for his lunch solves a problem that had baffled an illustrious general;[11] a sleepy courtier and a zealous bureaucrat betray a conspiracy by accident and alter the king's state of mind permanently. This is the logic of Ripley's facts and of many 'miscellaneous' items in the daily papers: a fire caused by spectacles left in the sun; a railway accident brought about by children flattening coins on the rails. The connection is preposterous, surprising; the causes seem much too small for such effects.[12] This is an unusual application of dramatic narrative, and it seems to be specifically Sallustian, but we do not find it in the works of the historian's medieval imitators.

Here and there, too, an isolated but sharply characterized scenic element appears, such as the room in which Catiline's fellow conspirators are executed:

> est in carcere locus, quod Tullianum appellatur, ubi paululum ascenderis ad laevam, circiter duodecim pedes humi depressus; eum muniunt undique parietes atque insuper camera lapideis fornicibus iuncta; sed incultu tenebris odore foeda atque terribilis eius facies est.
>
> (*Catilinae coniuratio* 55)

In the prison there is a dungeon known as the Tullianum, to which one comes after a short ascent to the left; built approximately twelve feet below the ground, it is protected all around by walls, and above

> by vaults of stone. It is squalid, dark, and filled with stench, and
> its appearance is frightening.

The perfect setting for an execution scene; but Sallust chooses to tell
us only that 'in eum locum postquam demissus est Lentulus, vindices
rerum capitalium, quibus praeceptum erat, laqueo gulam fregere' / 'After Lentulus had been taken down to that place, the executioners strangled him with a noose, as they had been ordered to do.'

AUERBACH AND EARLY MEDIEVAL NARRATIVE

Having considered these few dramatic passages of Sallust's work, we
have exhausted the case that can be made for his narrative as a model
for the new medieval manner, and we must agree that it is extremely
weak. On the other hand, his influence on medieval prose is overwhelming, particularly in historiography. Writers such as Gregory of
Tours, pure cultivators of narrative as a chain of scenes, quote Sallust
and obviously regard him as a prestigious, if not especially congenial,
model.[13] Other historians, however, such as Widukind of Corvey, can
combine the new manner with consistent imitation of the Roman
author. In his *Res gestae Saxonicae* Widukind has both the Sallustian
set speeches, phrasing, and verbal echoes, and the scenic structure,
direct speech, gestural staging, props and symbols of the medieval style.[14]
The fact that it is possible to imitate Sallust's lapidary and archaizing
prose while writing dramatic narrative confirms an important point
made briefly a few pages ago: prose style and narrative must be studied
separately, not as unconnected elements, but as discrete factors that
overlap only in certain respects.

The most influential modern analysis of early medieval narrative
technique is Erich Auerbach's study, in chapter four of *Mimesis*, of
Gregory of Tours' story of Sichar and Chramnesind.[15] The new elements of literary storytelling are outlined and interpreted there with
erudition and uncommon sensitivity. Auerbach, however, analyses
Gregory's prose and his narrative simultaneously, passing from the
indistinct use of Latin prepositions and the frequency of anacoluthon
to the division of the action into a succession of small scenes, and the
realistic use of direct speech. He finds the story extraordinarily vivid,
but incoherent and occasionally incomprehensible; the darkness of the
narrative he connects with the decline of classical syntax.[16] The argument is very persuasive and has had lasting influence; parataxis and

incoherent narrative appear yoked in the few investigations of early medieval narrative written after *Mimesis*.[17] The limited character of Sallust's influence suggests that the two aspects need not be coupled, since his imitators are able to borrow his language without taking over his narrative method.

Texts such as the murder of Praetextatus, or the passage in the *Liber historiae Francorum* where Fredegund takes her husband for her lover, for all their awkward language, convey a clear, comprehensible sequence of events. The gaps and omissions that I have pointed out in Gregory of Tours' narrative are possibly a matter of authorial choice; they in no way make the episode less coherent, but merely allow us to imagine it without explaining or interpreting the facts.

Auerbach's connection of shaky syntax and obscure narrative is based in good measure on the particular passage that he chose to analyse, one that had been discussed before, quite passionately, by two eminent historians of opposing views, and thus acquired a certain celebrity.[18] The story of Sichar and Chramnesind is an unusually confusing page of Gregory's book, one of those serial, escalating feuds of Germanic society that baffle us at times even in the lucid prose of the Icelandic sagas. It assumes knowledge of legal and genealogical facts that have not come down to us, which explains why specialists in Merovingian law and history had already paid so much attention to it. I would say with little hesitation that, by Gregory's standards and in spite of some unforgettable dramatic touches, it is a poorly told episode; the narrator even brings new characters into the fray without introducing them or explaining their relation to the ones we already know. It is also noticeable that Auerbach confines his analysis to the most confusing part of the story, the account of the origin and growth of the feud in book seven. The description of its bloody aftermath in book nine, which is crystal clear and shows the new narrative manner at its best, gets very little attention from him.

A LATE ANTIQUE MODEL?

In the discussion of the possible sources of early medieval narrative style we must give separate consideration to the influence that late antiquity and Christian literature may have had on the first medieval forms. It has been pointed out recently that the historiography of the late empire, and the work of Ammianus Marcellinus in particular, shows a pronounced tendency towards the anecdote and the sketching out of lively but not very relevant episodes, so that the classical distinction between historical discourse and antiquarian biography or memoir becomes a thing of the past, a discrimination no longer possible.[19] An evolution of that sort might conceivably have led to the medieval style we are studying here, which seems so new in the pages of Gregory of Tours and of Agnellus.

A reading of Ammianus in the light of early medieval historiography shows fewer common features than have been suggested by recent research, but also important similarities that have gone unnoticed. When Klaus Rosen, describing Ammianus' narrative style, tells us that 'historical events are a succession of scenes, and the historian is the eyewitness reporter,'[20] we should remember that the scenes he is talking about are not dramatic representations of transactions between individuals, which remain rare in the *Res gestae*, but tableaux of battles, sieges, marches, and imperial pageants, the familiar 'reality' of classical history, here presented with Ammianus' characteristic taste for exaggeration and grotesque detail. This paucity of scenes of the new sort is perhaps the reason that J. Vogt, who has stressed the novelty of Ammianus' style, refers pointedly to the story of a dignitary of the Eastern empire who defected to the Persians because his wife had been captured by their king (xviii.10 and xix. 9).[21] The incident seems to be entirely centred on the fate of the couple, and it is told in some detail, though without a single dramatic speech. However, the defection of Craugasius is not, as Vogt suggests, told for its own sake; Craugasius' action was encouraged by the Persian king because he thought it would allow him to capture Nisibis, the city of which the Roman was a standing official and which he had to abandon in order to rejoin his wife. In other words, the episode has reasons and consequences that tie it to the course of the war; though it is told at unusual length, it cannot be called gratuitous. As sole dramatic configuration, there is the moment when the Persians burst into the fortress where Craugasius' wife has taken refuge. The Persian king finds out the identity of her husband (though his questions on the subject are left out entirely), allows her to approach him in order to allay her fears ('uim in se metuentem prope uenire permisit intrepidam'), and has her covered with a long black veil as a sign that her virtue will be respected ('et uisam opertamque ad usque labra ipsa atro uelamine certiore iam spe mariti recipiendi et pudoris inuiolati mansuri benignius confirmauit'). All that can be said about Ammianus on the basis of this story is that he gives a much fuller account of episodes tangentially connected to the main action than a classical historian might have found necessary. We can imagine Sallust's version of the story of Craugasius: 'He de-

serted, crossing the Tigris to rejoin his wife, who had fallen into the
hands of the Persians.' The medieval attempt to visualize the action
and represent it dramatically hardly finds a precursor in the author of
this narrative, though the veiling of the lady does focus the scene
effectively on a symbolic object.

More interesting, in view of early medieval developments, is Ammianus' willingness to introduce arbitrary and irrational elements in
the description of his own experience. These are particularly noticeable
in accounts of his travels in time of war, where the luck of the road
often confronts him with wholly unexpected spectacles that cannot be
reduced to the logic of the episode as a whole. While riding from Nisibis
to Mount Izala in the retinue of his master Ursicinus, he comes upon
an abandoned child:

> qua causa ne occuparentur itinera, celeri cursu praegressi cum ad
> secundum lapidem uenissemus, liberalis formae puerum torquatum,
> ut coniectabamus, octennem in aggeris medio uidimus heiulantem,
> ingenui cuiusdam filium, ut aiebat; quem mater, dum imminentium
> hostium terrore percita fugeret, impeditior trepidando reliquerat solum.
>
> (xviii.6,10)

> On that account, fearing that the roads might be blocked, we marched
> on rapidly and, as we reached the second milestone from the city,
> came upon a handsome boy wearing a necklace, eight years old, as
> we thought, who stood crying in the middle of the road and declared
> himself to be the son of a gentleman; his mother, as she fled shaken
> by fear of the advancing enemy, had abandoned him in her agitation
> and terror.

Ammianus was ordered to take the boy back to the city, and it is not
surprising if the incident stuck in his mind. The episode is, however,
irrelevant to the history of the campaign in Mesopotamia and, even
more important, the boy is first described as he appears crying on the
road, with only a minimal attempt later to account for his presence
there. His necklace, his cries, even his good looks affect us as irrational
because they are displaced and do not connect with anything else in
the narrative. At other times, nevertheless, explanation not only precedes but even replaces description. While escaping on foot from Amida
after its capture by the Persians, Ammianus comes upon a horse dragging a dead man over the ground:

in qua statione leuius recreati cum ire protinus pergeremus et incedendi nimietate iam superarer ut insuetus ingenuus, offendi dirum aspectum, sed fatigato mihi lassitudine graui leuamen impendio tempestiuum. fugaci equo nudo et infreni calonum quidam sedens, ne labi possit, ex more habenam, qua ductabatur, sinistra manu artius illigauit moxque decussus uinculi nodum abrumpere nequiens per auia saltusque membratim discerptus iumentum exhaustum cursu pondere cadaueris detinebat, cuius dorsuali comprensi seruitio usus in tempore cum isdem sociis ad fontes sulphureos aquarum suapte natura calentium aegre perueni.   (xix.8,6–8)

Having rested a little at the post-station, we had started to march ahead, and I was already defeated by the effort of walking, to which as a man of rank I was not used, when I came upon a hideous sight which nevertheless brought me timely relief, undone as I was by fatigue and excessive effort. Some army servant, riding a runaway horse without saddle or bit, had tightly fastened the rein by which, as is usual, the horse was guided, around his left hand so as not to fall off, but then, thrown off soon afterwards and unable to untie the knot, he was torn limb from limb over rough country and through the woods, at the same time that the exhausted animal was held back by the weight of his corpse. I caught it, and availing myself opportunely of the use of its back, arrived with some difficulty and in the company of the same comrades at a source of sulphureous waters that were naturally hot.

Here the grisly encounter with the horse and the remains of its first rider is eclipsed by two explanatory schemes: how the fatigued narrator got himself a mount (the solution of a practical problem), and by what accident the horse came to kill its master (the reasons for an unpleasant sight that is assumed and never shown).

Another episode from Ammianus' own experience constitutes a scene of the kind we are familiar with in early medieval histories, and provides an impressive anticipation of a later style. Fighting with a Persian force on the way to Samosata, Ursicinus comes across a former officer of the household troops of the Roman governor of Mesopotamia who, pressed by debt, has gone over to the enemy.

denique ex ultima necessitate manibus iam conserendis, cum, quid agi oporteat, cunctaremur, occiduntur quidam nostrorum temere pro-

cursantes et urgente utraque parte Antoninus ambitiosius praegre-
diens agmen ab Vrsicino agnitus et obiurgatorio sonu uocis increpitus
proditorque et nefarius appellatus sublata tiara, quam capiti summo
ferebat honoris insigne, desiluit equo curuatisque membris humum
uultu paene contingens salutauit patronum appellans et dominum
manus post terga connectens, quod apud Assyrios supplicis indicat
formam, et 'ignosce mihi', inquit, 'amplissime comes, necessitate,
non uoluntate ad haec, quae noui, scelesta prolapso. egere me prae-
cipitem iniqui flagitatores, ut nosti, quorum auaritiae ne tua quidem
excelsa illa fortuna propugnans miseriis meis potuit refragari.' simul
haec dicens e medio prospectu abscessit non auersus, sed, dum eu-
anesceret, uerecunde retrogradiens et pectus ostentans.   (xviii.8,5–6)

At length, while we were faced with the absolute necessity of joining
battle, and delayed by deliberation as to what we should do, some
of our men, who had rashly pressed forward, were killed. As both sides
advanced, Antoninus, who was boastfully leading his troops, was
recognized by Ursicinus, who addressed him in a voice full of reproof
and called him a traitor and a scoundrel. Antoninus then removed
the diadem that he wore on his head as a sign of high rank, alighted
from his horse, and bowing down so that his face almost touched the
ground, he greeted Ursicinus calling him patron and lord and clasping
his hands behind his back, which among the Assyrians is a posture
of entreaty. He said: 'Forgive me, most generous lord, for it was need
and not my own will that drove me to this course of action, which
I knew to be a crime. As you are aware, I was forced to flee by immoral
creditors, against whose greed even your great fortune, which protected my wretchedness, could not avail.' When he had said this, he
withdrew from [our] sight, not turning his back, but humbly walking
backwards and presenting his breast [to us] until he disappeared.

For a moment, the Roman and Persian troops became a mere backdrop
for the meeting of two men, a loyal Roman and a traitor. Their dealings
begin with the loud invective of Ursicinus and lead, through the unexpected self-abasement of Antoninus, expressed with a wealth of gestures and ceremonial attitudes, to an explanation and apology in direct
speech that casts a new light on the traitor and makes him appear less
contemptible than before. Paradoxically, he humbles himself with the
manners of his new people, and shows that he remains a Roman at
heart by giving clear evidence that he is becoming an assimilated Persian. The scene closes with a gestural note ('pectus ostentans') that

underscores its unity of dramatic conception. Ammianus appears here, exceptionally, as the forerunner of writers such as Agnellus and Notker Balbulus, whose use of ceremonial poses and gesticulation gives a distinctive monumental quality to their narratives. Certainly, they would not have read Ammianus, who had no influence on early medieval historiography. But we may nonetheless consider him representative of a tendency towards the ritual dramatization of personal transactions that, as we shall see, was also characteristic of public life and of the visual arts in late antiquity, and that had far-reaching consequences for later narrative. We must remember, however, that other early medieval writers, such as Gregory of Tours and his continuators, display comparatively little interest in this ceremonial staging of human behaviour, and are capable of turning the most trivial and modest incidents into effective sequences of scenes without a touch of formal solemnity.

The generality and dryness of most late antique narrative is particularly pronounced in the Christian historians. While Eusebius of Caesarea, in his *History of the Church*, produces an intellectual chronicle populated by heresies and books rather than human characters, Orosius, in his *History against the Pagans*, remains in every way a moralizing orator. The former gives us the history of an institution and its doctrine, avoiding wherever possible individual lives and experiences but including transcripts of church documents and pertinent authors; the latter puts together a glorified check-list of the catastrophes that overcame humanity, and the Roman world in particular, before the triumph of Christianity under Constantine. Anecdotes are almost entirely absent, scenes few and done in the abstract manner of classical historiography. Representative of these very rare attempts at dramatic narrative is the following incident from the fifth book of Orosius' history, an episode of the first civil war, after a battle between the forces of Marius and Pompey.

> postera die cum permixtim corpora ad sepulturam discernerentur, miles Pompeianus fratris sui, quem ipse interfecerat, corpus adgnouit: in concursu enim utrique cognitionem uultus galea, considerationem furor ademerat; quamuis parum sit culpae circa ignorantiam, ut uideatur nescisse de fratre quem non ambigitur scisse de ciue. itaque uictor uicto infelicior, ubi et fratris corpus agnouit et parricidium suum, exsecratus bella ciuilia ilico pectus suum gladio transuerberans simulque lacrimas et sanguinem fundens super fraternum sese cadauer abiecit.   (v.19.12–13)

The following day, as the scattered corpses were being sorted out to be buried, a soldier on Pompey's side recognized the body of his brother, whom he himself had killed. In the rush of battle, the helmets covering their faces had prevented recognition on either side, and fury had blocked consideration. His ignorance takes away most of his guilt, for he had failed to identify him as his brother, though he certainly recognized him as a fellow citizen. The victor here turned out to be more wretched than the vanquished once he became aware of his brother's body and his own fratricide. Cursing civil wars, he immediately buried a sword in his breast, and shedding tears and blood at the same time, flung himself on his brother's corpse.

The technique is reminiscent of Livy, but a flat and colourless didacticism has replaced the Roman historian's varied range of dramatic devices. Although the episode is flooded with moralistic considerations, we are not allowed to hear the words with which the soldier himself cursed civil wars. His gestures are rendered obliquely, only through their aims or results, and often obscured by rhetorical ornaments ('shedding tears and blood at the same time') and by purely conceptual elements such as the parallel that balances 'cognitionem' and 'considerationem.' It is clear enough that the story is there only as an illustration of the horrors of war, true to the exemplary purpose of classical historical narrative.

A look at the biographical literature of the period is more rewarding, and it reveals the ways in which this genre was beginning to merge with historiography. The pagan imperial biographies of the *Historia Augusta* are still in the tradition of Suetonius and the *species*, an analytic, non-chronological scheme of each emperor's personality and government, the abstract categories of which are illustrated by specific details and events of his life. Christian productions, the lives of the early saints and desert fathers, on the other hand, display a strong interest in dramatic narrative. The tendency is not general: Pontius' life of Cyprian and Possidius' biography of Augustine are wholly discursive and rhetorical, long sermons using biographical incidents as their text. In his *Life of Saint Martin* and his *Dialogues*, Sulpicius Severus gives many examples of the tendency, already observed in the work of Ammianus, to animate a scene by focusing on ceremonial attitudes and conventional gestures. Thus, in chapter twenty of the *Life*, Martin of Tours, at a banquet in the palace of the usurper Maximus, drinks from a cup of wine and hands it to his attendant priest and not to his host, as he had been expected to do. And in the *Dialogues* the emperor Valentinian, who refuses to stand up before the saint, is forced to do so when his throne begins to burn (11.5), and Maximus' wife insists on serving Martin at table, like the humblest of servants (11.6).

The most surprisingly vivid and novelistic storytelling of the period is to be found in Jerome's short *Vitae patrum*, the lives of the hermits Paul of Thebes, Hilarion of Gaza, and Malchus which Jerome wrote as a preliminary exercise for a larger historical work that never saw the light. The following passage from the *vita* of Hilarion is a good instance of Jerome's originality. In it, the hermit addresses a demon who has entered a young woman by virtue of a love-charm placed under her door by a 'vicinus iuvenis.'

> 4. Illico insanire virgo et amictu capitis abiecto rotare crinem, stridere dentibus, inclamare nomen adulescentis; magnitudo quippe amoris se in furorem verterat. 5. Perducta ergo a parentibus ad monasterium seni traditur, ululante statim et confitente daemone: 'Vim sustinui, invitus abductus sum; quam bene Memphi somniis homines delude-bam! 6. O cruces, o tormenta, quae patior! Exire me cogis et ligatus subter limen teneor. Non exeo nisi me adulescens, qui tenet, dimiserit'. 7. Tunc senex: 'Grandis', ait, 'fortitudo tua, qui licio et lamina strictus teneris. Dic, cur ausus es ingredi puellam Dei?' 'Ut servarem', inquit, 'eam virginem'. 8. 'Tu servares, proditor castitatis? Cur non potius in eum, qui te mittebat, es ingressus?'. 9. 'Ut quid', respondit, 'intrarem in eum, qui habebat collegam meum amoris daemonem?'   (12.4–9)

> 4. Immediately the maiden began to rage; casting down the mantle that covered her head, she flung her hair about, gnashed her teeth, and cried out the name of the young man. The intensity of her love had turned to madness. 5. Her parents therefore took her to the mon-astery and handed her to the old man [Hilarion]. Right away, the demon began to howl and make himself known: 'I am enduring viol-ence; I have been brought here against my will. How well I was in Memphis, deluding men with dreams! 6. Oh what torture, what suf-ferings I endure! You force me to come out, and I am held in bonds under the threshold. I will not come out until the young man who keeps me tied there releases me.' 7. The old man then said: 'Your strength must be great indeed if you can be bound by a thread and a metal plate. Tell me, how did you dare come into a maiden consecrated to God?' 'So that I might preserve her virginity,' said the demon. 8. 'You would have kept her a virgin, you betrayer of chastity? Why

didn't you rather go into the man who was sending you to her?'
9. And the demon replied: 'Why should I have gone into him, when
he was already in the power of my colleague, the demon of love?'

The dialogue is animated and natural. The demon's comical lamentations and the ironic questions of Hilarion have a varied, changing
range of tones, as in a real conversation. The gestures of the possessed
woman are carefully described, and the charm, though it remains hidden, ties the motivation of the entire episode to one inanimate and
central object. Instead of concentrating on the ritual of the exorcism,
Jerome makes the dramatic movement of the scene light and informal,
omitting the hieratic ceremonial elements that characterize Ammianus and Sulpicius Severus.

The idea that early medieval developments in narrative technique
have their roots in the literature of late antiquity is appealing and
plausible, but it seems difficult to establish precise connections between writers of the two periods, even when their works show striking
similarities. An author such as Ammianus Marcellinus can be considered to illustrate a new direction in fourth-century literature that emerges
again with particular force several centuries later. But he was not read
by Agnellus and Notker, who must have derived their interest in ceremony from other sources, though Ammianus may be allowed to stand
as an early representative of the same stylistic current. Works such as
Jerome's *Vitae patrum*, which dramatize action as vividly as any of
the Merovingian histories, are known to be based on a tradition closely
related to that of the *Apophthegmata patrum*, the oral record of Egyp-
tian and Syrian asceticism, and it is likely that they owe their dramatic
traits to this source, and not to any properly literary development of
late antiquity.[22]

THE GOSPEL AS MODEL

A very likely source of the stylistic innovations we are discussing is
Scripture. Our early medieval historians were all in orders, and medieval education, until the twelfth century, was by and for the church
for the most part. Before Charlemagne, however, the cultural depres-
sion of Western Europe was so great that familiarity with the Bible,
even among the clergy, can easily be overrated.[23] There were two texts,
nevertheless, that all churchmen were required to know in order to
fulfil their duties in the liturgy: the psalter and the gospels.

The gospel narrative of the life of Christ shows every one of the
features that characterize the new narrative technique found in early

medieval historiography; it shows them, indeed, in a purer and more exclusive form, with less admixture of rhetoric and literary elaboration. If we consider but briefly the larger aspects of narrative procedure, we are struck first of all by the complete absence of authorial comments: no evangelist ever stops to tell us that Christ was good, or that his miracles were extraordinary. The rhetoric of the story is to be found in the actions it describes; the polemic against the Jews, for example, is carried out only in the acts and words ascribed to their leaders, and in the responses of Christ and the apostles. The fragmentation of the story into discrete scenic units or apophthegms unconnected by any tissue of general remarks is even more total and abrupt here than in any of our early medieval texts. The scenic units begin again and again with the same formulas and time-markers, though there is some variation from gospel to gospel. In the Vulgate version, Mark begins his scenes with 'et' plus indicative, 'et factum est' plus indicative; Matthew uses 'tunc' plus indicative, 'cum' plus subjunctive, 'cum autem' plus subjunctive, and sometimes an ablative absolute, while Luke frequently starts with 'factum est (autem)' plus subjunctive.

Though here and there, particularly in Luke and John, Christ preaches whole sermons, the overwhelming majority of the speeches are short and functional; direct speech is the rule, with very few exceptions. It is worth emphasizing that some of the most important utterances of Jesus are single sentences, brief orders, and exclamations, a few of which are even quoted in Aramaic: 'Talitha cum' to the daughter of Jairus, followed by a translation (Mark 5:42), or his last words on the cross. There is a new sense of the power of direct quotation at work here, an awareness that the force of spoken words is not tied to declamatory solemnity.

Emotions and moral qualities are often expressed by gestures: turning the other cheek, shaking the dust off one's feet, untying the strap of Christ's sandal. However, gesture is used most often to focus the action around which a scene revolves; it is at the critical moment of a given episode that a sick woman touches the hem of Christ's robe, Jesus writes with his finger in the dust or hands Judas a crust of bread, Judas kisses his lord, or Pilate washes his hands in public. The gestural staging of the healing miracles is particularly stable and familiar: the struggling and crying out of the possessed, and Christ's laying on of hands or simple touching of their bodies. Sometimes there is more than that:

32 et adducunt ei surdum et mutum
    et deprecantur eum ut inponat illi manum

33 et adprehendens eum de turba seorsum
    misit digitos suos in auriculas
    et expuens tetigit linguam eius
34 et suspiciens in caelum ingemuit et ait illi
    eppheta quod est adaperire   (Mark 7:32–4)

32. And they bring to him one deaf and dumb; and they besought
him that he would lay his hands upon him. 33. And taking him from
the multitude apart, he put his fingers into his ears, and spitting,
he touched his tongue. 34. And looking up to heaven he groaned, and
said to him: *Ephpheta*, which is, Be thou opened.   (Douay Bible)

It is not just the movements of the characters that are central to the
conception of the scene, but their postures and positions too: the beloved disciple sits reclining on Christ's breast at the Last Supper, the
woman with the jar of ointment kneels at his feet, the sick protagonists
of the healing miracles lie prone before him, while the sons of Zebedee
ask to be allowed to sit at his right and left; at the crucifixion, the
condemned thieves hang on either side of him.

Equally striking and frequent is the use of things as the dramatic
focus of narrative units. Generally they are the objects of an action
summarized in a single gesture: Christ shows the denarius to the men
sent by the Pharisees, hands out the loaves and fishes, breaks bread
and shares out the wine at the Last Supper; the high priest of the Jews
tears his robe in indignation at Christ's words. The very language of
the gospel is saturated with the symbolism of things: the cornerstone,
the lamps of the wise and foolish virgins, an old coat and a new, wine
and old skins, a light under a bushel. The trait is not only a dramatic
function, but belongs also to the rhetoric of the text; it pervades Christ's
parables as well as such non-didactic utterances as 'Take this cup away
from me.' The dramatic role of objects is, however, fundamental, especially in the gospel of Mark, which displays the simplest, most radical version of this narrative manner. In Mark the object need not be
symbolic to become the vivid centre of a moment in the story. Between
the arrest of Jesus and his appearance before the high priest, the following minimal anecdote takes shape around the fate of the protagonist's cloak:

51 Adulescens autem quidam sequebatur illum amictus
    sindone super nudo
    et tenuerunt eum

52 at ille reiecta sindone nudus profugit ab eis   (Mark 14:51–2)

51. And a certain young man followed him, having a linen cloth cast
about his naked body; and they laid hold of him. 52. But he, casting
off the linen cloth, fled from them naked.   (Douay Bible)

A more complex effect involving clothes, remotely akin to the appearance of Charles the Bald in symbolic regalia in the pages of Agnellus, is to be found in the scene where Christ is dressed as king of
the Jews by his executioners. Even though the sense of parody and
ritual inversion present in the gospel narrative has no place in the *Liber
pontificalis*, both episodes make dramatic use of ceremony and treat
garments, royal or not, as more than mere accessories.

CHARACTERISTICS OF ORAL-TRADITIONAL NARRATIVE

This would seem, then, a simple, logical solution to the problem of
sources and models: the clergy of the period knew the gospel, quite
often by heart, and they made use of its simple and effective form to
tell the history of their own times, the legends of their saints, and the
lives of their temporal and spiritual rulers. But this explanation, for a
number of reasons, is too narrow to be fully satisfactory. In the first
place, it is obvious that many episodes of early medieval historical
narrative have nothing in common, either in subject matter or in tone,
with the gospels. Incidents of murder and adultery are told, nevertheless, in a manner that can come very close to that of the evangelists.
To take the gospels as the direct source of the new narrative style
would require the hypothesis of a long, undocumented period of elaboration in the course of which the style of the gospels became available
for every kind of narrative purpose. But there is a second and more
serious objection: the specific traits we are discussing here are not only
found in scripture, but are in fact typical of all oral prose narrative. By
'oral prose' I mean prose of oral origin, whether or not it has known a
written stage later and undergone some adaptation to literary standards.
If the text remains fundamentally faithful to oral form, we shall find
in it discontinuity, brief dramatic units, frequent and realistic use
of direct speech, gestures, and significant objects as the focus of the
scenes. Rather than document the various points of this description one
by one, I will consider here three samples of oral narrative, of very diverse origins: an anecdote about St Anthony from the fourth-century
Apophthegmata patrum,[24] a Hasidic story collected in the United States
in the 1960s with an obviously brief existence in tradition,[25] and a

passage from one of the taped stories of the Moroccan raconteur Mohammed Mrabet, from the collection *Harmless Poisons, Blameless
Sins*, published in 1976.[26]

> A hunter in the desert saw Abba Anthony amusing himself with the
> brethren. Wanting to satisfy him that it was necessary sometimes
> to condescend to the brethren, the old man said to him, 'Put an arrow
> in your bow and bend it [the bow].' So he did. The old man then said,
> 'Bend it further,' and he did so. Then the old man said, 'Further,'
> and the hunter replied 'If I bend my bow beyond measure I will break
> it.' Then the old man said to him, 'It is the same with the work of
> God. If we bend the brethren beyond measure they will soon break.
> Sometimes it is necessary to come down to meet their needs.' When
> he heard these words, the hunter was pierced by compunction and,
> greatly edified by the old man, he went away. And the brethren,
> strengthened, went back to their own place.

> The Rebbe had to travel from Haifa to Jerusalem during the war in
> order to make papers to come to America. F. wanted to come along
> and the Rebbe said that it was too dangerous. However, after the
> liberation[27] the Rebbe leaned his head in his arms on the doorpost and
> said, 'You can come if you will lie on the floor of the taxi.'
> The whole way the Rebbe didn't say anything and the road was
> full of shooting. Then the Rebbe asked F. to sit up, and pointed to an
> Arab on the hill who was aiming directly at their car. The Rebbe
> said, 'He wants to shoot but he can't.' He stood there frozen and was
> unable to shoot.

> As a boy Hadidan Aharam lived in the country with his parents. His
> father owned a very large farm with many miles of wheatfields.
> When he was fourteen he ran away to live in the nearest town, but
> he often came back to visit his family. One day he returned and
> found his father working in the field with the peasants. When the old
> man looked up and saw him, he merely said: Ah, there you are, my
> son. Tell your mother to kill the biggest white hen, will you?
> Hadidan Aharam turned and set off for the house. As he went he
> was thinking of his father. He hasn't seen me for two months and he
> doesn't get up to greet me, he said to himself. He walked more slowly,
> pulled out his kif pipe, and began to smoke. A hen, he thought angrily.
> He passed a herd of cows and stood looking at them for a time.
> When he got to the house his mother ran to him and kissed him.
> Have you seen your father? she said.

> I just saw him, Hadidan Aharam told her. He said to tell you to
> have the men kill the biggest white cow.

Among the salient features common to all three texts is the presence
of direct speech, realistic and close to everyday usage, neither formal
nor purely declarative in purpose. Most often the speeches are inseparable from the action; they are commands ('Bend it further' in
the apophthegm; 'you can come if you will lie on the floor of the
taxi,' phrased conditionally in the Hasidic story; 'Tell your mother
to kill the biggest white hen, will you?' in Mrabet's story) or questions ('Have you seen your father?'). Hadidan's thoughts are presented throughout as direct speech. Speeches are among the things
that *happen* in these stories; events as much as words, they allow
the plot to unfold.

Gestures are central in every case, whether omitted and yet decisive,
as when Hadidan's father does not get up to greet him, implicit, like
the actual bending of the bow by the hunter or the frozen aim of the
Arab soldier, or expressive and carefully described, like the Rebbe leaning his head against his arms, perhaps bracing himself for the trip, or
deciding to run a certain risk. This variety must not blind us to the
sheer frequency and functional importance of gestural elements.

Objects are also significant: the bow in the first story, the gun we
assume the Arab to be holding in the second, Hadidan's kif pipe in the
third, all are essential props. The bow is treated as a simile and placed
at the very centre of the episode; the pipe works as a symbol of Hadidan's malice, independence, and anger, all attributes of the kif smoker
in Mrabet's world; the gun is simply an instrument.

Time and place are indefinite in Mrabet's narrative, while the two
religious stories make claims to some historical accuracy, though without describing the stage of the incident or fixing the moment at which
it took place. This vagueness constitutes the most important difference
between the style of early medieval historiography and that of oral
storytelling; the basic claims of historiography suffice to explain the
relatively greater precision of medieval authors in matters of setting
and time.

The distinctive traits of the oral style result from the conditions
under which oral prose narrative is produced. The oral storyteller must
take account of two sorts of difficulty: that which he may experience
in generating and sustaining a narrative sequence, and that which his
public may have following him or keeping their attention on his words.
Unlike the classical historian, the oral narrator tries to become transparent, to vanish from the scene or from his listener's awareness; by

appealing primarily to their dramatic imagination, he invites them to follow an action that does not include him as judge, critic, or interpreter. His audience is illiterate, indifferent to rhetorical display, and that is just as well, because by performing brilliantly according to the literary norm he would only call attention to himself and underscore his constant presence and manipulation of the narrative. For his listeners, this personal involvement of the narrator would soon become an element of monotony and the possible cause of distraction.

All this is not to say, however, that the oral storyteller's public does not have standards of its own: it appreciates vivid imagery and dramatic recital, the narrator's power to make his audience transcend the moment of performance. Between the powerful single images, gestures, and dialogues that constitute the scenes, and that give him an opportunity to mime and act out his story, he cannot weave the tissue of logical and rhetorical continuity typical of literary narrative. Easily bored and confused, his public needs numerous new beginnings, a breaking up of the action, comic-strip-wise, into many short, discrete chapters, each with one dramatic element or more as its focus. The constraints of performance also favour the simple linear addition of narrative units. The narrator can rarely, for example, place a small episode within a larger one, an elementary procedure in literary storytelling (for example, flashbacks, simultaneous narratives) because it is a strain on his memory and control of the plot to have to go back and finish the longer sequence after he has closed the smaller one. Even if he feels equal to the task, his audience may lose the thread and, in any case, fail to appreciate his effort.

The fact that at least fifteen centuries yawn between the apophthegm of St Anthony and the Hasidic story demonstrates the extraordinary stability of oral narrative style. This brings us back to a point of the introduction: if I can discuss the new features of early medieval narrative as if they had not evolved in the course of five centuries, it is because they are taken from this unchanging model, because their source is a traditional form unaffected by literary fashions. The only developments and individual variations that the style undergoes among the various early medieval writers who use it are determined by their readiness and ability to combine literary techniques taken over from the classics with the basic structures of the oral manner. Wherever learning and classical models become more available, the narrative, though more 'correct', turns almost automatically less dramatic and more difficult to visualize.

The narrative manner of preliterate societies was never as vigorously present and influential in Western Europe as in the time after the Migrations, when entire nations of pagan and semi-pagan illiterates became objects of the missionary work of the church, when their leaders founded states around the Mediterranean and took power over the Latin population and its clergy. The sources of much of what we read in Paul the Deacon and Agnellus of Ravenna must have been oral accounts, some of them family history, many others local or regional tradition. The literary history of the period, however, involves not only the rise of the new style and next to it the preservation and reproduction of the classical models, but the merging of the two currents, and the literary posterity of the oral style in the hands of gifted writers.[28] Here again, the interview between Charles the Bald and George of Ravenna, as described by Agnellus, provides an excellent illustration. The expressive 'freeze' that immobilizes king and archbishop so that the narrator may describe the robes of the one and the gestures and attitude of the other is inconceivable both in the classical tradition and in oral narrative. The insignia of royalty have no direct consequences for the development of the story, nor are they connected with anything previously described; Sallust or Livy would have thought it trivial and useless to dwell on them at such length. The aim of Agnellus in this strongly marked pause of the action is to convey an important scheme embodied by the two actors at that moment: royalty as defender and corrector of the church, and the archbishop as a figure of fallen spirituality. In Roman historical writing such general points emerge gradually from the course of the action itself, the oratory of the leading characters, or the interjected comments of the author. As to oral narrative, though it may describe extraordinary attire and unusual gesticulation, it never uses them to make abstract statements, but for the sake of the garments and gestures themselves, to delight the imagination of the audience. That such a scene as this can occur in a work of the ninth century is the effect of a unique symbiosis of traditional and literary possibilities.

The attempt to explain the most important characteristics of the new narrative style by referring back to an oral tradition that can never be known first-hand may be taken as an especially bad case of *ignotum per ignotius* and of the tendency, rightly deplored by critics of oral theories, to solve any problem in the history of literature by turning to anthropology and comparative folklore. The difficulty of providing evidence for oral-traditional claims is increased in this instance because what is postulated is a tradition of prose, one whose existence, by definition, cannot be established by such tokens of orality as formulas and formulaic systems, the familiar criteria for oral poetry.[29]

In spite of such objections, however, the case for an oral prose tradition as basic model for early medieval narrative is neither vague nor excessively speculative. The argument is not that Gregory of Tours and Paul the Deacon composed their histories orally, but that they adopted the techniques of oral narrative and used them in their own literary production, adding to them considerably in the process. Narratives that are chains of brief dramatic units, realistic dialogue in direct speech, scenes staged by means of gestures and props: these features are found only exceptionally in classical historiography, while late antique narrative develops certain kinds of gestural staging and neglects the other elements, and dialogue in particular. On the other hand, every known kind of oral narrative, from accounts of personal experiences taped by social scientists for linguistic analysis to the performances of professional storytellers throughout the world, presents these traits consistently and in full.[30] In every tradition of oral narrative, the performer's need to act out the incidents he describes[31] leads him automatically to exclude his personal voice and opinions from the story, and this in turn leaves him free to take illusion as far as possible and make his audience feel that they are seeing it all take place.[32] Biblical narrative and the Icelandic sagas operate along these lines, and are widely believed, on that account, to derive from traditions of oral storytelling in prose, though here, as with early medieval historiography, oral techniques have undergone considerable changes on becoming part of a literary style.[33]

Finally, oral tradition in the early middle ages is no unsubstantiated hypothesis, because the writers of the period refer to it frequently and, as might be expected, historians more often than anyone else.[34] Some of these references are commonplaces of historical discourse, an easy way to give emphasis and credibility to any given assertion by proclaiming that we have it from our ancestors, or from the elders of the community.[35] But in other cases the reference is much too specific to be dismissed as a mere phrase. Among these allusions to orality and its manifestations, an important text that has gone unnoticed by students of medieval literature is Agnellus of Ravenna's prologue to his *Liber pontificalis*, a good part of which is dedicated to a discussion of oral sources and their value.

Non solum quod eorum facta perspexi, verum etiam ex auditu, quae mihi seniores nostri retulerunt, vestris auribus patefaciam. Moises etenim praecellentissimus vir, inspirante Deo, Genesis librum descripsit. Ipse enim ait: 'Interroga patres tuos, et annunciabunt tibi, seniores tuos, et dicent tibi' (Deut. 32, 7), et Iob: 'Interroga generationes pristinas, et diligenter investiga patrum memoria' (Iob 8, 8). Ex stirpe enim Abrahae Moyses descendit, et antequam Abraham nasceretur, totius huius mundi fabrica a Deo facta fuisse memoratur. Marcus etiam, Petri apostoli discipulus et in baptismate filius, non corporaliter Domini secutus fuit vestigia, neque ulla miracula ab eo facta vidit, sed Petro enarrante euangelium exaravit. Lucas vero, Pauli apostoli ministrator, inbutus ab eo doctrina, euangelii aperuit fontem. Multi etenim alii ex auditu rerum volumina condiderunt; sicut in Vitas patrum legitur: 'Narravit mihi quidam senex' etc. Nonne Gregorius sedis Romanae ecclesiae antistes in plurimis locis librûm Dialogorum retulit dicens: 'Narravit mihi ille et ille homo' et reliqua?

I shall make known to your ears not only what I have seen of their work [the work of the bishops of Ravenna], but also what I know from hearing, as it was told to me by our elders. Moses, that outstanding man, wrote the book of Genesis through God's inspiration. He says: 'Ask your parents and they will make you know; ask your elders and they will tell you' (Deut 32:7), and Job: 'Ask the former generations, and study diligently the tradition of the fathers' (Job 8:8). Moses was descended from the race of Abraham and commemorates how, before Abraham was born, the frame of this entire universe was made by God. Mark, indeed, who was the disciple of the apostle Peter and his son by baptism, never followed in the flesh the footsteps of the Lord, and did not see any of the miracles he performed, but wrote the gospel from Peter's account. Luke, however, the assistant of the apostle Paul and steeped by him in knowledge, opened up the source of the gospel. And many others wrote books on various subjects from what they had heard, so that we read in the Lives of the fathers: 'A certain old man told me... ' etc. And does not Gregory, bishop of the church of Rome, say in various parts of his *Dialogues*: 'This and that man told me the following story' and other such things?

Agnellus is placing his written text as a mere link in the transmission of knowledge from ear to ear: 'ex auditu ... vestris auribus.' A fuller and more reverent awareness of orality as embodied in literary tradition is hardly conceivable; we find here the Old Testament and the New, hagiography, and Gregory the Great's *Dialogues* as precedents for what Agnellus is undertaking in his own book. What these works have in common that allows him to claim their authors as ancestors of a sort is not their religious content, but their relation to oral narrative.

IN CONCLUSION

The rare episodes presented in scenic form by classical historians can show remarkable similarities to the early medieval style outlined above. At the centre of the scene of Tarquin's usurpation we find Servius' question, the only speech quoted directly, a short and simple utterance that would be far less surprising in an early medieval story than in this classical text, where it stands surrounded by majestic oratory in indirect speech. The debate between Jugurtha and the sons of Micipsa, as described by Sallust, has as its focus well-defined ceremonial positions. In spite of such important formal analogies, and without ruling out the possibility that these and similar passages from classical historiography did manage to influence the narrative style of the early medieval period to some extent, we consider it impossible that the primary source of the new style could be found in classical models. The central difficulty lies in the *rarity* of scenic narrative in classical literature, and not in the form of its infrequent scenes. When the scene is an exception, a dramatic break in an otherwise indirect and discursive report, its entire nature changes. It becomes a mark of emphasis, and as such an indicator of how that particular moment in the narrative must be interpreted. It can also, as in Sallust, serve as an indirect comment on the oddity of the events described. It is one more sign of the power of the narrator.

Late antiquity can provide some closer approximations, though not in the flow of scenes or the use of realistic dialogue. What distinguishes such authors as Ammianus Marcellinus and Sulpicius Severus from classical historians and biographers is the design of individual scenes, which often follows the lines of familiar ceremonies, or focuses on symbolic objects. The Christian authors of this period, if not Ammianus, were widely read between 500 and 1000 AD, and their ritualism and interest in props have clearly influenced the early medieval manner. Still, these writers constitute an insufficient model, especially where direct speech is concerned, and it would be very difficult to understand from their narrative practice how it is that Gregory of Tours, in the late sixth century, can let so many of his characters speak out credibly in direct form. When, as in Jerome's hagiographies, we come visibly closer to early medieval narrative, it is because Jerome himself has put aside classical standards and is writing under the influence of an oral tradition.

An important limitation of my argument so far is that it is based entirely on the analysis of historical and biographic narratives. Early medieval historians could easily have found inspiration in other genres. In late antiquity alone the conversion scene in book eight of Augustine's *Confessions*, or the more melodramatic moments in the works of the Greek and Latin novelists, particularly Heliodorus and Apuleius, provide impressive illustrations of dramatic narrative. But even setting aside the difficult question of their availablity to early medieval writers, these seem less likely models for the style of Gregory of Tours and his fellow historians than any of the texts I have considered above.[36] There is simply no resemblance at all between them.

We are left with scripture, and particularly the gospel, the form of which resembles early medieval narrative more closely than anything else we have seen so far, both in the frequency of scenic units and in their individual composition. It is clear, however, that those features which gospel narrative might be thought to have passed on to early medieval writers are common to all oral-traditional narrative in prose. Since early medieval culture, with its impoverished and insufficient literary resources, was confronted with wave upon wave of native and alien orality, the hypothesis that oral form may be the primary model of the new style seems worthy of serious consideration. It is, nevertheless, necessary to remember that sources, or a model, do not provide a full answer to the question of origins. Just as important as the source itself are its reception and interpretation, as well as the reasons that led the writers of a given culture and period to adopt a specific model. These factors almost invariably result in a transformation of the original impulse, at times so radical that the new works it inspires can only be traced back to it by way of hypothesis and speculation.

2 Scenes and Speeches

If we go back far enough in the search for origins, even the rare scenes in classical narrative may turn out to be a borrowing, an oral trait assimilated from popular tradition.[1] The crucial fact in the development of early medieval narrative, however, is the breaking of the oral flow of scenes into literature. Gregory of Tours himself, the most consistently scenic narrator of the period, remains capable of stretches of indirect authorial reporting that mark his *Libri historiarum* as literary work. Nevertheless, the line between authentic oral storytelling and its literary offshoots becomes at this time almost impossible to draw. The differences between the two are clearly perceptible, if often slight, but they vary from one author to another among the many influenced by oral form: where one comments openly on the course of the action, another betrays his literary training by rendering all or most speeches in indirect form (*oratio obliqua*), or by making the characters speak at great length, and in the language of oratory.

Once naturalized, the scene functions primarily as a ploy of narrative, one more instrument in the rhetoric of the text, which here invites us to 'see for ourselves.' The immediate appeal to the visual and dramatic imagination of the reader, addressed most often to a 'sight' and 'hearing' of the mind, indicates that the invitation is illusionistic in purpose and effect. Today scenic narrative dominates fiction, though it has been given up by most historians. It is therefore necessary to keep in mind that we are in the grip of the scenic gesture ourselves, even now under the illusion it encourages. Before engaging in any analysis or discussion of the early medieval scene, we must become fully aware that the design of the story as a series of scenes is a narrative strategy, as purely rhetorical as the author-bound reports of classical history, and that the recourse to imagination is a device of oral performance and the written page, calling upon our eyes and ears only at a remove.

The intent of the new style becomes manifest in the design of the scene. We may compare it usefully with the more purely illusionistic medium of photography, and point out that the presence in photographs of those unplanned, involuntary details that capture the viewer's attention as manifestations of the irreducible reality behind the picture (what Roland Barthes calls the *punctum* – for example, the big hands and dirty fingernails of Tristan Tzara in his portrait with monocle) is matched in the narrative of our period by the deliberate inclusion of very 'lifelike' and prominent details that seem nevertheless irrelevant.[2] Describing how Egidius, bishop of Rheims and counsellor of Childebert II, was almost lynched by rebellious soldiers, Gregory of Tours closes his brief account with the following image: 'Attamen lassatis sociorum equis, solus pertendit episcopus, tanto timore perterritus, ut unam caligam de pede elapsam collegare non curaret.' / 'However, the horses of his comrades became tired and fell behind, so that the bishop was the only one to get away, and in such terror that he did not trouble to fasten one of his boots, which fell off as he rode' (*HF* VI.31). A clear attempt on the part of Gregory to make us feel that we are witnessing an unedited slice of life, the falling boot functions as a make-believe *punctum* to introduce a fake imbalance in the composition of the scene. The narrator uses this apparent lack of critical control to efface the traces of his own activity: the facts are speaking to us 'by themselves.'

The medium of the scene is narrative time. In Livy's account of the fall of Servius a slowing down of narrative pace is effected as much by time-indicators ('celeriter ... celeriter ... Tum vero in dies ... Postremo ... ') as by an increase in descriptive detail as we come closer to the usurpation: the seduction of Tarquin by Tullia and the murder of their consorts get far less attention than Tullia's later speeches, where she exhorts Tarquin to take power. Narration practically grinds to a halt with the scene at the Forum, which thus appears not only as the undoubted climax of the sequence, the crisis of this particular turn of historical fate, but also as a ripple in narrative time, a moment of full description that opens up the text to the reader's imagination.

The far greater frequency of scenes in early medieval narrative, which allows very little or no preparation for individual units, or explicit interconnection between them, eliminates the sense of a continuous chronological sequence created by the classical narrator's summaries, connective passages, and rationalizations. The broken, scene-to-scene rhythm of the new form can dispense almost entirely with authorial comments. This tendency explains the fragmentary, disjointed appearance of much early medieval historiography, sometimes compensated for by elaborate chronologies, computations of the age of the world, or dynastic tables, helpful additions which usually remain separate from the narrative proper, and do not shape or order it in the least.[3]

Though unheralded, the early medieval scene remains a segment of time, that is, it preserves its unity as a single occasion, as 'one time that ... ', whatever other unity it may be missing. (Unity of space and action are not to be counted on, and the very cast of characters sometimes changes halfway through a scene.) The narrative sequence often comes close to being purely additive, a series of discrete occasions. The narrator may routinely repeat the scenic gesture: 'one day that ... '; 'and the following morning ... '; 'he then went to see ... ' In the end, these occasions only come to be considered parts of a unified narrative time because of the implicit narrative chronology that makes them a sequence. Now and then the individual scene is introduced by an abstract time-word or -phrase ('interea', 'alia autem die'), by an ablative absolute ('Conlucutione facta ait Chilpericus rex ... ') or other participial construction ('Quod cernens, Brunichildis regina dicit ... '), or most commonly, by a temporal clause with 'cum', 'dum,' or 'tunc' marking the relative position of the events in time, their posteriority or simultaneity to other events ('Igitur, cum die sancto Paschae hic legatus Toronus advenisset, sciscitati sumus, utrum nostrae religionis esset.' / 'Therefore, when the envoy arrived in Tours on Easter Sunday, I asked him whether he was of our faith' [HF vi.40]). None of these expressions serves exclusively to introduce scenes; they are also used to report new events in the authorial summaries. Writers tend to show a marked preference for one or another of them: Gregory of Tours makes heavy use of ablative absolutes and temporal clauses, while Agnellus, perhaps because he is closer to oral tradition, having written his book ostensibly to read it aloud, is more likely to open his scenes with time-phrases such as 'quadam die dominico,' 'post aliquantos dies,' 'in ipsa denique nocte' / 'One Sunday,' 'A few days later,' 'That same night.'[4]

SEQUENCE AND COMPOSITION

The scene of the usurpation in Livy is quite long. It involves a variety of elements: speeches, gestures, and one significant object (the throne),

all of them carefully introduced and interpreted by the narrator. One
may say that the scene is painstakingly composed: there is, for example,
a clear sense of a climax when Servius challenges Tarquin from the
vestibule. His words brand the young man's act as a crime, an impiety,
and thereby carry the moral weight of the scene; the ejection of the
lawful king after that, though dramatic, is only a moment of waning
intensity, a working out of what we by now expect.

Early medieval scenes are rarely composed in this sense, and their
analysis presents specific difficulties caused by this lack of formal
clarity. Let us take another episode from Gregory of Tours to illustrate
this feature; it describes the death of Waddo, count of Saintes, at the
hands of the angry servants of a country estate.

> 1–4 Beretrudis vero moriens filiam suam heredem instituit, relinquens
> quaepiam vel monastiriis puellarum, quae ipsa instituerat, vel aecle-
> siis sive basilicis confessorum sanctorum. Sed Waddo, cui in superiore
> libro meminimus, quaerebatur, a genero eius equos suos fuisse direptus;
> cogitavitque accedere ad villam eius unam, quam reliquerat filiae
> suae, qui infra Pectavo termino erat, dicens: 'Hic a regno alterius
> veniens, diripuit equos meos, et ego auferam villam eius'. Interea
> mandatum mittit agenti, ut se adveniente omnia quae erant ad
> expensam eius necessaria praepararet. Quod ille audiens, coniunctis
> secum hominibus ex domo illa, se ad bellum praeparat, dicens: 'Nisi
> moriar, non ingreditur Waddo in domum domini mei'.
> 5–8 Audiens autem uxor Waddone, adparatum scilicet belli instaurari
> contra virum suum, ait ad eum: 'Ne accesseris illuc, care coniux;
> morieris enim, si abieris, et ego cum filiis misera ero'. Et iniecta manu,
> voluit eum retenire, dicente praeterea tum filio: 'Si abieris, pariter
> moriemur, et relinques genetricem meam viduam orfanusque ger-
> manus'. Sed cum eum haec verba paenitus retenire non possint, furore
> accensus contra filium et timidum eum mollemque exclamans, proiecta
> secure paene cerebro eius inlisit. Sed ille in parte excussus, ictum
> ferientis evasit.
> 9–16 Ascensis denique equitibus, abierunt, mandans iterum acturi,
> ut, domum scupis mundatam, stragulis scamna operiret. Sed ille
> parvi pendens mandatum eius, cum turbis, ut diximus, virorum ac
> mulierum ante fores domini sui stetit, operiens adventum huius. Qui
> veniens, statim ingressus domum, ait: 'Cur non sunt scamna haec
> operta stragulis aut domus scupis mundata?' Et elevans manum cum
> sica, caput hominis libravit, caeciditque et mortuus est. Quod cer-
> nens filius hominis mortui, emissa ex adverso lanceam, contra Wad-

donem dirigit; cuius mediam alvum ictu penetrans, a tergo egressa
falarica, ruens ad terram, advenientem multitudinem, qui collecta
fuerat, lapidibus obrui coepit. Tunc quidam de his qui venerant cum
eo inter imbres saxeos accedentes, coopertum sago ac populo mitigato,
heiulante filio eius, eumque super equum elevans, adhuc viventem
domui reduxit. Sed protinus sub lacrimis uxoris ac filiorum spiritum
exalavit. Explicita igitur tam infilicem vitam, filius eius ad regem
abiit resque eius obtenuit.   (HF ix.35)

Before dying, Beretrude appointed her daughter her heir, and made
some bequests to the nunneries that she had founded and to the ca-
thedrals and churches of the saints. But Waddo, whom I mentioned
in an earlier book, claimed that her son-in-law had taken some of
his horses; he therefore made up his mind to visit an estate she had
left to her daughter, and which was within the boundaries of Poitiers,
saying: 'He came here from another kingdom and took my horses,
so I will have his estate!' Meanwhile he sent orders to the bailiff to
prepare all things necessary to receive him on his arrival at the
estate. When he heard this, the bailiff gathered about him all those
who lived in the estate, and prepared to do battle, saying: 'Waddo
will not come into my master's house, if it costs me my life.'

Hearing of these preparations for violence against her husband,
Waddo's wife said to him: 'Do not go there, dearest husband; you will
be killed if you go, and I and your sons shall live on miserably.'
Stretching out her hand, she tried to detain him, while his son added:
'If you go we shall all die; you will leave my mother a widow and
my brother an orphan.' These words were unable to hold him back;
full of anger against his son and calling him weak and effeminate, he
flung his axe at him and almost brained him. But the son, jumping
aside, was able to dodge the blow.

They got on their horses and rode away, sending ahead one more
message to the bailiff that he should have the house swept clean
with brooms and put covers on the benches. But he cared little for
such orders and stood, as I said before, with the gathered men
and women of the estate, at the door of his master's house waiting
for Waddo to arrive. As soon as he got there he walked into the
house and asked: 'Why are the benches not covered and the floors
unswept?' Raising his hand, he struck the man on the head with his
dagger, so that the bailiff fell on the ground dead. Seeing this, the
dead man's son cast his spear at Waddo; the missile pierced his
stomach and came out through the back, and as he fell the gathered

crowd began to pelt him with stones. Then one of the men who had
come with him, coming to his aid among a shower of rocks, covered
him with a military cloak; the crowd was pacified and, while Waddo's son wept loudly, his men raised him on his horse and took him
back home still alive. Shortly thereafter, however, he expired among
the tears of his wife and children. After his ill-starred life had ended
thus, his son went to see the king and obtained the right to inherit
his father's property.

The story is told in sixteen sentences, and it contains more than one
scene, making it possible to observe not only the design of individual
units, but also the construction of the narrative sequence. From the
start we are confronted with problems of classification. The first sentence, on Beretrude and her will, is clearly authorial; it provides the
context of what is to follow without any attempt to represent the events
for the reader. The second could be described in the same terms up to
the 'dicens,' which introduces Waddo's speech in direct form. Should
this be considered a minimal scene, since we get to hear the character's
own words? The occasion of the words is not indicated, and we do not
know by whom they were meant to be heard. Is Waddo speaking to
himself, or is this an artificial monologue purely for the benefit of the
reader? Impossible to tell. The following sentence is again authorial,
but the fourth presents us with the same problem as the second, being
a speech without circumstances, this time helped along by certain
references to the speaker's activity: the bailiff has gathered the servants
of the house and is preparing to fight. The ablative absolute 'coniunctis
secum omnibus' before his words makes it seem likely that he is speaking in the presence of the assembled men. As it stands, his speech has
an occasion and probably an audience, but no imaginable physical
stage.

The next four sentences, five to eight, constitute a fully developed
scene between Waddo, his wife, and one of his sons, with speeches,
gestures, and one eloquent object: Waddo's 'securis' flying through the
room. The narrator is absolutely neutral and interprets nothing. The
scene is brief and highly dramatic, but it shows no recognizable principle of composition. The initial 'Audiens autem uxor Waddone ... ait ... '
opens the scene by placing it in time relative to the bailiff's threat.
After that, the dramatic elements follow one another without an in-
terval: the wife's pleading, made more pathetic by her manner of address with 'care coniux' and by the gesture of her outstretched hand,
the son's dire prophecy, Waddo's savage rejoinder with the axe, and

the boy's leap aside. Impossible between them, and in the minimal format of the scene, to determine a climax. The whole is rather like a succession of possible climaxes, all competing for the reader's attention and held in place by an equality of tension between them. Each gap in the sequence between scenes and potential scenes is filled, as we have seen, by no more than one sentence of authorial report.

The second full scene follows after the authorial summary of sentence nine, and it covers from ten to fourteen. Sentence ten, in providing a sketchy mise-en-scène (the front of the house, the gate, the gathered people) introduces a dramatic resource that had been missing in the previous scene. Waddo's absurd questions about the benches and the cleaning of the house are supremely worth quoting, for they reveal the stupidity and arrogance of the man even better than his immediate murder of the bailiff; however, they also define a symbolic object with a function equivalent to that of Servius' throne in Livy. In the aggressor's mind, the benches become the symbol of successful usurpation, a reading suggested also by his previous messages to the bailiff insisting on these particular tokens of submission. The length and extreme violence of the fighting that follows, rich as it is in movement, compromises the centrality of Waddo's words as a possible climax, waters down the pathetic irony of the scene, and produces once again the unresolved tension of elements met earlier in the story. One of Waddo's companions has only to cover his corpse with a cloak for the crowd suddenly to become peaceful. The two actions are juxtaposed to suggest a causal connection between them, and to bring out the irrationality of the multitude who, like angry animals, grow violent at the mere sight of blood, becoming calm again as soon as it is hidden.

The presentation of Waddo and his opponent is consistent in that the two manifest the same simple qualities throughout: Waddo's first speech expresses his resolve to take over the property. In the scene with his wife and son, he threatens the boy with the same unthinking, explosive brutality with which he kills the bailiff later. The text is too short for us to speak of characterization, but there is a unity of design in these figures. The decision to quote Waddo's last question about the benches and the cleaning shows an awareness that it is possible to illustrate and even expose character in these minimal dramatic units, however partial and schematic the revelation. The characters' speeches carry the dramatic brunt of the story here, though in the end we are distracted by spears flashing and by showers of rocks.

It is common, particularly in Gregory's anecdotes, for a speech to occupy the undisputed centre of the scenic frame, but then it stands so much by itself, it is so obviously the one thing we are invited to notice, that there can hardly be any talk of composition or of climax. A fine example of this simple structure is an exchange between Gunthchramn and his recently widowed sister-in-law Fredegund, as reported by Gregory. The king protects his ruthless kinswoman and extends hospitality to her, exposing himself to certain surprises:

> Quadam vero die, dum pariter ad mensam epolarentur, regina consurgens et vale dicens, a rege detenebatur, dicente sibi: 'Adhuc aliquid cybi sume'. Cui illa: 'Indulge', inquid, 'depraecor, domini mi, quia iuxta consuetudinem mulierum contigit mihi, ut pro conceptu consurgam'. Haec ille audiens, obstipuit, sciens, quartum esse mensem, ex quo alium ediderat filium; tamen permisit eam consurgere.
>
> (*HF* vii.7)

> One day, when they were eating together, the queen rose and begged to be excused. The king tried to detain her, asking: 'Won't you have something more to eat?' She replied: 'Please excuse me, my lord, because as so often happens with women, I have become pregnant and must rise now.' Hearing this, he was amazed, knowing that she had given birth to a son only four months earlier. However, he allowed her to get up and leave.

This tiny scene gravitates around the queen's announcement, which is ambiguous and possibly scandalous. Fredegund's words, in their formality and affected modesty, tell us that she is on her best behaviour for the time being, though without losing any of her effrontery. A remark such as the king's 'Adhuc aliquid cybi sume,' in its utter artlessness and insignificance, represents nonetheless an entirely new possibility in literary dialogue.[5] Our discussion must now turn to what the characters say, and how they say it.

SPEECH

Two features of early medieval style that immediately stand out as characteristic are the frequency with which dialogue is quoted in direct form, and the informal, 'spoken' quality of many of the speeches.

Turning to the first point, we may ask ourselves how prevalent direct form is, and how significant it can be considered from the point of view of style.[6] Indirect speech is used quite often in early medieval narrative, both in the Greek East and Latin West. The ratio of its employment relative to direct speech varies widely among individual writers, most often in direct proportion to their classical training: Gregory of Tours and Agnellus of Ravenna rarely have recourse to it, Paul the Deacon more often than not. Though not a distinctive feature of the new narrative manner, it is not incompatible with it. A fully scenic, illusionistic text, with dialogue in direct form, dramatic gestures, symbolic props, and a marked absence of authorial participation, can also contain one or two speeches in *oratio obliqua*. Two important questions arise here: first, what difference does it make whether a speech appears in *recta* or in *obliqua*? In what way does this choice condition the effect of the words? Second, when do early medieval narrators use one and not the other? Does their selection of either of these forms follow any rationale? It is perhaps safest to ask these questions of a specific text.

Qui rex [Alboin] postquam in Italia tres annos et sex menses regnavit, insidiis suae coniugis interemptus est. Causa autem interfectionis eius fuit. Cum in convivio ultra quam oportuerat aput Veronam laetus resederet, cum poculo quod de capite Cunimundi regis sui soceris fecerat reginae ad bibendum vinum dari praecepit atque eam ut cum patre suo laetanter biberet invitavit. Hoc ne cui videatur inpossibile, veritatem in Christo loquor: ego hoc poculum vidi in quodam die festo Ratchis principem ut illut convivis suis ostentaret manu tenentem. Igitur Rosemunda ubi rem animadvertit, altum concipiens in corde dolorem, quem conpescere non valens, mox in mariti necem patris funus vindicatura exarsit ...   (*HL* II.28)

After ruling Italy for three years and six months, King Alboin was slain through the treachery of his wife. The murder, however, had a specific cause. While he sat drinking at a banquet in Verona, longer than was good for him, he ordered the beaker that he had had made from the skull of his father-in-law, King Cunimund, to be offered to the queen to drink wine with, and invited her to drink joyfully with her father. This may sound impossible to some, but I am speaking Christ's own truth: I myself saw the beaker when on a feast day prince Ratchis showed it to his guests, holding it in his hand. Rosimund, when she heard this thing, experienced a deep pain in her heart. Unable to suppress it, she was soon raging to avenge her father's death by the murder of her husband.

If we examine Paul's well-known account of the incident that led to the murder of King Alboin by his wife Rosimund and her accomplices, we notice immediately that the fatal speech of the king, which seals his fate from the outset, is given in indirect form. When the drunken ruler invites his wife to drink from a beaker made from her father's skull, Paul writes: 'eam ut cum patre suo laetanter biberet invitavit,' and what follows is all a consequence of this gruesome joke.[7] Paul seems to have preserved to a considerable extent the words attributed to Alboin in the traditional Langobardic narrative that was his source. Alboin still makes the macabre pun that is the point of his whole speech: 'cum patre suo' with a 'cum' that means 'in company with,' but also 'by means of.' If it is possible to quote his line this faithfully in indirect form, what difference can it make to the scene whether Alboin uses direct or indirect speech? Would it be a very different episode if he were to say 'Bibe laetanter cum patre tuo'? The dramatic conception is as full in Paul's text as it would be with a speech in direct form, because the narrator has imagined and conveyed Alboin's actual words.

Is direct quotation then merely a stylistic red herring? We may ask ourselves just that when we consider the rest of the story. Rosimund, pretending to be her own serving maid, copulates in the dark with one of Alboin's squires in order to blackmail him into helping her out in her revenge. When she discloses her identity, her words are in direct form: 'Nequaquam ut putas, sed ego Rosemunda sum.' / 'It is not at all as you think. I am Rosimund.' Both parts of the story are believed to go back to the same source in oral tradition, so we can dispense with the hypothesis of a mixture of styles in the original narrative.[8] Why *oratio recta* at this point? It cannot be to mark the importance of the speech, since Alboin's far more critical words were rendered in *obliqua*. Do we have here a purely mechanical stylistic change, meant to give a more varied texture to the passage? There is no indication that Paul avoids sustained use of either form in the dialogue of his narratives. Here, as so often in the writing of our period, we can discover no consistent criterion for the distribution of indirect speech.

As to the effect of indirect speech on the scene of the invitation to drink, my answer would be that it undermines the dramatic illusionism which early medieval narrative shares with oral storytelling. The author may have imagined the scene in the same detail, with the same actions, gestures, and words that it would have involved had the dialogue been in direct form, but he interposes his voice, his point of view, ultimately his presence. He puts a subjective frame on what would otherwise be a transparent, objective picture. Paul is torn between the

form of his oral source or sources and the demands of his early Carolingian literary background. To the economically drawn but fully imagined scene he has added not only his own voice in the indirect quotation
of Alboin's speech, but also moral comment (the king had sat drinking
'longer than was good for him'), and he interrupts the narrative bluntly
and defers Rosimund's reaction to assure us that the cranium-beaker
is no fantasy, because he has seen it himself. The carefree shattering
of the dramatic illusion involves more than just *oratio obliqua* in this
case, but it is clear that *obliqua* would have been enough. The presence
of speeches in indirect form sets a distinct limit to the reader's ima-
ginative response: he can no longer follow the events of the scene as
they develop, but must now be guided by the voice of the unmistakably
present narrator, who describes those events for him.

THE 'SPOKEN' TONE

The unassuming simplicity, even triviality, of much of the dialogue,
its lack of formality and rhetorical ornaments, leaves a first impression
of total spontaneity which must be qualified in two ways at least. In
the first place, like all literary simplicities, it is not really artless.
Though it gives up the postures of oratory and the more obvious constraints of literary form, this rhetoric of the ordinary has devices of its
own, which are susceptible of analysis. Held up to the reality of spoken
language, compared with an actual transcript of ordinary speech, it will
reveal principles of artistic selection and exaggeration, the systematic
omission of many genuine traits of colloquial expression, the effects
of an implicit literary formula for spontaneity. That a stylistic analysis
of this language can be outlined at all goes far to prove that it has a
rhetoric of its own; ordinary conversation would be impossible to dis-
sect with terms of art, void as it is of composition and deliberate effects.

The second qualification made necessary by the persuasive naturalism of this dialogue is a reminder that highly stylized speeches are
possible as well, and that the formal range of direct speech in early
medieval narrative covers the extremes of solemnity and artifice. We
need only recall the words of Charles the Bald to the humiliated bishop
of Ravenna, spoken with the pompous delivery of public address and
adorned with an elaborate grammatical rhyme ('O tu pastor, si in te
istud permanet nomen, cur reliquisti ecclesia tibi commissa et plebem,
quam afflixisti, non recuperasti, sed per longinquo itinere, ut videres
praelium, venisti?'), to realize that hieratic formality is quite possible
within the new style, and available to a narrator as unpretentious and

close to oral form as Agnellus. Let us examine first the stylization that can be found in the more simple and spontaneous-sounding dialogue, considering one by one the features we might look for in an ideally 'natural' elocution to see whether they are present in the speeches and conversations quoted in our texts.

Brevity is a salient characteristic of much early medieval dialogue. Gunthchramn asks the pregnant Fredegund, 'Won't you have something more to eat?' From the sixth century on we hear characters say 'Do not kill me!', 'Give me some food,' 'What are you doing here?' The novelty of this can only be appreciated in contrast with the style of the classical historians. The customary speeches in classical historiography are much too long for casual delivery; their length serves to explain why so many scenes are staged as declamations at the senate or on the battlefield, before a captive and inactive audience.

In early medieval history, direct speech is too frequent to have an emphatic function such as Livy gives to Servius' few words at the Forum by quoting them. No exchange is too unimportant for the words of the actors to be reproduced. Agnellus describes the arrival of the priest Theodore at the monastery of St Andrew the Apostle; he has come to see his relative the archdeacon Theodore with the purpose of organizing a revolt of the clergy against the tyrannical archbishop of Ravenna:

> Pulsante eo ostium ianua, venerunt famuli domum, percussorem ligni inquirere, quis esset. At illi dedit notitiam, quia: 'Ego sum'. Illi autem citius abeuntes narraverunt, dicentes: 'Theodorus archipresbyter ostium pulsat, vult ad te ingredi'. Rapidissimus alius venit et dixit, quia in monasterio erat. Et archidiaconum ait: 'Quid prodest, quod loquimur, quia ad effectum non pervenimus'? Dixerunt ei domestici sui: 'Quid est hoc, quod irascetis? Caro tua proxima est, si tunc tuus est, loquere cum eo; non separemeni. Quod si pontifex contra te saevierit, ille pro te quomodo verba proferat'?   (LPR 121)

> When he knocked at the door, the servants of the house came to ask who it was. He answered: 'It's me.' They went quickly and told the archdeacon: 'Theodore the archpriest is at the door and wishes to see you.' Another man came running in and said that Theodore was already in the monastery. The archdeacon asked: 'What good will it do if we talk, since our words can have no effect?' His servants replied: 'Why are you angry in this way? He is your kin, your own flesh. Therefore speak with him, and do not be separated from each

other. Otherwise, if the bishop should rage against you, how could he have anything to say in your favour?'

The transaction at the door, which the reader could easily be allowed to imagine for himself, including the priest's inane 'Ego sum', is carefully represented. Important matters too can be discussed with the most businesslike brevity. According to an apocryphal story about Justinian told by Fredegar, the emperor's mistress (here called Antonia, though obviously Theodora is meant), watching over his sleep once in the days when Justinian was only a *comes cartarum*, saw an eagle fly down to protect him from the sun with the shadow of its wings.[9]

> Quod cum, Antonia vigilante, fuisset repertum, sperans hoc signum, Iustinianus imperium adsumerit, expertum a somno, dicens ei: 'Si imperatur effectus fueris, erit digna ancilla tua tibi concubito'. Et ille subridens, cum ei fuisset difficile hoc esse honore dignum, dixit ad eam: 'Si imperatur effectus fuero, tu mihi eris agusta'. Commutantis ab invicem anolis, ait Iustinianus ad Bellesarium: 'Scias inter me et Antunia placuisse, si ego efficior imperatur, ipsa sit mihi agusta. Anolis commutantis hoc foedus inivimus'. Dixitque Antunia: 'Si soror mea tibi agusta, ego Bellesario matrona efficiar'. Dicensque Bellesarius divino noto: 'Si Antunia agusta efficitur, tu estratus mei matrimonium sociaris'. Idemque anolis commutandis abierunt.
>
> (*CF* ii.62)

Antonia saw this as she watched over his sleep, and believed it to be a sign that Justinian would assume imperial power. When he awoke, she said to him: 'If you should become emperor, would this servant of yours be worthy of your bed?' And he, smiling, since that honour seemed very difficult for him to achieve, said to her: 'If I am made emperor, you will be my empress.' They exchanged rings, and Justinian said to Belisarius: 'You must know that Antonia and I have decided that if I am made emperor she will be my *augusta*. We have sealed this agreement by exchanging rings.' And Antonia [Belisarius' future wife Antonina is meant] said: 'If my sister is to be your empress, than I shall be Belisarius' wife.' Guided by Providence, Belisarius said to her: 'If Antonia becomes empress, you will come into my bed as my wife.' They too exchanged rings and then left.

This playful agreement between young men and courtesans is obviously more important than it seems, since Providence plays a hand in it. Two engagements and the fate of the late Roman empire are settled, according to the story, by these casual words.[10]

Clearly, then, whenever early medieval narrative tries to make dialogue sound like spoken language, it uses brevity as one of its characteristic features. Long speeches are synonymous with a display of rhetorical organization, periodic structure, and logical reasoning. The vivid, naturalistic long speech is a contradiction in terms. A statement by the Merovingian king Gunthchramn quoted by Gregory of Tours manages to sustain the colloquial tone rather longer than usual. It represents the king's table-talk at a banquet which Gregory attended. Gunthchramn had just signed a treaty with his nephew Childebert, but was planning to preserve his alliance with Chlothar II, another nephew of his and an enemy of Childebert.

> Dictis igitur missis, convivio nos adscivit, quod fuit non minus oneratum in fercolis quam laetitia opulentum. Semper enim rex de Deo, de aedificationem aeclesiarum, de defensionem pauperum sermonem habens, ridebat interdum, spiritali ioco delectans, addens etiam, unde et nos aliquid laetitiae frueremur. Dicebat enim et haec verba: 'Utinam mihi nepus meus promissa costodiat! Omnia enim quae habeo eius sunt. Tamen si eum scandalizat illud, quod legatus Chlothari nepotis mei suscipio, numquid demens sum, ut non possim temperare inter eos, ne scandalum propagetur? Novi enim eum magis incidere quam in longius promulgare. Dabo enim Chlothario, si eum nepotem meum esse cognovero, aut duas aut tres in parte aliqua civitatis, ut nec hic videatur exheredari de regno meo, nec huic inquietudinem praeparent, quae isti reliquero.' His et aliis locutus, dulci nos affectu fovens ac muneribus onerans, discedere iobet, mandans, ut ea semper Childebertho regi insinuentur, quae vitae eius comoda fiant.
>
> (*HF* ix.20)

After mass had been said, he invited us to a banquet which was no less lavish in courses than in good spirits. The king spoke continually about God, the building of churches, and the protection of the poor. Now and then he laughed, delighting in witty repartee, so that we too might enjoy the happy mood. He spoke as follows: 'I hope my nephew will keep his promises to me! All I have belongs to him. He may be shocked because I receive the envoys of my other nephew, King Chlothar, but am I perhaps mad in my attempt to make peace between them, so that the contention will not become general? I am sure that it is better to suppress it than to allow it to go on. If I

can recognize Chlothar as my nephew, I shall give him two or three
cities somewhere, so that he may not seem disinherited of his part
in my kingdom. That way, what I leave to the one will not make the
other unhappy.' Having said this and other things, he treated us with
warm affection and loaded us with gifts. He bid us farewell, admonishing us always to give King Childebert such advice as would make
his life happier.

The king speaks five sentences in all, the first, second, and fourth
extremely short. The first is in the optative subjunctive, the direct
expression of a wish; the second serves as a promise or a deed of gift,
rather than a declarative statement; the third, rather longer, ends unexpectedly in a question introduced by the rhetorical and rather exaggerated 'Numquid demens sum?' / 'Am I perhaps mad?' After the
simple statement of the fourth sentence, Gunthchramn lapses into
specifics of his political planning in the fifth. It is not only the inelegant
variety and discontinuity of these parts but also the weakness of their
logical connection that creates the illusion of spoken language. The
king's pronouncements do not lead one to the other, and cannot do so,
for they express conflicting aims. His words stray strategically in two
different directions, though they manage to communicate a definite
attitude and state of mind: he is trying to convince his listeners and
perhaps himself that there is nothing dubious about his plans, that his
relations with both nephews are perfectly straightforward.

Much later in our period, the revival of learning under Charlemagne
gave new vitality to the classical models, bringing forth mixed and
sometimes inconsistent styles in direct speech. Widukind of Corvey,
a post-Carolingian, is capable of brief, naturalistic dialogue, as in the
following exchange between a Saxon and a Thuringian during the siege
of the Thuringian fortress Burg Scheidungen by the Franks and their
Saxon helpers:

Interea urbe ex pace promissa securiore reddita, egressus est quidam
cum accipitre victum quaeritans supra litus fluvii supradicti. Emisso
vero volucre, quidam ex Saxonibus in ulteriore ripa ilico eum suscepit.
Quo rogante, ut remitteretur, Saxo dare negavit. Ille autem: 'Da',
inquit, 'et secretum tibi sociisque utile prodam'. Saxo econtra: 'Dic,
ut accipias quod quaeris'. 'Reges', inquit, 'inter se pace facta decre-
tum tenent, si cras inveniamini in castris, capiamini aut certe occi-
damini'. Ad haec ille: 'Serione haec an ludo ais?' 'Secunda hora', ait,
'sequentis diei probabit, quia vos oporteat sine ludis agere. Quaprop-

ter consulite vobis ipsis et fuga salutem quaerite'. Saxo statim emittens
accipitrem, sociis retulit quae audivit.   (*RGS* i.10)

Meanwhile, after the population of the citadel had been reassured by
the promised peace, one of them went out with a hawk, hunting
for food on the shore of the aforementioned river. As he sent out the
bird, however, a Saxon on the other bank immediately caught it.
When the man asked to have it back, the Saxon refused to hand it
over. The Thuringian, however, said: 'Give it back to me, and I shall
tell you a secret vital to you and to your people.' The Saxon replied:
'Tell it to me [now], so that you may get back what you are asking
for.' The other said: 'The kings have made peace, and agreed that
if tomorrow you are found in your camp you will be captured or put
to death.' The Saxon asked: 'Do you speak seriously or in jest?'
'Tomorrow the second hour of the day will show you that you cannot
afford to be led by jests. Be guided by good advice, and seek safety
in flight.' The Saxon immediately returned the hawk and told his
fellow warriors what he had heard.

Thus notified that a secret peace between Thuringians and Franks has
been made, and that the new allies are preparing to turn against the
Saxons, the warrior alerts his people and they begin to look for a way
out of their dangerous predicament. Urging his fellow Saxons to take
matters in their hands and to face the Franks with a *fait accompli* by
wiping out the Thuringians immediately, the old warrior Hathagat,
'qui merito bonarum virtutum pater patrum dicebatur,' / 'who on account of his good qualities was called father of fathers,' makes a speech
which falls clearly within the traditional Germanic category of the
exhortation to fight (German *Reizrede*), but which has the form and
tone of a Sallustian address worthy of Marius or Catiline, even if it
remains much shorter than their average performance. The most likely
explanation here is that the short dialogues are taken over almost
directly from tradition, while the long speeches are the author's own
creation.[11] There probably was some native tradition about Hathagat
and his words of courage to the Saxons, but Widukind either did not
know it, or decided that he could do better on his own. The grizzled
fighter begins his address with the following eloquent lines:

'Hucusque inter optimos Saxones vixi, et ad hanc fere ultimam
senectutem aetas me perduxit, et numquam Saxones meos fugere vidi;
et quomodo nunc cogor agere quod numquam didici? Certare scio,

fugere ignoro nec valeo. Si fata non sinunt ultra vivere, liceat saltem, quod michi dulcissimum est, cum amicis occumbere'.   (*RGS* i.11)

'Until today I have lived among noble Saxons. Life has brought me to extreme old age, and I have never yet seen my Saxons flee. How can I be required now to perform what I never learned? I know how to fight, but am ignorant and incapable of flight. If fate does not allow us to live longer, let me do, at least, what seems sweetest to my mind: to lie dead among my friends.'

The literary style of the passage is marked by parallelisms and neat oppositions of terms ('certare' − 'fugere'), and particularly by the figurative discussion of courage as a subject of instruction. We recognize characteristically Roman formulas and pathos, however international the range of heroic sentiment from which they are drawn.

Another distinctive feature of the colloquial speeches is the simplicity of their syntactic form and vocabulary. The nineteenth-century editors of these writers have said so much about their incapacity to write correct Latin that we have to ask ourselves whether this simplicity is a matter of choice, that is, whether our early medieval narrators could have made their characters speak more articulately if they had wanted to. In my opinion there can be no doubt about it. All our authors, and particularly Gregory of Tours and Gregory the Great, are able to write Latin of various degrees of complexity and elegance, even if their language remains unclassical. Though by no means as systematic as the stylistic levels of Byzantine Greek, these degrees are readily identifiable: they frequently appear juxtaposed within one work, and stand out the more clearly for the contrast. We need only compare Gregory of Tours' language in the prologues to the various books of his history, or, for a more clear-cut case, in the speeches that he attributes to himself, with the words he ascribes to those characters of whom less eloquence must be expected. Here we have the beginning of Gregory's adlocution to the bishops gathered for the trial of Praetextatus in Paris. He speaks as a highly placed ecclesiastic to his peers, trying to warn them against all collaboration with the king in his persecution of their fellow prelate.

Quibus intentis et ora digitis conpraementibus, ego aio: 'Adtenti estote, quaeso, sermonibus meis, o sanctissimi sacerdotes Dei, et praesertim vos, qui familiariores esse regi vidimini; adhibite ei consilium sanctum atque sacerdotalem, ne exardiscens in ministrum Dei pereat ab ira eius et regnum perdat et gloriam'. Haec me dicente, silebant omnes.

Illis vero silentibus, adieci: 'Mementote, domini mi sacerdotes, verbi
prophetici, quo ait: *Si viderit speculatur iniquitatem hominis et non
dixerit, reus erit animae pereuntes* (Ez. 33, 6). Ergo nolite silere, sed
praedicate et ponite ante oculos regis peccata eius, ne forte ei aliquid
mali contingat et vos rei sitis pro anima eius'.   (*HF* v.18)

As they sat there, tense and pressing their fingers to their lips, I said:
'I beg you to pay attention to my words, saintly priests of God, and
particularly those of you who are closest to the king: offer him your
holy and priestly counsel, so that in his rage against this minister
of God he may not perish by his own wrath, and lose both his kingdom
and good fame.' They said nothing, and I added while they sat in
silence: 'Remember, my lord bishops, the words of the prophet who
said: *'If the watchman sees the evil of mankind and gives no warning, he will be guilty for the soul that perishes'* (Ez 33, 6). Do not
remain mute, but preach and bring the king's sins before his eyes,
lest he meet with some evil and you be held guilty for the loss of his
soul.'

The elaborate formulas of address, the long subordinating periods, the
scriptural quotation, all make the speech worthy of the bishop of Tours
and the solemn occasion. A good speaker to compare with Gregory is
Gunthchramn, a royal Frank of minimal literacy. Summoned to Paris
by the widowed Fredegund to stand as godfather to a posthumous son
of Chilperic, and angry at not finding the child on his arrival in the
city, he speaks in public as follows:

'Germanus meus Chilpericus moriens dicitur filium reliquisse, cuius
nutritores, matre depraecante, petierunt, ut eum de sancto lavacro
in dominici natalis solemnitate deberem excipere, et non venerunt.
Rogaverunt deinceps, ut ad sanctum pascha baptizaretur, sed nec
tunc adlatus est infans. Depraecati sunt autem tertio, ut ad festivitatem
sancti Iohannis exhiberetur, sed nec tunc venit. Moverunt itaque
me per tempus sterile de loco ubi abitabam. Veni igitur, et ecce!
absconditur nec ostenditur mihi puer. Unde, quantum intellego, nihil
est quod promittitur, sed, ut credo, alicuius ex leudibus nostris sit
filius. Nam si de stirpe nostra fuisset, ad me utique fuerat deportatus.
Ideoque noveritis, quia a me non suscipitur, nisi certa de eo cognus-
cam indicia'.   (*HF* viii.9)

'It is said that when my brother Chilperic died he left behind a son
whose guardians, acting on his mother's wishes, asked me to receive

him at the baptismal font on Christmas day. But they did not come.
Once more they begged me to have him baptized, on Easter Friday,
but again the child was not brought to me. A third time they requested
that he be presented on St John's day. Yet again he did not appear.
Now they have made me leave my home in this stifling weather. I am
here and, behold, the child is kept hidden and not shown to me. As
far as I can tell, all that is said about him is false. I believe he is the
son of some vassal of ours. If he were of our blood, he would already
have been brought to me. Know, therefore, that I will not receive
him unless I am shown true tokens of his identity.'

The short, blunt sentences, their very plain vocabulary, the lack of any
form of address or other oratorical gesture, undoubtedly characterize
the king as a very different kind of speaker. From many remarks in his
history of the Franks, it becomes clear that Gregory had a keen sense
of the common tongue. Though very modest about his own language,
he recognized many levels of vulgarity below his usage. Of a false
prophet who came to see him at Tours he says: 'Erat enim ei et sermo
rusticus et ipsius linguae latitudo turpis atque obscoena; sed nec de eo
sermo rationabilis procedebat.' / 'His speech was uncouth and he made
abundant use of coarse and indecent expressions; what he said made
no rational sense' (HF ix.6). The prophet later turns out to be the
escaped servant of another bishop, proving thereby that even in the
sixth century you could tell a man's class by his language.[12]

An equally varied range of styles can be found in the works of Gregory
the Great, whose Dialogues are written in a Latin markedly simpler
than that of his theological and homiletic books. Different levels are
recognizable within the Dialogues themselves between on the one
hand the expository speeches of Gregory to the deacon Peter, explanations of the nature of dreams, the function of purgatory, and other
more or less theoretical matters, and on the other hand the plain little
anecdotes of saintly men and women that make up the bulk of the
work. Speculation and theory cannot be dealt with in the simplest
language; for the anecdotes, however, Gregory insists on staying close
to the oral form in which he heard them at first: most often they had
been communicated to him by friends or neighbours of the saints in
question.[13] His awareness of the difference between spoken and written
language is clearly expressed at the beginning of book one, where Gregory, commenting on this fidelity to his sources, remarks to Peter:
'Hoc uero scire te cupio quia in quibusdam sensum solummodo, in
quibusdam uero et uerba cum sensu teneo, quia si de personis omnibus

ipsa specialiter et uerba tenere uoluissem, haec rusticano usu prolata stilus scribentis non apte susciperet.' / 'I want you to know that in some parts I give only the sense [of my sources], in other both the sense and the words. For if I had wished to preserve the exact words of all the characters, my pen would not have been able to produce rustic expressions.' Later examples will show that in certain respects, the short hagiographic narratives of the *Dialogues* can go further in the imitation of ordinary speech than anything attempted by Gregory of Tours.

In some texts, the word-order of the speeches is closer to the Romance languages than to Latin. This transitional quality, perhaps not always deliberate, is particularly noticeable in a narrative from the *Liber historiae Francorum*, the story of how Fredegund, servant to Queen Audovera, brought about a separation between her mistress and King Chilperic by suggesting that Audovera, in her husband's absence, stand godmother to her own newborn daughter. The queen did not remember the prohibition of marriage between the parents and godparents of a child, which was in force at the time.

> Cumque episcopus adfuisset, non erat matrona ad presens, qui puellam suscipere deberet. Et ait Fredegundis: 'Nunquam similem tuae invenire poterimus, qui eam suscipiat. Modo tumet ipsa suscipe eam'. Illa vero haec audiens, eam de sacro fonte suscepit. Veniens autem rex victor, exiitque Fredegundis obviam ei, dicens: 'Deo gratias, quia dominus noster rex victoriam recepit de adversariis suis, nataque est tibi filia. Cum qua dominus meus rex dormiet hac nocte, quia domina mea regina commater tua est de filia tua Childesinda?' Et ille ait: 'Si cum illa dormire non queo, dormiam tecum'. Cumque introisset rex in aulam suam, occurrit ei regina cum ipsa puella, et ait ei rex: 'Nefanda rem fecisti per simplicitatem tuam; iam coniux mea amplius esse non poteris'.   (*LHF* 31)

The bishop arrived, and no lady could be found to receive the little girl from the font. Fredegund said to Audovera: 'We shall never find one as fine as you to receive her. Therefore receive her yourself.' Hearing this, the queen received her from the holy font. When the victorious king came home, Fredegund went out to meet him and said: 'Praised be God that our lord the king is victorious over his enemies. A daughter has been born to you. With whom will my lord the king sleep tonight, since my lady the queen is godmother to your daughter Childesinda?' He said: 'If I may not sleep with her, I shall sleep with you.' As the king entered his hall, the queen came towards him with the little girl, and he said to her: 'You have done a terrible thing through your simple-mindedness; from now on you can no longer be my wife.'

As is well known, Fredegund then took over her mistress's place. Her question to Chilperic, 'Cum qua dominus meus rex dormiet hac nocte?' is used, very colloquially, to make a statement ('You will have to sleep with somebody else tonight'), and the interrogative pronoun coming after 'cum', as in French 'avec qui?', marks the norm of the speaker, if not that of the whole text, as proto-Romance.

When we consider vocabulary, it becomes less easy to find evidence that dialogue follows an artifically simplified standard. In general it is safe to say that rare or literary words, if they are used at all, appear less frequently in naturalistic 'spoken' dialogue than in third-person, or authorial, narrative. What conclusions may we draw from this tendency? How deliberate is the use of this simpler language? Our authors rarely betray an awareness of stylistic levels in vocabulary, the most interesting exception being Agnellus' anecdote about the reception of Charlemagne by the saintly but unlearned Archbishop Gratiosus of Ravenna in 787 (*LPR* 165). Gratiosus had promised to his monks and helpers that he would not open his mouth, but seeing that the royal visitor had barely touched his food, he encouraged him with the words 'Pappa, domine mi rex, pappa.' Charlemagne, expressing surprise and incomprehension ('admiratus rex'), asked the monks: 'Quis est hic sermo, quem vates loquitur, pappa, pappa?' / 'What is this word that the bishop is saying, pappa, pappa?' and they obligingly translated for him the rustic imperative: 'ut comedatis et iocundemini' / 'that you should eat and make merry with us.'[14] Exotic dialect words such as *pappa* are, however, rare, and the absence of the more ambitious literary words must be considered a better index of the style of direct speech.

The obscurity of much spoken language when recorded or transcribed can be explained by its lack of all context. Not only does the setting, the specific situation in which the utterance is made, allow the speaker to use pronouns and demonstratives without further clarification, but the speaker's gestures, facial expressions, and tone of voice, as well as the course of action in which he and his interlocutors find themselves engaged, narrow down the possible meanings of many broken, incomplete, or ambiguous statements. No wonder, then, that in the literary representation of spoken language, however realistic it may be, speech tends to become far more explicit than it ever has to be in real life, and at the same time more independent of the situation in which it occurs. Classical historiography goes very far in this direction, achieving an almost total divorce of words and context. Most often, while a speech is being made there is no other action to account for; what the orator says is fully intelligible in itself, and would make almost as much sense if it were spoken in a very different set of circumstances. Speech, in fact, becomes an alternative to any other kind of activity: when Marius pronounces an oration, the war against Jugurtha comes to a temporary stop. Commands, calls, exclamations, and in general the kind of language that is itself action are rare if not wholly absent in the classical histories; description and reasoned exposition are dominant.

Under the influence of oral narrative, early medieval writers moved towards a coordination of words and action, speech and context. The close interdependence of dialogue and physical activity in the following passage from Gregory of Tours illustrates what could be achieved in this direction. The text describes a violent quarrel between Fredegund and her daughter Rigunth.

> Rigundis autem, filia Chilperici, cum saepius matri calumnias inferret diceritque, se esse dominam, genetricemque suam servitio redeberit, et multis eam et crebro convitiis lacesserit ac interdum pugnis se alapisque caederent, ait ad eam mater: 'Quid mihi molesta es, filia? Ecce res patris tui, quae penes me habentur, accipe et utere ut libet'. Et ingressa in registo, reseravit arcam monilibus ornamentisque praetiosis refertam. De qua cum diutissime res diversas extrahens filiae adstanti porregeret, ait ad eam: 'Iam enim lassata sum; inmitte tu', inquid, 'manum et eiece, quod inveneris'. Cumque illa, inmisso brachio, res de arca abstraheret, adpraehenso mater operturio arcae, super cervicem eius inlisit. Quod cum in fortitudine praemeret atque gulam eius axis inferior ita adterreret, ut etiam oculi ad crepandum parati essent, exclamavit una puellarum, quae erat intrinsecus, voce magna, dicens: 'Currite, quaeso, currite; ecce! domina mea a genetrice sua graviter suggillatur'.   (*HF* ix.34)

Chilperic's daughter Rigunth, however, often spread slanderous stories against her mother and said that she herself was the mistress, and that Fredegund should go back into service. She often attacked her mother with all sorts of insults, and sometimes the two came to blows and slaps. Once Fredegund said to her: 'Why do you annoy me so much, daughter? Look, here are those of your father's treasures which are left in my possession. Take them and enjoy them as you please.' She went to her treasury and opened a chest full of precious objects and ornaments. For a long time she stood there, taking out a great many things and handing them to her daughter, who stood next to her. Finally she said: 'I am tired of this now. Reach in with your own hands and pull out whatever you find.' When Rigunth, with her arms in the chest, was helping herself to the contents, Fredegund took hold of the lid, slammed it down on her neck, and started to press upon it with great strength. The edge of the chest was cutting into Rigunth's throat, so that her eyes were about to burst out of her head. Then one of the maids, who was outside, cried out loudly: 'Hurry! Hurry! My lady is being strangled by her mother!'

Fredegund does not need to specify what she is tired of doing, or where her daughter should reach in with her own hands. Earlier in the scene, when she asks Rigunth why she annoys her so much, she does not have to indicate what prompts her to raise the question. Her short speeches have no logical autonomy in the text: they are conceived as parts of the action, and make little sense in isolation.

The stage itself, its physical disposition, its properties, the actors other than the speaker in their various groupings, can be sketched out without the direct intervention of the narrator by making the speaker refer to them. This can be handled very skilfully, so that it sounds natural and 'spoken,' but is nevertheless quite artificial: a use of the characters' voices for expository purposes. It is Gregory of Tours again who supplies an excellent instance of this device. When Mummolus, the count of Auxerre, decides to betray his fellow-conspirator Gundovald and hand him over to the king's men, he addresses his intended victim with the following treacherous words: 'Nihil tibi fallaciter loquimur; sed ecce! viros fortissimos stantes ad portam tuum opperientes adventum. Nunc autem depone balteum meum aureum, quod cingeris, ne videaris in iactantia procedere; et tuum adcinge gladium meumque restituae.' / 'We are telling you no lies. See the powerfully armed men at the gates, waiting for you. Now then, take off my golden baldric, which you are wearing, so that you may not seem to go forth vaingloriously; gird on your own sword and give me back mine' (*HF* VII.38). Neither the bravoes at the gate, nor the golden baldric, nor the swords to be exchanged are present in the scene except through this speech. Our image of stage and action arises from what the actors themselves say, though to this end they are made to talk in an unnaturally clear descriptive manner.

To enliven his dialogue, the early medieval narrator frames speeches with gestures, which occasionally are only implicit in the spoken words. When in the pages of Notker Balbulus an arrogant bishop interrupts his sermon to have a spectator brought by force to the pulpit because he has kept his hat on and, turning to the congregation, comments on the now bareheaded offender's appearance, exclaiming: 'Ecce videtis, populi, rufus est iste ignavus' / 'Behold, you people, this wretch has red hair!' (*DKR* I.18), the reader is tempted to add various gestures of scorn and denunciation to the scene, all entirely conjectural. Most often, however, our authors delight in the direct description of gesture, even where it does not appear wholly necessary. In the chronicle of Fredegar, a soldier, noticing an old friend among the fleeing enemy on the battlefield, calls out to him: 'Veni sub clepeum meum; de hoc periculo te liberabo.' / 'Come under my shield! I shall save you from this danger' (*CF* IV.90). Though the actual raising of the shield that accompanies his words can be easily imagined by the reader, the author feels called to inform us that, 'cumque ad eum liberandum clepeum aelevassit' / 'as he was raising his shield to protect him,' the ungrateful friend struck him with his sword.

The most common way of tying a gesture to a character's words is to formulate it as an ablative absolute or a participial clause, followed by the customary 'ait' or 'dicit.' A murderer asks for St Martin's help: 'elevata contra basilica manu, ait ... ' / 'with his hand raised in the direction of the church, he said ... ' (*HF* VII.29). Childebert I begs for the lives of his nephews: 'lacrimis respersa facie, ait ...' / 'with his face bathed in tears, he said ... ' (*HF* III.18). The nun Chrodield denounces her abbess and a lover she attributes to her: 'indicans eum digito [ait]: "En ipsum" '/ 'pointing at him with her finger, [she said]: "That one" ' (*HF* x.15). Charlemagne addresses the lazy children of the nobility, who have not studied enough: 'vultum contorquens et flammante intuitu conscientias eorum concutiens, hyronice hęc terribilia tonando potius quam loquendo iaculatus est in illos ...' / 'with a contorted face and a fiery look that shook their conscience, thundering rather than speaking, he scornfully cast these terrible words at them ...' (*DKR* I.3). Archbishop Hildebert of Mainz hands a ceremonial sword to Otto I during his coronation: 'accedens ad altare et sumpto inde gladio cum balteo, conversus ad regem ait ...' / 'going to the altar and taking from it the sword and baldric, he turned to the king and said ...' (*RGS* II.1).

Two characteristics of real-life communication that are automatically dismissed by listeners as soon as they have understood a speaker, and which all but the most realistic or experimental of modern writers leave out of their dialogue, are redundance and incoherence. We should not expect early medieval narrators to reproduce the redundance of ordinary speech in any significant proportion; however, the feature finds some unusual applications in their work. It turns up, of course, in predictable contexts such as commands, to express emphasis and an intensity of determination. When Notker's high-handed bishop orders his sexton to drag the red-haired irreverent to the pulpit, he cries out: 'Attrahe illum, cave ne dimittas! Velis nolis huc debes venire' / 'Drag him here! Don't let him escape! You must come whether you want to or not!', adding as the poor man comes closer: 'Accede propius, appropinqua etiam!' / 'Come nearer! Step up closer!' (*DKR* I.18). A more interesting use of redundance can be found in the fourth book of the *Dialogues* of Gregory the Great, where the author describes the ecstatic deaths of several monks and nuns. The last words of these saintly persons, often addressed to an invisible presence, are extremely redundant, probably to suggest the inexpressible beatitude of a dialogue only one side of which can be quoted: 'Bene ueniunt domini mei, bene ueniunt domini mei. Quid ad tantillum seruulum uestrum estis dignati conuenire? Venio, uenio. Gratias ago, gratias ago.' / 'Be welcome, my lords; be welcome, my lords. Why have you deigned to gather around the meanest of your servants? I come, I come. I give thanks, I give thanks' (IV.12); also, more simply: 'Ecce, domina, uenio. Ecce, domina, uenio.' / 'Behold, my lady, I come. Behold, my lady, I come' (IV.18). We must not forget that in the oral tradition in which these anecdotes circulated at first, such utterances probably came under the special category of 'last words,' and ecstatic last words at that. Whether this led to a more reverent transmission of what was actually said or whether redundant form was already established in tradition as the conventional expression of ecstatic agony is difficult to say. In Gregory's stories, at least, these final speeches are always redundant, which in my view gives some force to the second possibility.[15]

As for incoherence, that is to say the broken and rambling surface of spoken language of the most careless sort, there is no attempt to represent it this early. It is only much later, at the very end of the middle ages, that Chaucer will daringly allow the Wife of Bath to lose the thread of her thought for a moment: 'But now, sire, lat me se, what shal I seyn? / A ha! by God, I have my tale ageyn' (*Canterbury Tales*; D 585–6).

MORE FORMAL TONES

Brevity, syntactic and lexical simplicity, the coordination of speech with action and physical expression: these are new qualities in literary dialogue. They characterize many of the speeches we have looked at so far, and it is tempting to take them as a common denominator for the form of direct speech in the narratives of the period. However, as I pointed out some pages back, the confrontation of Charles the Bald and George of Ravenna proves that there were some alternatives to naturalistic dialogue for the writers of the first medieval centuries. In that episode as Agnellus describes it, the words of the ruler are unlike ordinary speech in two fundamental ways. In the first place, they rhyme and are too highly organized for spontaneous delivery. Secondly, they are placed in a context where they would not occur naturally. Charles has just won the battle of Fontenoy; he is also furious at the bishop. This is clearly the wrong moment for him to strike the majestic pose Agnellus attributes to him. There is no denying, on the other hand, that the scene is eloquent in its own way, and that in its rigidity and artifice we recognize an expressive power that is characteristically early medieval.

Dialogue in the more hieratic register is not always as successful as Agnellus makes it in that particular scene. To illustrate the contrast between 'spoken' and formal styles, I shall first use two deathbed episodes, since we have already seen what Gregory the Great can make of them in the naturalistic range. Both are examples of the sort of formality that arises from the words themselves, from diction and rhetoric rather than from the situation in which the speech is made. A deathbed is undoubtedly solemn, but here it is the form of the speeches rather than their occurrence in such a scene that marks the presence of a more stylized quality. The gravity of the situation does not of itself dictate a more formal tone, since there are equivalent scenes in the most colloquial mode.

A Spanish Visigothic text of the seventh century describes the death of Augustus, a youth of the Catholic community of Mérida, 'ephoebus ... insons simplex et inscius litteris' / 'an innocent and simple youth, ignorant of letters' (VSPE I.1). The narrator, a deacon in the local church of St Eulalia who speaks throughout as an eyewitness, asks the ailing Augustus how he feels and gets the following answer:

'Equidem, quantum ad praesentis pertinet vitae spem fatoer ita iam omnes corporis mei artus resolutos ut nihil virium omnino artus mei remanserit. Quantum vero pertinet ad spem vitae aeternae non solum spem habere me gaudeo, verum etiam ipsum vitae aeternae auctorem dominum Ihesum Christum cum angelorum catervas atque omnium sanctorum innumerabiles multitudines me vidisse confiteor'.   (1.5)

'For my part, as far as the hope of earthly life is concerned, I must say that all the limbs of my body are weakened to such a degree that no strength at all is left in them. Where the prospect of eternal life is concerned, however, I not only rejoice in the hope of it, but confess that I have seen the author and lord of eternal life, Jesus Christ himself, with bands of angels and the countless multitudes of all the saints.'

If the boy's simplicity is borne out by his unremarkable vocabulary, it is roundly contradicted by the balanced opposition of clauses in his reply: 'ad praesentis pertinet vitae spem' – 'pertinet ad spem vitae aeternae,' as well as by the objective infinitives 'habere me gaudeo' and 'vidisse confiteor' balanced within the construction 'non solum' – 'verum etiam.' This is highly organized expository language; instead of displaying his ectasy or his loss of strength by using broken syntax, Augustus becomes a teacher and model of holy dying, and explains what a Christian's disposition at that time must be, both towards the life he is giving up and towards the one that is beginning. This first statement is followed by a very long, orderly, and detailed account of a vision of the hereafter, which the boy is later asked to repeat for the benefit of an abbot.

An equally artificial rendering of a deathbed speech, this time on a political subject, is provided by Widukind of Corvey when he describes the last interview between the moribund Conrad I and his brother Eberhard.

Cumque [rex] se morbo sensisset laborare pariter cum defectione primae fortunae, vocat fratrem, qui eum visitandi gratia adierat, quemque ita alloquitur: 'Sentio', inquit, 'frater, diutius me istam vitam tenere non posse, Deo, qui ordinavit ita, imperante, gravique morbo id cogente. Quapropter considerationem tui habeto, et quod ad te maxime respicit, Francorum toto regno consulito, mei adtendendo, fratris tui, consilio. Sunt nobis, frater, copiae exercitus congregandi atque ducendi, sunt urbes et arma cum regalibus insigniis et omne quod decus regium deposcit preter fortunam atque mores. Fortuna, frater, cum

nobilissimis moribus Heinrico cedit, rerum publicarum secus Saxones summa est. Sumptis igitur his insigniis, lancea sacra, armillis
aureis cum clamide et veterum gladio regum ac diademate, ito ad
Heinricum, facito pacem cum eo, ut eum foederatum possis habere
in perpetuum. Quid enim necesse est, ut cadat populus Francorum
tecum coram eo? ipse enim vere rex erit et imperator multorum
populorum'. His dictis frater lacrimans se consentire respondit.

(*RGS* 1.25)

When the king found himself a prey to illness and sensed that fortune
had turned against him, he called to his side his brother, who had
come to visit him, and spoke to him as follows: 'Brother, I feel that I
cannot stay alive much longer. God has so ordained, and a grave
illness makes it inevitable. Therefore take stock of your predicament
and, what must concern you above all, consider the best interest of
the entire Frankish kingdom, keeping in mind the advice that I, your
brother, give you. We have, oh brother, great armies that we can
summon and lead; we possess cities and arms, as well as the royal
insignia and everything the majesty of kings requires, except good
fortune and character. Good fortune, my brother, and the noblest
disposition belong to Heinrich. The well-being of the state is to be
found with the Saxons. Take therefore these insignia, the sacred
spear, the golden bracelets and the tunic, the sword and crown of the
ancient kings; go to Heinrich and make peace with him, so that you
may always have him as an ally. What need is there that the entire
nation of the Franks should fall with you before him? Indeed, he will
be king and emperor over many nations.' When he had said this, his
brother, weeping, answered that he agreed.

Here too the balance of ablative absolutes in the first sentence and of
imperatives in the second give the passage a literary ring. The enumeration of forms of wealth and power, which are then proclaimed to
be useless without a good character, gives the speech a homiletic tone,[16]
and the introduction of fortune, whether personified or not, strikes a
decidedly rhetorical note. The king would have had to be extraordinarily collected to express himself like this while wounded and sick.
His statement is also remarkable for the variety of arguments and
reasoning that it uses, some purely rhetorical, some moral, and some
political. It is, of course, possible that Conrad has long thought out
the instructions he wishes to give his brother on such a vital issue as
the succession; nevertheless, the very careful formulation of this tes-

tament adds to the effect of its literary phrasing to disqualify it as credible living speech. We are very far from the ecstatic repetitions of Gregory the Great's dying monks. The effect of this language, however, is not to be described in negative terms only; neither Widukind nor the Visigothic hagiographer was aiming at the natural. The hereafter and the royal succession called for a tone more exalted that that of spoken language, a nobler form than ordinary conversation.

The fullness of statement in the speech of Conrad I adds to the effect of unusual formality in an unlikely context, and thereby compromises his role as dying man and the general credibility of the scene. The king makes a very brief reference to the state of his health; after that, the artful and varied logic of his final dispositions suggests a council of state rather than a deathbed. The same feature appears marginally in the words of Augustus of Mérida: his liminal position between life and death allows him to play the part of instructor; people are brought to hear him, and his double role distances the figure of the boy excessively from the ostensible context of the scene, the circumstance of death.

One classical aim of formal elocution is missing in these texts. From the point of view of ancient oratory, formality and fullness of statement would be considered manifestations of eloquence. When in early medieval narrative characters display either or both of these traits in their speech, the point is very rarely to make them seem eloquent persons. Formality and fullness are determined rather by the importance of the subject on which they talk, by the social or moral status of the speaker and, sometimes, by the availability to the author of classical and late antique models. A passage from the *Liber historiae Francorum* shows how fullness can be dictated solely by the nature of the subject. The author has given a lively account of Clovis' wooing of Chrodechild, full of naturalistic dialogue between the princess and Clovis' emissaries. After the marriage has taken place, the Frank says to his wife, 'Postola quod vis, et ego concedam.' / 'Ask for anything you want, and I will grant it.' She replies:

> 'Primum peto, ut Deum caeli, Patrem omnipotentem credas, qui te creavit. Secundo confitere dominum Iesum Christum, filium eius, qui te redemit, Regem omnium regum, a Patre de caelis missum; tertio Spiritum sanctum confirmatorem et inluminatorem omnium iustorum. Totam ineffabilem maiestatem omnipotentiamque coeternam agnosce et agnitam crede et idola vana derelinque, qui non sunt dii, sed sculptilia vana, incendeque ea et ecclesias sanctas, quas succendisti, restaura. Et memento, queso, ut requirere debeas porcionem genitoris

mei et genetricis meae, quos avuncolus meus Gundobadus malo ordine
interficit, si sanguinem eorum Dominus vindicetur'.   (*LHF* 12)

'I ask first that you should believe in God in heaven, the almighty
Father who created you. Second, that you acknowledge Jesus Christ
his son, who redeemed you, the King of all kings, sent down from
heaven by the Father. Third, [that you believe in] the Holy Ghost, who
strengthens and enlightens all the just. Acknowledge their inexpressible majesty and coeternal omnipotence, and having acknowledged,
believe in it. Abandon your useless idols, which are not gods but
vain images. Burn them, and rebuild the holy churches you once set
on fire. And I beg you to remember that you must get back the estate
of my father and mother, who were murdered by the evil initiative
of my uncle Gundobad. In this way the Lord may avenge their blood.'

The shift in style is so violent here that it must be considered a flaw;
the organized, comprehensive statement of Trinitarian orthodoxy and
the conditions of conversion stands in open defiance of its anecdotal,
romantic context. The serious and businesslike tone generated by enumeration ('Primo ... secundo ... tertio ... et memento, queso ... ') ignores
wholly the irony of Chrodechild's last requirement, and imposes an
ecclesiastical gravity on her shrewdness. But for the Franks of the
eighth century there were few subjects of greater seriousness than the
definition of the Trinity, even though for the historical Clovis the issue
at stake had been conversion from paganism and not the acceptance
of orthodox definitions.[17] Confronted with such lofty subject matter,
the anonymous Neustrian author makes Chrodechild recite her demands in words that are strongly reminiscent of the Catholic symbols
and professions of faith of the period.

Another aspect of the context of speeches that we need to consider
here is the matter of interlocutors. Discussing Gregory of Tours' story
of Waddo and the bailiff, we found that the first speeches of the protagonists were not addressed to anyone in particular; on reading them
we cannot tell whether they only represent the speaker's thoughts, or
stand for actual speeches that are being heard by unspecified persons.
Ideally, a naturalistic speech is justified by the presence of one or more
interlocutors, and by being aimed at that particular audience in its
tone, subject, and practical consequences. In this sense, for example,
Fredegund's invitation to her daughter to reach into the chest of treasure shows a flawless insertion in the scene. Narrative of a more hieratic,
stylized sort often presents a clear disjunction between formal and real

interlocutors. The dying Conrad I repeatedly addresses his brother; Chrodechild is apparently talking to her husband in private. The effect of their words, however, is that of a public statement or a proclamation; their speeches are really addressed to the readers of the book and to the public that will hear their stories.

SOME CONVENTIONS OF DIRECT SPEECH

The dramatic illusionism that underlies the conception and design of many scenes in these historical narratives is supported by a number of practical conventions. Groups of people, sometimes large crowds, are made to speak with a single voice. Describing the revolt of the Ravenna clergy against their archbishop, Agnellus reports that the tyrannical prelate, defeated when his priests did not come to escort him to mass on Christmas morning, sent emissaries of peace to the dissidents gathered at the church of St Apollinaris in Cesarea, halfway between Ravenna and Classe.

> His ita peractis, statim pontifex misit nobiles viros cum velocissimis equis, ut satisfacti omnes ad ecclesiam reverterent. Illi vero, cum vidissent eos ad se venientes, mox levaverunt se omnes, submissi humo vultibus, et magna voce, antequam legati pontificis locuti fuissent, dixerunt: 'Recedite, quia non habemus pastorem, sed interfectorem. Quando in hunc regressus est ovile, non talem, ut facit, dedit promissa. Surge, sancte Apolenaris, celebra nobis missam die nativitatis Domini. Te nobis dedit sanctus Petrus pastorem. Ideo tui sumus oves. Ad te cuncurrimus, salva nos. Non hic consecrationem accepisti, sed ipse apostolus suis te beavit manibus et Spiritum sanctum tribuit; ad nos direxit, et nos tuam recepimus praedicationem. Ad gubernandum missus es, non ad delendum. Tu ante acquissimum iudice stas, certa pro nobis, confringe ora cruenta lupi, ut nos deducere valeas per amoena pascua Christi'.   (LPR 122)

These matters transacted, the bishop sent out noblemen on swift horses so that all [the clergy], reconciled, might come back to the church. The priests, however, when they saw them coming, stood up at once with downcast faces and said loudly before the bishop's envoys could speak: 'Turn back, for we do not have a shepherd, but a murderer. When the fold was handed over to him he promised quite different things from what he has performed. Rise, St Apollinaris, celebrate for us the mass of the Lord's nativity. St Peter gave you to us as shepherd; therefore we are your sheep. We gather around you; save us. You were not consecrated here; the apostle himself blessed you with his hands and consecrated you. He directed you to us, and we listened to your preaching. You were sent to rule, and not to exterminate. You stand now before the fairest of judges: fight on our behalf, crush the bloody jaws of the wolf, that you may lead us to the pleasant meadows of Christ.'[18]

I do not quote their *deploratio* in its entirety, but the passage is long enough to make clear that a speech of this sort could not have been uttered chorally by a crowd. That no individual speakers are singled out in this scene can probably be explained by Agnellus' wish to mark the unanimity of the assembled priests. A more animated use of the same device is made by Gregory of Tours when he stages the lynching of the tax-collector Parthenius by a crowd of angry Franks in a church in Trier. Having found asylum in the church, and knowing that it will not be respected by his pursuers, Parthenius has the priests hide him in a chest for liturgical objects and robes. After his enemies have checked every other part of the building, one of them suggests looking in the chest.

> Dicentibus vero costodibus, nihil in ea aliud nisi ornamenta eclesiae contenere, illi clavem postolant, aientes: 'Nisi reservaveritis velocius, ipsi eam sponte confringemus'. Denique, reserata arca, amotis lintiaminibus, inventum extrahunt, plaudentes atque dicentes: 'Tradidit Deus inimicum nostrum in manibus nostris'. Tunc caedentes eum pugnis sputisque perurguentes, vinctis postergum manibus, ad colomnam lapidibus obruerunt.   (*HF* III.36)

> The keepers said that there was nothing inside it except the ornaments of the church, but they demanded the key, saying: 'Unless you unlock it right away, we ourselves shall break it open.' As soon as the chest was open, moving aside the vestments, they found the man and pulled him out, rejoicing and saying: 'God has delivered our enemy into our hands.' After striking him often with their fists and spitting all over him, they bound his hands behind his back, tied him to a pillar, and stoned him to death.

In this scene the mob is active as one man; because their words are brief and closely coordinated with the action of the moment, they are more credible than the laments of the Ravenna clergy.

A more ingenious way of making a crowd talk is to invent a dialogue between anonymous individuals in it, in order to illustrate a reaction or state of mind in which every person present is assumed to share. The author of the *Liber historiae Francorum* places one such scene in his account of the war between Neustrians and Austrasians after the murder of Chilperic I. At night, the troops of Fredegund move forward camouflaged under a forest of branches, after having fastened tiny bells to their riding gear.

> Cum autem custodes hostium Austrasiorum ramis silvarum quasi in montibus in agmine Francorum cernerent et tinnitum tintinnabulorum audirent custodes, dixit vir ad socium suum: 'Nonne crastina die in illo et illo loco campestria erant, quomodo silvas cernimus?' Et ille inridens, dixit: 'Certe inebriatus fuisti, modo deleras. Non audis tintinnabula equorum nostrorum iuxta ipsam silvam pascencium?'
>
> (*LHF* 36)

> The watchmen of the Austrasian army saw branches gathered as in a forest in the middle of the Frankish camp, and heard the jingle of the bells. One of them asked his companion: 'Weren't there open fields yesterday in this place and in that one there? How come we now see woods?' The other one, laughing, replied: 'You must have been drunk, and now you are raving! Can't you hear the bells of our horses that are grazing by the forest?'

The error of these two guards serves to explain how the Neustrians managed to fool all those Austrasians who were not asleep.

Even more artificial is the use of envoys and ambassadors: the narrators present the text of the messages they carry as if the sender were speaking directly. Gregory of Tours tells of one embassy sent by King Childebert to his uncle Gunthchramn in Paris, requesting that various treatises between them be implemented:

> Sed cum eum [Childebertum] Parisiaci recipere nollent, legatos ad Gunthchramnum regem diregit, dicens: 'Scio, piissime pater, non latere pietati tuae, qualiter utrumque usque praesens tempus pars obpraesserit inimica, ut nullus de rebus sibi debitis possit invenire iustitiam. Idcirco supplex nunc depraecor, ut placita, quae inter nos post patris mei obitum sunt innexa, custodiantur'.   (*HF* VII.6)

> Since the Parisians refused to receive Childebert, he sent messengers

to King Gunthchramn and said: 'I know, most pious father, that it
has not escaped your pious understanding how both of us until now
have been the victims of a hostile party, so that neither of us has
been satisfied in his just expectations. Therefore, I beg of you humbly
that the agreements be kept that were made between us after my
father's death.'

The message is introduced by 'dicens' and not 'dicentes'; this is Childebert himself addressing his uncle, and the point of this convention
must be to represent such mediated communication as if it were direct.
The messengers, mere carriers of their master's voice, are not worth
noticing, and the scene can be understood only as a long-distance confrontation between the two rulers. All sense of place is lost; is this
Childebert talking to his messengers, the messengers relaying his words
to Gunthchramn in Paris, or both?

The least common of these literary conventions at the time has had
perhaps the greatest success and remains an essential narrative artifice
today: I mean the rendering of private thoughts as direct speech. Gregory of Tours, who uses the device now and then, introduces interior
monologues with 'haec ad se reversa, ait ... ' / 'turning to herself, she
said ... ' (*HF* ix.33) and, borrowing a phrase from the Vulgate psalter,
with 'dixitque in corde suo ... ' / 'and he said in his heart ... ' (*HF* ix.19).

VOICE AND CHARACTER

A major issue which we have not touched upon is the use of direct
speech in characterization; in other words, the possibility of suggesting
a personal voice, emotions, changing states of mind, through a character's words. We tend to assume in medieval literature a lack of interest in the individual personality, though we probably have an
exaggerated sense of this indifference. In historiography, however, where
much is made to depend on individual figures and their motives, we
may expect some effort to tailor speech to personality.

A first problem in studying this particular function of dialogue is
that very few of our authors portray individuals in action over long
periods of time, so that there is no occasion for a whole personality to
emerge, but only the emotions of a few moments. With the exception
of book two, a biography of St Benedict, Gregory the Great's *Dialogues*
contain only brief anecdotes about many different saints. Agnellus'
Liber pontificalis dedicates a few chapters to each of the archbishops
of Ravenna and his administration. Fredegar and the *Liber historiae*

Francorum describe the adventures of a great many kings and princes without dwelling on any one of them for long. Fortunately, there are two important exceptions to this tendency: Gregory of Tours' *Libri historiarum*, which follows the careers of Clovis, Chrodechild, Fredegund, and Gunthchramn, among others, in sufficient detail, and Notker's collection of stories about Charlemagne.

A reading of Gregory reveals basic limitations of early medieval narrative where psychology is concerned. This judgment may surprise at first, given the intensely emotional quality of so many of the episodes that we are discussing: murder, revenge, martyrdom, political confrontation. The fact is, however, that even in these passages the emotions are implicit in the scenes, and not in the characters. The scene is a type-scene, or at least falls within a certain category, a dramatic range, and it is the category, the type, that determines what emotion is expressed. The loosely episodic form of so much of this writing, in which scene is added to scene, fractures any sense of a unified personality, or of a continuity of character and motivation in the protagonists; they react according to a formula, not to a temperament conceived independently of the demands of the scene.

In a book published in 1940, Gustavo Vinay developed an interesting reading of Gregory of Tours' history of the Franks.[19] According to this interpretation, the entire history is about the appearance of a new factor in European history: the Frankish *feritas*, a quality until then unknown, manifested by the greatest leaders of the Franks. Gregory admires this *feritas*, especially when it is allied to orthodox Catholicism, and he understands it enough to judge it according to a new standard rather than apply the general Christian anathema on cruelty and violence. The bishop of Tours, with the political insight of the Gallo-Roman senatorial class, realizes that the future belongs to this quality, which he has probably come to consider a national or racial characteristic of the Franks. This fierce disposition only reaches full expression in given moments of individual lives (for example, it appears only very seldom in the career of Gunthchramn, far more often in that of Clovis).

Vinay's thesis is enlightening; it gives a theme to Gregory's book and adds meaning to many single episodes. The personality of Fredegund, which I wish to consider here, would seem to be a pure instance of *feritas* in all its blind energy and power. She tries to choke her own daughter with the lid of a chest; she makes her husband murder his former wives Gailswintha and Audovera, as well as some of his children from earlier unions; the defiant Bishop Praetextatus is killed before the altar at her command. Her speeches are either harsh orders or

melodramatic exhortations to Chilperic or to her courtiers and later
protectors to murder enemies of hers (as when she asks for her foe
Leudast to be eliminated: 'Prostrataque pedibus regis, adiecit: "Vae
mihi, quae video inimicum meum, et nihil ei praevaleo." ' / 'Lying at
the feet of the king, she added: "Oh misery, that I see my enemy before
me, and can do nothing against him!" ' [HF vi.32]. The scene takes
place in a church, before Sunday mass). However, when after the deaths
of two of her children she feels that she is being punished for her sins
and invites her husband to repent with her and cancel a new scheme
of taxation, her words are as solemn and sanctimonious as those of
any sermonizing prophet or prelate come to admonish a sovereign.[20]

> 'Diu nos male agentes pietas divina sustentat; nam sepe nos febribus
> et aliis malis corripuit, et emendatio non successit. Ecce! iam perdimus
> filios. Ecce! iam eos lacrimae pauperum, lamenta viduarum, suspiria
> orfanorum interimunt, nec spes remanet cui aliquid congregemus.
> Thesaurizamus, nescientes, cui congregemus ea. Ecce thesauri rema-
> nent a possessore vacui, rapinis ac maledictionibus pleni! Numquid
> non exundabant prumptuaria vino? Numquid non horrea replebantur
> frumento? Numquid non erant thesauri referti auro, argento, lapidibus
> praeciosis, monilibus vel reliquis imperialibus ornamentis? Ecce quod
> pulchrius habebamus perdimus! Nunc, si placet, venite; incendamus
> omnes discriptionis iniquas, sufficiatque fisco nostro, quod sufficit patri
> regique Chlothario'.   (HF v.34)

'For a long time now divine mercy has borne with our evil doings.
Often it has chastised us with fevers and other illnesses, but there
has been no improvement on our part. Now we have lost our children!
Behold, the tears of paupers, the lamentations of widows, the sighs
of orphans have killed them! No hope is left now of an heir for whom
we might gather anything. We store up treasures, not knowing for
whom we are saving them. And our wealth will be left behind without
an owner, haunted by thefts and curses! Did our cellars not overflow
with wine? Were the granaries not packed full of grain? And our store-
rooms, were they not filled with gold, silver, precious stones, jewels,
and other royal ornaments? Now we have lost our most precious
possession! Come, therefore, and let us set fire to these iniquitous
tax-lists. Let what was enough for King Chlothar, your father, suffice
for our exchequer!'

Neither the sentiment nor the very clerical rhetoric of her speech,
which the queen delivers 'pugnis verberans pectus' / 'beating her breast

with her fists,' has anything to do with the *feritas* and *saevitia* of her behaviour in other episodes. This fragmentation of her character is no reflection of the emotional discontinuity and self-contradiction that are part of human nature, but a direct consequence of early medieval scenic narrative. When Fredegund plots a crime and sends her murderers out with careful instructions and poisoned knives, she is the representative of national ruthlessness. Here, she is acting out a scene of repentance; her words echo the texts used by medieval preachers to bring their audience to a realization of guilt, and to make them see their misfortunes as punishment for past crimes. Her use of figurative language ('lacrimae pauperum,' 'lamenta viduarum,' and 'suspiria orfanorum' as agents of the death of her children) and her balancing of parallel clauses and symmetrical questions are suited to what she says, but not to what she is.[21]

Notker's Charlemagne illustrates another variety of this narrative schizophrenia: personal anecdotes show him talking like a shrewd, prosaic peasant, with crude humour and a relative simplicity of expression. When he appears as the emperor, however, every hint of naturalism disappears and he is stylized into a likeness of God the Father, thundering away in majestic periods. He speaks colloquially in his private capacity, as when he comments on the shortness of Frisian cloaks: 'Quid prosunt illa pittaciola? In lecto non possum eis cooperiri, caballicans contra ventos et pluvias nequeo defendi, ad necessaria naturę secedens tibiarum congelatione deficio.' / 'What good are these little tunics? In bed I can't cover myself with them; on horseback they do not defend me from the wind and rain; when I sit down to relieve my bowels I perish from the freezing of my shins' (*DKR* 1.34). The colloquial 'pittaciola' and the mention of the 'necessaria naturę' define the tone of his remarks, though the neat balancing of the three last clauses somewhat restrains their informality by adding a sententious ring to the short speech. On the other hand, Charlemagne appears at his most superhuman in the scene where he praises some children of modest parents because they have studied well, and condemns the young aristocrats who have accomplished nothing in the same time. Appropriating for the state the symbolism of divine judgment, he has the good students placed at his right and the bad ones at his left, like the sheep and the goats. After praising the diligent, he turns to the noble drones:

'Vos nobiles, vos primorum filii, vos delicati et formosuli, in natales
vestros et possessionem confisi, mandatum meum et glorificationem

vestram postponentes, litterarum studiis neglectis, luxurię ludo et
inercię vel inanibus exercitiis indulsistis'. Et his praemissis solitum
iuramentum, augustum caput et invictam dexteram ad çelum con-
vertens, fulminavit: 'Per regem celorum! non ego magni pendo nobi-
litatem et pulchritudinem vestram, licet alii vos admirentur; et hoc
procul dubio scitote, quia, nisi cito priorem neglegentiam vigilanti
studio recuperaveritis, apud Karolum nihil unquam boni acquiretis'.

(DKR 1.3)

'You noble ones, sons of my leading vassals, you delicate and pretty
ones, trusting in your birth and possessions and neglecting my commands and your own improvement, you put aside the study of letters
and dedicated yourselves to the enjoyment of play, idleness, and
foolish amusements.' Having said this, he turned his noble head and
his unvanquished right hand towards the heavens, and thundered
this oath against them: 'By the heavenly king! I do not care much for
your nobility and elegance, whether others admire them or not. Know
without any doubt that unless by diligent study you soon make
up for your former negligence, you will never receive anything of value
from Charlemagne!'

The contrast here is not to be explained by the normal difference between relaxed private behaviour and the more solemn language and
gestures of imperial ceremony. Notker's portrayal of Charlemagne in
state is wholly symbolic; it represents an abstract role and leaves all
psychology aside. The democratic sentiments of his admonition are
supported by his ability to switch occasionally to the equally stereotyped bluntness of his remarks on the uses of the 'pittaciola.'

In given scenes we may find now and then impressive revelations
of character, often about secondary figures. Yet even these are not
disclosures of individual psychology, but accurately observed manifestations of human nature at its most general. Gregory of Tours describes the behaviour of Leudast, count of Tours, after Fredegund publicly
refuses to forgive his offences. The count, characterized by Gregory as
'incautus et levis' / 'imprudent and frivolous,' does not realize that the
queen's bullies are already looking for him.

Igitur regresso rege cum regina de eclesiam sanctam, Leudastis usque
ad plateam est prosecutus, inopinans, quid ei accederit; domusque
negutiantum circumiens, species rimatur, argentum pensat atque
diversa ornamenta prospicit, dicens: 'Haec et haec conparabo, quia

multum mihi aurum argentumque residit'. Ista illo dicente, subito
advenientes reginae pueri, voluerunt eum vinci catenis. Ille quoque,
evaginato gladio, unum verberat; exinde succensi felle, adpraehensis
parmis et gladiis, super eum ruunt.   (*HF* vi.32)

After the king and queen left the church, Leudast followed them to
the street, not realizing what was going to happen to him. He went into
the shops of various merchants, examined their wares, counted his
money, and looked closely at some ornaments. He said: 'I will buy this
and this, for I have a great deal of gold and silver.' As he spoke, the
queen's servants arrived and tried to put him in chains. Leudast,
drawing his sword, struck one of them, and the others, much angered,
took their shields and swords and fell upon him.

A fool's death has a peculiar pathos, and it is Leudast's foolishness and
vanity that are revealed by his irrelevant remark as much as by his
carefree shopper's attitude; the words are both psychologically true and
dramatically effective.[22] And yet we recognize the effect: this is something that Gregory has already done with Waddo of Saintes, whose last
words are an inane question whether the house has been swept and
the benches covered.[23] Even closer to Leudast's attitude before dying
is that of Magnovald, murdered by order of King Childebert II.

Stante infra Mettensis urbis palatium rege et ludum spectante, qualiter
animal caterva canum circundatum fatigabatur, Magnovaldus arcessi-
tur. Quo veniente et nesciente quae actura erant, cum reliquis dissolutus riso, prospicere pecudem coepit. At his cui iussum fuerat, cum
viderit eum spectaculum intentum, librata secure caput eius inlisit.
                                                                (*HF* viii.36)

The king was staying at his palace in Metz, and amused himself by
watching how a wild animal, surrounded by a pack of hounds, was
harried by them. Magnovald was summoned and came, not knowing
what was to happen; he began to laugh with the others and watch the
beast. A man there had been given specific orders; when he saw
Magnovald absorbed by the spectacle, he swung his axe and split his
skull.

Here the victim is given nothing to say, but the phrase 'dissolutus riso'
is sufficient to create the same sense of pathos compounded by fatal
ignorance and frivolity. The common ground of this scene and the

arrest of Leudast is marked by the phrases 'inopinans, quid ei accederit' and 'nesciente quae actura erant.' We may feel that Magnovald remains opaque in death, that in his case there is pathos but no disclosure, since he does not speak. The irony of his predicament is reinforced, however, by a suggested parallel between him and the harried animal. The similarities among the three scenes remind us that however incisive or revealing speeches and brief character notes may seem, we must not underestimate the importance of dramatic stereotypes and formulas in the literature of this period.

Elaborate attempts to characterize the speaking voice can be based on the most familiar clichés: here is Charlemagne's wife Hildegarde trying to persuade her husband to give a bishopric to a protegé of hers rather than to the promising young clerk whom he has already chosen for it:

> Cumque ille peticionem eius iocundissime susciperet, dicens se nihil ei velle aut posse denegare, nisi quod clericulum illum fallere dedignaretur, ut est omnium consuetudo feminarum, ut consilium suum et votum virorum decretis praeponderare velint, dissimulata iracundia mente concepta et grossa voce in exilem conversa gestibusque languidulis inconvulsos imperatoris animos emollire temptata, dixit ad eum: 'Domine mi rex, quid puero illi episcopatum illum ad perdendum? Sed obsecro, domine dulcissime, gloria mea et refugium meum, ut detis illum fideli famulo vestro, clerico meo illi'. (*DKR* I.4)

> He heard her request with pleasure, and said that he neither would nor could refuse her anything, but that he would not disappoint that young clerk. It is the tendency of all women to impose their opinions and desires against the decisions of men. She therefore repressed the anger that she felt inwardly. Making her loud voice delicate and adopting fluttering gestures, she attempted to weaken the emperor's unwavering resolution and said: 'My lord, what does it matter if that boy does not get the bishopric? I beg you, my sweetest lord, my glory and my refuge, to give it to my own cleric, who is also a faithful servant of yours.'

The flattering feminine note is communicated by the empress's own words ('Domine mi rex,' 'domine dulcissime, gloria mea et refugium meum') and reinforced by the descriptive notes ('grossa voce in exilem conversa,' 'gestibusque languidulis'). The observation 'ut est omnium consuetudo feminarum' / 'It is the tendency of all women,' however, gives the whole game away. This is not Hildegarde speaking, but Woman, as she, from the beginning of time, has sought to influence Man's judgment against his better knowledge. In Notker's work no other page recalls this episode and its caricature of gender, but the schematic nature of his portrayal of the empress is no less obvious for that.[24]

DIALOGUE IN THE BYZANTINE LOW-STYLE NARRATIVES

Byzantine literature provides fewer insights on the subject of dialogue and direct speech than on other topics. This is because characterization and the choice between naturalism and a more stylized rhetoric are closely determined in each work by the level of style chosen by its author. The Latin writer can move within a certain range in a single story, and go from the formal language of a solemn introduction, or of the brief admonition to a king or a sinner ascribed to the saint or hero of the narrative, to the simple, short statements of an exchange of insults between warriors. Greek levels of style do not allow for much variation; once chosen, a given style determines every aspect of the text, including the way in which characters express themselves.[25] In the high style, any effort of characterization is precluded by the uniformly artificial, rhetorical quality of the speeches. The less assuming middle style and the low seem open to some expressive variety, but far less than is possible and common in Latin. These stylistic constraints are observed so consistently that the presence of two levels side by side in the same work is usually a good indication that the piece has been put together from sections of different narratives.

In Leontios of Neapolis' *Life of Simeon the Fool*, a hagiographic work of the first half of the seventh century, the hero and his friend Ioannes, while still adolescents, decide to leave the κοινόβιον of Abba Nikon and withdraw to the desert.[26] They have adopted the monastic habit only very recently. As they are making their way out of the monastery in the still of the night, they come upon Nikon, their spiritual father, and give him praise and thanks for his guidance:

> 'We thank you, father, and do not know what to offer in return to
> God and to your venerable head. Who would have hoped to see us
> worthy of such gifts? What king would have been able to honour
> us with such a distinction? What earthly treasures could make us rich
> so suddenly? The use of what baths could thus have purified our
> souls? What family might so love and save us? What hospitality or gifts
> could have had the power to bestow forgiveness of our sins as

instantly as you do, honoured father? In place of all our parents and families, you are our father and mother in Christ. You ruler, you unifier, you leader, you guide, and so many things the tongue is unable to tell.'

This is only the first part of an oration full of heavy parallelism, repetition, and enumeration. The tone is that of prayer, but also of public oratory; these are hardly the accents of private devotion. There is no action; the speakers are frozen in attitudes of thanksgiving. No wonder that Nikon, to whom the speech is addressed, reacts with wonder and admiration.

The shepherd was astounded and amazed, seeing those who had been ignorant two days before, now reason thus because they had taken on the divine [monastic] habit.

Only a few pages later, after Simeon, returned from the desert, has begun his career as holy fool in the city of Emessa, he is falsely accused by a servant girl of making her pregnant. His first reaction, on hearing the charge from the girl's mistress, is to tell her, with clownish gestures of the head and hands: 'ἄφες, ἄφες, ταπεινή, ἄρτι γεννᾷ σοι καὶ ἐσχάνεις μικρὸν Συμεῶνα.' / 'Let it be, let it be, wretched one! Soon she will bear you [a child], and you will have a little Simeon!'[27] Later on we learn that, having befriended some loose women and trained them to be chaste, he would exclaim whenever one of them had yielded to the flesh: 'παρέβης, παρέβης. ἁγία, ἁγία, δὸς αὐτῇ' / 'You went astray! You went astray! Holy Virgin! Holy Virgin! punish her!' The grotesque effect of 'μικρὸς Συμεών,' the repetition of single words, the habit of addressing interlocutors as 'ταπεινός,' 'σαλός,' or 'ἔξηχος,' the brevity of these speeches, all serve to characterize the speaker, a humble saint in the guise of village idiot expressing himself with ludicrous coarseness while he conveys a hidden truth. An expressive range that includes both the very artificial prayer of thanks of the young monks and these brief 'mad' utterances of the older saint is broader than we can allow for a single Byzantine text, and it is one among several features that indicate that the Emessa adventures of Simeon must have been taken without much revision from a πατερικόν, or popular collection of anecdotes about religious men, and incorporated by Leontios into his stylistically more ambitious life of the saint.[28]

In a religious narrative, the low style makes possible a greater range of expression and characterization through speech because the genre has developed from a well-established oral tradition of storytelling connected with the lives and sayings of great ascetics, miracle-workers, and religious leaders. In this tradition, as documented in the *Apophthegmata patrum*, naturalistic dialogue is the rule. Secular narrative at this humblest literary level shows far more limited means of expression and marked technical insecurity in making characters talk. It is probably the weakness of the secular oral tradition, or its absence, that makes the figures of Byzantine historiography in the low style waver between awkward, unnatural formulas and a more believable human tone.[29] In his *Chronographia*, written in the late sixth century, Ioannes Malalas has the Augusta Pulcheria announce to her brother Theodosius II that she has found him a bride:

> 'I have found you a young woman, very beautiful, refined, well bred, eloquent, of Greek origin, a virgin, the daughter of a philosopher.'
>
> (Book XIV)

Nothing less credible dramatically than this lifeless inventory. But what is interesting about Malalas, who is here relating events recent enough that they cannot be entirely shaped yet by the oral mode of presentation, is that he has no consistent manner.[30] Here and there he can make his actors talk with a surprisingly natural sound, which avoids rigid formulas such as Pulcheria's enumeration of qualities and goes beyond the limited dramatic schemes of the oral tradition. Theodosius' intended bride, the Athenian virgin Athenais (later Eudoxia), becomes empress. She had originally come to Constantinople seeking legal help against her brothers, who refused to share with her the paternal inheritance.[31] Once married to Theodosius, she elevates these brothers to important positions in the administration and explains her kindness to them with the following words:

> 'If you had not used me badly, I would not have been forced to go and become empress. You gave me the rank of empress, which did not correspond to my birth. It was my good fortune that made you unjust to me, and not your ill-will.'   (Ibid)

Word-order and vocabulary have the simple 'spoken' ring, and communicate effectively the placid, forgiving tone of the young woman.[32] If the narrative as a whole shows the lack of a definite manner in its dialogue, this may also be explained in part by the predominance of indirect speech and non-scenic, discursive presentation. In spite of the very popular level of Malalas' writing, *oratio recta* is far less frequent in his work than in that of his Latin contemporaries.[33]

Independently of the manner in which it is represented, the act of speech often acquires in these narratives an uncommon significance. Words constitute a *littera* (German *Wortlaut*), a text to which the speaker will be held in the most narrow sense, with no latitude of interpretation whatsoever. Because of the dangers that can arise from speaking when our utterances are taken so literally, words are presented as risks and also as traps, frequently fatal however harmless and trivial they may have seemed when spoken. Widukind provides an excellent illustration of this kind of understanding and use of words in a tale about an equivocal oath. Archbishop Hatho of Mainz is assigned the task of delivering the rebellious Count Adalbert of Bamberg into the king's hands. Hatho rides alone into Adalbert's stronghold and takes an oath that either he will make peace between him and the king or he will bring him back to his fortress uninjured. As they are leaving, Adalbert offers the archbishop some lunch, but the latter refuses. As soon as they are outside the city gates, however, he pretends to change his mind: ' "Proh", inquit, "saepius petit, qui oblata spernit; taedet me longioris viae tardiorisque horae. Nam ieiuni tota die non possumus ambulare." ' / ' "Alas," he said, "he who refuses what he is offered often has to beg for it later on. I am anxious about the long way we have to go, and the lateness of the hour. For we cannot travel all day without eating" ' (*RGS* 1.22). The proverbial sound of 'saepius petit, qui oblata spernit' underscores Hatho's nonchalant manner, put on to deceive the count, since this moment is the turning point of his stratagem. They all go back into the citadel to eat, and here Hatho considers himself released from his oath, since he has complied with it by bringing Adalbert back unharmed: 'Pontifex in urbem reversus cum Adalberto liberatur a lege iuramenti, ut sibi videbatur, eo quod incolumem eum loco suo constituisset' (ibid). After lunch, he takes Adalbert to the king and hands him over to be executed.

But the scope of early medieval literalism is by no means restricted to equivocal oaths, or to characters like Hatho, of whom Widukind writes that he was 'obscuro genere natus ingenioque acutus, et qui difficile discerneretur, melior consilio foret an peior' / 'of humble origin and extremely cunning; it is hard to say whether his advice did more evil or good' (ibid). The holiest men may use this reductive interpretation of their own words in fulfilment of spiritual and ecclesiastical duties, as a form of *reservatio mentalis*, or equivocation. Gregory the Great tells the story of Libertinus of Funda, a monk who, having been beaten by his abbot with a footstool until he is black and blue all over, forgives his superior the undeserved blows, teaching him a lesson in magnanimity and meekness. He does not wish to expose the injustice and violence of his master, so when his fellow monks ask him about the bruises on his face, he is forced to make a very curious statement in order not to lie: 'Hesterno die sera, peccatis meis facientibus, in scabillo subpedaneo inpegi adque hoc pertuli.' / 'Yesterday evening, on account of my sins, I collided with a footstool and suffered this harm' (*Dialogues* I.2).

Some of the stories seem to imply that God himself shares this standard of interpretation, and that he will hold us to the letter of anything we say, even if we have said it in a flight of rhetoric or a moment of emotional abandon. Agnellus, having told the story of his ancestor, the scholar Johannicius, who was tortured to death by order of Justinian II, adds that Johannicius' sister, while she was lamenting his death, exclaimed that if she could only look upon the tyrant's severed head once in her life, she would not mind dying immediately after. A revolution took place and Justinian was beheaded. His head was handed down the streets of the city, stuck on the point of a spear.

> Factum est autem, cum per singulas plateas duceretur iam dictum capud in summitate lanceae fixum, nunciatum est ad praefatam feminam, quod truncatum capud inde sit ferendum. Quae subito in superiora ascendit domus, per fenestram respiciens, stare illum portatorem rogavit; et cum diutissime idem intueretur, lacrimis obortis pectusque replevit, agens gratias Deo, quia quod desideravit cunspexit. Et dum vellet se ad fenestram deflectere, cecidit retro et quassata mortua est.   (*LPR* 142)

> It happened, however, that as the head was being paraded down the various streets, stuck on the point of a spear, the aforesaid lady was told that the severed head was being brought that way. Immediately, she withdrew to an upper floor of the house and, looking out through the window, begged the bearer to stop. She looked at the head for a very long time; her tears welled over, bathing her breast, and she gave thanks to God for the sight that she had so desired. As she was

moving away from the window, she fell backwards and died from
the fall.

If God did not overlook the lady's effusion, neither does he punish the
wiles of those who swear equivocal oaths to mislead and deceive their
fellow men.

Words spoken in anger or drunkenness are often found to play a key
role in early medieval stories, as manifestations of the destructive
power of language and the irrevocability of the *littera*. Paul's history
of the Langobards contains a very good instance of the danger of angry
words in the story of Ferdulf, duke of Friuli, and Argait, one of his
vassals (*HL* vi.24). Argait allows some Slavic cattle-thieves to escape
after a raid on Friulan territory, and the enraged duke says to him:
'Quando tu aliquid fortiter facere poteras, qui Argait ab arga nomen
deductum habes?' / 'When have you done anything with courage, you
whose very name Argait is derived from *arga*?' In Langobardic *arga*
meant 'perverse, homosexual' as well as 'weak' and 'effeminate'; these
are not just angry words, but words about words, an etymological insult. Later, on the occasion of a large incursion of Slavs, Argait reminds
his lord of this ill-advised insult: 'Memento, dux Ferdulf, quod me esse
inertem et inutilem dixeris et vulgari verbo arga vocaveris. Nunc autem
ira Dei veniat super illum, qui posterior e nobis ad hos Sclavos ac-
cesserit.' / 'Remember, Duke Ferdulf, that you said I was a weakling
and a useless fellow, and called me 'arga' in our common language.
Let the wrath of God now fall on him who is last to reach the Slavs.'
He then leads him on a wildly exposed charge against the enemy in
the course of which the Langobardic nobility of Friuli is wiped out
entirely.

The consequences of words carelessly spoken and overheard by the
wrong parties are brought home to us no less dramatically. Paul has a
pointed anecdote about the usurper Alahis, who wrested the Langobardic kingship from Cunincpert, the rightful heir. Having come to
power with the help of Aldo and Grauso, wealthy noblemen of Brescia,
he was no sooner victorious than he began to plan the destruction of
his allies. One day he was counting coins in the presence of one of
Aldo's young children. A coin fell to the floor and was handed back to
him by the boy. Alahis, believing the child would not understand him,
said: 'Multos ex his genitor tuus habet, quos mihi in proximo, si Deus
voluerit, daturus est.' / 'Your father has many of these, which he soon,
God granting, will hand over to me' (*HL* v.39). That evening, the boy

repeated the king's words to his father at home, and they eventually led to Alahis' expulsion and death and to the return of the ousted Cunincpert. The story as told by Paul emphasizes the trivial, everyday occasion on which the fatal words were uttered, as well as the apparent harmlessness or insignificance of the child who heard them, ironies meant to teach us that no words are unimportant, that what we say can always turn against us and destroy us.

3 Gestures

Speeches are not an absolute requisite of the scene. They often constitute the climax, or at least the most conspicuous element in the filling of the scenic frame, and, particularly when rendered in the more vivid, naturalistic style, they mark an early medieval innovation in narrative technique. But there are alternatives to speech, and our narrators knew them well.

In the third book of his history of the Langobards, Paul the Deacon describes a royal betrothal. After the death of King Authari, his subjects decide to let his widow, the Bavarian princess Theudelinda, who had made herself beloved among them, choose their next ruler by taking him as her husband. Her choice falls upon Agilulf, the duke of Turin, and she has him summoned immediately.

> Qui cum ad eam venisset, ipsa sibi post aliquod verba vinum propinari fecit. Quae cum prior bibisset, residuum Agilulfo ad bibendum tribuit. Is cum reginae, accepto poculo, manum honorabiliter osculatus esset, regina cum rubore subridens, non deberi sibi manum osculari, ait, quem osculum ad os iungere oporteret. Moxque eum ad suum basium erigens, ei de suis nuptiis deque regni dignitate aperuit.
>
> (*HL* iii.35)

> When he appeared before her, she, after a few words, had some wine served. Drinking first, she offered what was left to Agilulf. As he took the cup, he respectfully kissed the queen's hand, but she, blushing and with a smile, said that the man ought not to kiss her hand whom

it befitted to kiss her lips. Straightway she raised him up to kiss her, and annouced to him their marriage and his royal dignity.

The text quoted here adds up to a full scene. The narrative is in the style of the period: brief in the extreme and thoroughly dramatized, with no intrusion or comment from the narrator. What is most remarkable, however, is that it is staged entirely by means of gestures. The sequence: T drinks – T offers the cup to A – A takes the cup – A kisses the hand of T – T blushes and smiles – A kisses T on the lips, tells us all we need to know. The queen's remark, given in indirect form, serves as a clarifying gloss on the action, and does not seem really necessary. If we wished to reduce the scene to its bare essence, we might well take the words 'eum ad suum basium erigens'; put in those terms, that action conveys the sense of the whole episode. Already, however, we see the close interdependence of gesture and phrasing. Few movements and gestures have a fixed meaning unaffected by the words used to describe them. Everything here depends on the range of 'erigens,' which makes it possible to read Agilulf's political elevation from duke to king into his change of physical posture.

If we analyse the sequence outlined above, it will appear that its various elements work in different ways. Theudelinda's blush and her smile are immediately comprehensible as natural reactions. Expressive gestures of the most primary, symptomatic sort, they reveal emotions without the mediation of any cultural code. Not so the two kisses, which reflect a social convention, an etiquette of which we must be aware to interpret their import and even the sense of the queen's remark. The kiss on the lips, furthermore, is the osculum sponsalicium of late antique and medieval law, an element of legal ceremony and gestural symbolism.[1] Theudelinda's offer of the cup is the most complex movement in the scene: it can be taken as a simple action, a practical step to provide her guest with refreshment, consistent with a universal custom of hospitality. If we consider it in the context of Germanic narrative, however, and specifically in connection with the traditional feminine roles in the legends of the Migration period, we will have to place her cup of wine next to the one offered by Hiltgunt to the hero in Waltharius (lines 224–5): 'Illa mero tallum complevit mox pretiosum / porrexitque viro qui signans accipiebat ... ' / 'She soon filled a costly cup with wine, / and handed it to the man, who crossed himself as he took it ... ', next to the beaker brought by Gudrún to her husband Atli in the Eddic 'Atlakvíða,' as he returns from killing her brother (stanza 33): 'Út gecc þá Gudrún   Atla í gogn / med gyltom kalki   at reifa giǫld rognis ...' / 'Then Guðrún went out to meet Atli, / with a gilded beaker to give the prince his reward ... ', and next to the many cups brought around by Queen Wealhþeow to her husband's guests in *Beowulf* (lines 620–4): 'Ymbēode þā   ides Helminga / duguþe ond geogoþe   dæl æghwylcne, / sincfato sealde,   oð þæt sæl ālamp, / þæt hīo Bēowulfe,   bēaghroden cwēn / mōde geþungen   medoful ætbær ... ' / 'Then the lady of the Helmings went round / among all the warriors and the young men, / offering [drink in] costly beakers, until it happened / that the bejewelled queen of noble disposition / brought to Beowulf a cup of mead ... ' Her offer of wine puts Theudelinda in the traditional attitude of the royal hostess, the lady of the hall, the heroine.[2] Her gesture here is coloured and modified by the fact that she has drunk first from the cup. For the time being, she is the head of state and must express her position by this assumption of privilege. The offer of a shared cup, nevertheless, is already a proposal of marriage. She had been served by a domestic (present but invisible, like the stage attendants of the Kabuki), and could have had wine poured for Agilulf by somebody else. She is not performing a merely practical action; her behaviour is variously coded.

Scenes staged primarily in gestural terms can also function on the basis of more artificial symbolic and iconographic associations, with little or no help from blushes, tears, and other natural manifestations of emotion. A good instance of such staging is the climax of Agnellus' story about the *cubicularius* Lauricius. Commissioned by the Emperor Honorius to build him a palace in Cesarea, a suburb between Ravenna and Classe, Lauricius raised instead a basilica in honour of St Lawrence. His master finally came to inspect the finished building.

> Qui dum ex longinquo itinere Honorius augustus a Caesaream pervenisset, vidensque sublimia aedificia, placuit valde sibi; qui cum intus fuisset ingressus, veloci cursu Lauricius fugiens post sanctam aram, ut evadere potuisset. Quem cum iussisset Honorius cunprehendere, cecidit in faciem suam pronus in terram, et factus in extasim, preciosissima gemma, quam in corona capitis habebat, infixa est in una ex lapidibus. Solumque caput sursum erigens, post nebulatis oculis visumque receptum, vidit post ipsum altare beati Laurentii, quod beatissimus papa consecraverat Iohannes, stantem praedictum Lauricium et athleta Christi Laurentius manum super Lauricii colla tenentem. Tunc imperator Lauricium iustiorem se iudicavit, et relicta iracundia, acsi patrem eum venerare coepit et secundum se inter omnes in palatio habuit.   (*LPR* 35)

After a long journey, the Emperor Honorius arrived in Cesarea and, seeing the lofty buildings, felt very pleased. When he went into [the church], Lauricius ran swiftly and took refuge behind the holy altar in order to escape. Honorius ordered his arrest, but as he did so he fell on his face, flat on the ground. He lay there in a trance, and the precious gem which adorned his crown was thrust into one of the flagstones. After the fog that had dimmed his eyes disappeared and his sight returned, Honorius raised his head only and saw behind the altar of St Lawrence, which the blessed Bishop Johannes had consecrated, Lauricius standing and Christ's champion Lawrence with his hand on Lauricius' neck. Then the emperor judged Lauricius to be a better man than himself. Giving up his anger, he began to respect him as if he were his father, and made him second in importance to himself among all the people in the palace.

Clearly, speech is dispensable here. Honorius' order to arrest the hero is not quoted, even indirectly, but merely indicated ('Honorius ordered his arrest'); his praise of Lauricius in the end is summarized in the most general terms ('judged Lauricius to be a better man than himself'). There are two climactic moments in the scene as it stands: first the emperor's fall, and in particular the collision of the jewel in his diadem with the marble floor, a symbolic humiliation of imperial arrogance before sanctity, expressed as a clash of objects rather than persons. The second crucial moment takes place when the fallen emperor raises his head and sees St Lawrence and Lauricius before him, the saint with his hand resting on the pious builder's neck, in a conventional attitude of patronage and protection.[3] Here the point is put across by the familiar symbolism of certain gestures and positions: the raising of one's head to behold a revelatory vision, Honorius prone before the standing Lauricius, St Lawrence's hand 'Lauricii colla tenentem.'

Scenes where the gestures, or simply the physical behaviour of individuals, whether expressive or not, are described in some detail constitute something of a novelty in European narrative. If we recall Sallust's Ligurian soldier creeping over the fortress wall in search of snails, it is mainly because such pictures are uncommon in classical history. Livy expresses the general sense that such details are trivial and not worthy of serious history when, describing the fight between young Titus Manlius and a huge Gaul who had challenged the entire Roman nobility, he excuses himself for including the most striking gestural note in the whole episode.

Armant inde iuuenem aequales; pedestre scutum capit, Hispano
cingitur gladio ad propiorem habili pugnam. Armatum adornatumque
aduersus Gallum stolide laetum et – quoniam id quoque memoria
dignum antiquis uisum est – linguam etiam ab inrisu exserentem
producunt.   (VII.10)

The youth, armed by his comrades, takes a foot-soldier's shield and
girds on a Spanish sword, suitable for closer combat. They lead him out
thus armed and adorned to meet the Gaul, who rejoices foolishly
and – the ancients considered even this worthy of commemoration –
sticks out his tongue in ridicule.[4]

Early medieval narrative changes the stylistic balance altogether; though
speech remains more frequent than physical action, it becomes possible
occasionally to do without speech, or almost. And beyond mere action,
expressive movements can be articulated into an alternative language
to convey concepts and emotion.

FOCUS AND PUNCTUATION

Scenes articulated exclusively or primarily by gestures, like the two
we have examined, are, as we might expect, unusual; they represent
a possibility within the style of the period, but one that is seldom used.
A more economic and varied distribution of significant elements is the
rule, so that in the most common type of scene gesture appears linked
with direct and indirect speeches, with props and symbolic objects,
and the summarizing remarks of the narrator, to form a chain of heterogeneous items. In this more frequent sort of narrative sequence, the
gestures can be placed in a variety of ways, of which two are perhaps
the most effective: as the focus of a scene, or scattered throughout it
to form a kind of dramatic punctuation. In the first type of arrangement
the gesture stands at the centre of the episode on account of either its
causal function or some more superficial, flamboyant quality of its
own. The other elements of the scene, and particularly all reactions
to the gesture itself, whether verbal or not, together with the narrator's
own observations, serve to comment on this gestural focus and interpret it. A good example of this scenic type is an anecdote of the Byzantine court told by Notker, and typical of the line of invidious
comparisons between the Frankish empire and Byzantium that fill the
second half of his book.[5] Charlemagne sends an ambassador to the

Greeks, and the man is invited to dinner by the emperor. Coming from
a more rational court, he is unaware of an extravagant local custom.

> Tunc rex vocavit eum ad convivium suum et inter medios proceres
> collocavit. A quibus talis lex constituta erat, ut nullus in mensa
> regis, indigena sive advena, aliquod animal vel corpus animalis in
> partem aliam converteret, sed ita tantum, ut positum erat, de super-
> iori parte manducaret. Allatus est autem piscis fluvialis et pigmentis
> infusus, in disco positus. Cumque hospes idem, consuetudinis illius
> ignarus, piscem illum in partem alteram giraret, exurgentes omnes
> dixerunt ad regem: 'Domine, ita estis inhonorati sicut numquam
> anteriores vestri'. At ille ingemiscens dixit ad legatum illum: 'Obstare
> non possum istis, quin morti continuo tradaris. Aliud pete, quod-
> cumque volueris, et complebo'. Tunc parumper deliberans cunctis
> audientibus in hęc verba prorupit: 'Obsecro, domine imperator, ut
> secundum promissionem vestram concedatis mihi unam peticionem
> parvulam'. Et rex ait: 'Postula quodcumque volueris, et impetrabis,
> praeter quod contra legem Grecorum vitam tibi concedere non possum'.
> Tum ille: 'Hoc' inquit 'unum moriturus flagito: ut quicumque me
> piscem illum girare conspexit, oculorum lumine privetur'. Obstupe-
> factus rex ad talem conditionem iuravit per Christum, quod ipse hoc
> non videret, sed tantum narratibus crederet. Deinde regina ita se cępit
> excusare: 'Per lętificam theotocon sanctam Mariam, ego illud non
> adverti'. Post reliqui proceres, alius ante alium, tali se periculo exuere
> cupientes, hic per clavigerum çeli, ille per doctorem gentium, reliqui
> per virtutes angelicas sanctorumque omnium turbas ab hac se noxa
> terribilibus sacramentis absolvere conabantur. Tum sapiens ille
> Francigena vanissima Hellade in suis sedibus exsuperata victor et sanus
> in patriam suam reversus est.   (DKR II.6)

Then the king invited him to his table and placed him among his
leading nobles. In this company the following law was in force: no
one at the king's table, whether native or foreigner, could turn over any
animal or part of an animal, but only eat from the top of it, as it
had been set before him. A fresh-water fish was served, cooked in spices
and placed on a dish. When the guest, ignorant of that custom, turned
the fish over, all the men arose and said to the king: 'Lord, you have
been insulted as none of your predecessors.' The king said mournfully
to the ambassador: 'I cannot go against these men. You must be handed
over to be executed right away. Therefore ask for something, anything
you want, and I shall grant your wish.' After reflecting for a moment,

the ambassador spoke the following words in the hearing of all there: 'I beg, lord emperor, that according to your promise you will assent to one small request.' The king said: 'Ask for anything you want and you will get it, except that I cannot go against the law of the Greeks and let you live.' He replied: 'This is all I ask before I die: that whoever saw me turn over the fish may lose the light of his eyes.' Astounded by the request, the emperor swore by Christ that he had seen nothing, but only believed what others told him. Then the queen began to excuse herself: 'By the blessed mother of God, St Mary, I did not see it.' Then the other nobles, one after another, wishing to escape this dangerous predicament, tried to excuse themselves by swearing tremendous oaths: one swore by the celestial doorkeeper, the other by the apostle of the pagans, the rest by the angelic host and by the company of all the saints. The clever Frank, having defeated the foolish children of Hellas on their own ground, went back hale and victorious to his native country.

Though Notker pays most attention to the Frank's clever evasion and to the ridiculous oaths and excuses of the queen and courtiers, these are all responses to the turning over of the fish, the innocent and ordinary action which sets off the chain of events. As performed by the Frank, this is a mere practical action rather than a gesture, but we have been told its meaning and consequences in advance, so that when it happens we are aware of it as an offence, an insult in the code of Byzantine etiquette. It becomes clear that the expressive value or the significance of a gesture as used in narrative need not be made to depend on the intention or purpose of the character who performs it. The extremely arbitrary interpretation attached to this movement at the Greek court is an important part of the meaning of the scene, designed to bring out the relativity of such codes (what is correct or meaningless at Aachen is a serious insult in Constantinople) and the perverse foolishness of the Byzantines. Since the act, by nature neutral, does not carry its consequences implicit in itself, it has to be noticed and reacted to, undergoing a public 'reading' of sorts, and the speeches of the courtiers serve to decipher it in this way, giving a sense to what obviously has none.[6]

Far more often gestures, instead of being the subject of dialogue, serve as a complement to the speeches. The importance of such complements can vary widely; on occasion the accompanying gesture can turn the meaning of a character's words into their logical opposite, or serve as a negation. Most frequently, however, these brief gestural notes are used for emphasis or emotion, to indicate schematically the narrator's dramatic conception of the scene. Here the natural expressive functions of gesture predominate over its code-dependent, civilized values; they add immediacy and a minimum of visual reality to the narrative, but do not affect its basic sense. We find gestures used in this way in Gregory of Tours' account of the trial of Praetextatus, falsely accused by Chilperic I of conspiring to commit regicide. Deceived by promises of royal mercy if he will only plead guilty to the charges, the accused prelate appears before the king and a jury of his peers.

> Cumque haec altercatio altius tolleretur, Praetextatus episcopus, prostratus solo, ait: *'Peccavi in caelo et coram te* (Luc. 15, 18), o rex miserecordissime; ego sum homicida nefandus; ego te interficere volui et filio tuo in solio tuo eregere'. Haec eo dicente, prosternitur rex coram pedibus sacerdotum, dicens: 'Audite, o piissimi sacerdotes, reum crimen exsecrabile confitentem'. Cumque nos flentes regem elevassemus a solo, iussit eum basilicam egredi. Ipse vero ad metatum discessit, transmittens librum canonum, in quo erat quaternio novus adnixus, habens canones quasi apostolicus, continentes haec: *Episcopus in homicidio, adulterio et periurio depraehensus, a sacerdotio divillatur.* His ita lectis, cum Praetextatus staret stupens, Berthechramnus episcopus ait: 'Audi, o frater et coepiscope, quia regis gratiam non habes, ideoque nec nostram caritatem uti poteris, priusquam regis indulgentia merearis'.   (*HF* v.18)

The argument went on and on, and then Bishop Praetextatus, prostrating himself on the floor, said: *'I have sinned against heaven and against you* (Luke 15:18), most merciful king; I am a miserable murderer; I planned to assassinate you and set your son on the throne.' After he had spoken, the king threw himself at the feet of the bishops and said: 'Hear, most pious bishops, how this guilty man confesses his terrible crime!' Weeping, we raised the king from the floor, and he ordered Praetextatus to leave the cathedral. The king went to his dwelling and sent us a copy of the canons with a new four-page fascicle which contained what seemed to be apostolic canons. It read: *'A bishop found guilty of homicide, adultery, or perjury will be stripped of his bishopric.'* This was read out and, as Praetextatus stood there dazed, Bishop Bertram spoke to him: 'Listen, brother and fellow bishop, you have lost the king's favour. You cannot benefit from our mercy before you have deserved the king's forgiveness.'

Prosternations and tears add to the general gloom of the scene, but tell us nothing that we did not know already. Chilperic's kneeling before the clergy only underscores his manifest hypocrisy, since Gregory has told us earlier that the false promises of mercy had been conveyed to Praetextatus at his command, though anonymously. The bishop's dumbfounded expression on hearing the canons read is a clever touch, perhaps essential from the dramatic point of view, but it is already clear enough from the narrative that he has been fooled.[7] The scene would not be the same without these vivid observations, but they do not determine or affect the course of events.

A far more effective and important method of dramatic punctuation consists in staging a given scene around the repetition of one or two gestures, sometimes with considerable variation in the form and meaning of the repeated element. Gregory of Tours is a master of this technique. Early in his history of the Franks, in an excursus about the Arian persecution of Catholics in Africa, he tells of the defeat of an Arian bishop who, to compete with the numerous healing miracles of his Catholic rivals, attempts to fake the cure of a blind man.

> Quod cernens ille nequam Arrianorum episcopus, vocatum ad se quendam hominem ab illo quo ipse vivebat errore, ait: 'Non patior, quod hi episcopi multa in populos signa depromunt illosque cuncti, me neglecto, secuntur. Adquiesce nunc his quae praecipio, et acceptis quinquaginta aureis, sede in platea, per qua nobis est transitus, et manum super clausus oculus ponens, me praetereunte cum reliquis, exclama in magna virtute, dicens: "Ad te, beatissime Cirola, nostrae relegiones antestes, depraecor, ut respiciens manefestis gloriam ac virtutem tuam, ut oculos meos aperiens merear lucem videre quam perdedi".' Qui iussa conplens resedensque in platea, transeunte heretico cum sanctis Dei, iste qui Deum inridere cogitabat exclamat in magna virtute, dicens: 'Audi me, beatissime Cyrola, audi me, sanctae sacerdus Dei, respice caecitatem meam! Experear ego medicamenta, quae saepe caeci reliqui a te meruerunt, quae lebrosi experti sunt, quae ipsi mortui praesenserunt. Adiuro te per ipsam virtutem quam habes, ut mihi desideratam restituas lucem, quia gravi sum caecitate percussus'. Veritatem enim nesciens, verum dicebat, quia caecaverat eum cupiditas, et virtutem Dei omnipotentis inridere per pecuniam aestimabat. Tunc hereticorum episcopus paululum se divertit, quasi in virtute triumphaturus, elatus vanitate atque superbia, posuit manum super oculos eius, dicens: 'Secundum fidem nostram, qua recte

Deum credimus, aperiantur oculi tui'. Et mox ut hunc nefas erupit, risus mutatur in planctum, et dolus episcopi patefactus in publico; nam tantus dolor oculos miseri illius invasit, ut eos digitis vi comprimeret, ne creparent. Denique clamare coepit miser ac dicere: 'Vae mihi misero, quia seductus sum ab inimico legis divinae! Vae mihi, quia Deum per pecuniam inridere volui et quinquaginta aureos accepi, ut hoc facinus perpetrarem!' Ad episcopum autem aiebat: 'Ecce aurum tuum, redde lumen meum, quod dolo tuo perdidi! Vos quoque rogo, gloriosissimi christiani, ne despiciatis miserum, sed velociter occur-rite pereunti! Vere enim cognovi, quia *Deus non inridetur* (Gal. 6, 7)'. Tunc sancti Dei misericordia moti: '*Si*', inquiunt, '*credis, omnia possibilia sunt credenti* (Mark 9, 22)'. At ille clamabat voce magna: 'Qui non credederit Christum Filium Dei et Spiritum sanctum ae-qualem habere substantiam atque deitate cum Patre, hodie quae ego perfero patiatur'. Et adiecit: 'Credo Deum Patrem omnipotentem, credo Filium Dei Christum Iesum aequalem Patri, credo Spiritum sanctum Patri et Filio consubstantialem atque coaeternum'. Haec illi audientes et se invicem honore mutuo praevenientes, oritur inter eos sancta contentio, quis oculis eius signum beatae crucis inponeret. Vindimialis vero ac Longinus Eugenium, ille autem eos exorat, ut manus inponerent caeco. Quod cum fecissent et manus suas super capud eius tenirent, sanctus Eugenius crucem Christi super oculos caeci faciens, ait: 'In nomine Patris et Fili et Spiritus sancti, veri Dei, quem trinum in unam aequalitatem atque omnipotentiam confite-mur, aperiantur oculi tui'. Et statim ablata dolore, ad pristinam rediit sanitatem.   (*HF* ii.3)

Seeing [the miracles of the Catholics], that evil bishop of the Arians called to him a certain man who believed the same heresy as he and said: 'I cannot suffer that these bishops should perform so many wonders among the people, so that they are followed and I neglected. Do as I will tell you and you will get fifty pieces of gold: go sit on the street down which we usually walk. Place your hand over your closed eyes and as I pass by with the others, cry out as loud as you can: "I beg you, most blessed Cirola, bishop of our religion, to look upon me and manifest your glory and your power, that my eyes may be opened and I may deserve to see the light that I have lost." ' The man obeyed his command and sat down on the street. As the heretic walked by with the holy priests of God, he, wishing to make a mockery of God, cried out loudly: 'Listen to me, most blessed Cirola! Listen to me, holy priest of God! Look upon my blindness! Let me obtain such a cure as other blind men have deserved of you, lepers have experienced, and even the dead have felt. I implore you in the name of your own power to restore to me the light of my eyes, for which I pine, for I am stricken with total blindness.' Though he did not know the truth, he spoke truthfully, for greed had blinded him, and he was planning to act in scorn of the almighty for the sake of money. Then the bishop of the heretics stood aside for a moment, as if triumphing in his great power, elated by vanity and arrogance. He placed his hand over the man's eyes and said: 'In the name of our faith, which we rightly believe, let your eyes be opened.' As soon as he had uttered this blasphemy, the joke was turned to tears and the bishop's hoax was laid bare before all, for the eyes of the wretch were filled by such a terrible pain that he had to press down on them with his fingers so that they would not burst. At last the fool began to cry out: 'Woe upon my misery, for I have been seduced by the enemy of God's law! Woe upon me, for I decided to mock God for money, and took fifty pieces of gold in payment for performing this evil act.' To the bishop he said: 'Here, take your gold back and give me my sight, which I lost through your deceptions! And you, most glorious Christians, I beg you not to despise this poor wretch, but help me promptly, before I perish! I have truly found out that *God is not mocked* (Galatians 6:7).' The holy men of God, moved by compassion, said: '*If you believe, all things are possible to the believer* (Mark 9:22).' He exclaimed in a loud voice: 'May whoever does not believe that Christ the Son of God together with the Holy Ghost shares one substance and divinity with the Father experience this very day what I am suffering now.' And he added: 'I believe in God the Father almighty; I believe in Jesus Christ, son of God and equal to the Father; I believe in the Holy Ghost, consubstantial and coeternal with Father and Son.' When they heard these words, they offered each other in turn the honour [of the cure], and a holy debate arose between them as to who should make the sign of the holy cross over the man's eyes. Vindimialis and Longinus begged Eugenius, he in turn implored them to lay their hands on the blind man. They did so, and as they held their hands over his head, St Eugenius made a cross over the blind man's eyes and said: 'In the name of the Father, the Son, and the Holy Ghost, true God, whom we believe to be one in three persons, omnipotent and equal, let your eyes by opened.' Immediately the pain disappeared and he was restored to his former health.

Every gesture here, except for the Arian's turning aside ('paulolum se divitit'), is a variation on the laying on of hands or the other common gesture of healing, making the sign of the cross over the affected part of the body.[8] When the false healer tells his collaborator to sit with his hands over his eyes ('manus super clausus oculos ponens'), the protective gesture is meant to identify him as a blind man, but it has the same form as the Arian's healing touch ('posuit manum super oculos eius') and contrasts ironically with its repetition by the now really blind man, who this time presses down on his smarting eyes to keep them from bursting ('eos digitis vi comprimeret, ne creparent'). The contrast between fraudulent and true healing is marked when the Catholic bishops cure the Arian's penitent accomplice with signs functionally identical but formally different from the one performed by Cirola: a placing of their hands on the man's head ('manus suas super capud eius tenirent') and a sign of the cross over his eyes ('crucem Christi super oculos caeci faciens'). Constant variation within repetition makes this an admirable instance of the schematism characteristic of hagiographic narrative; the gestures spell out by themselves the lesson of the story, though they could not be understood as a statement on Arianism and Catholicism without their narrative context.[9]

An equally fine example of gestural repetition, this time without variation, occurs later in the same work. Accused of having murdered King Chilperic, his treasurer Eberulf takes refuge in Gregory's own church in Tours under the right of asylum. He is a dissolute and impulsive man who soon assaults Gregory with abuse, slander, and complaints. His host, however, has an ominous warning to give him in an account of a premonitory dream.

> His diebus vidi somnium, quod ipsi in sancta basilica retuli, dicens: 'Putabam me quasi in hac basilica sacrosancta missarum solemnia caelebrare. Cumque iam altarium cum oblationibus palleo syrico coopertum essit, subito ingredientem Gunthchramnum regem conspicio, qui voce magna clamabat: "Extrahite inimicum generationis nostrae, evellite homicidam a sacro Dei altario". At ego, cum haec audirem, ad te conversus dixi: "Adpraehende pallium altaris, infelix, quo sacra munera conteguntur, ne hinc abiciaris". Cumque adpraehenderis, laxa eum manu et non viriliter detenebas. Ego vero, expansis manibus, contra pectus regis meum pectus aptabam, dicens: "Noli eiecere hunc hominem de basilica sancta, ne vitae periculum patiaris, ne te sanctus antestis sua virtute confodeat. Noli te proprio iaculo interemere, quia, hoc si feceris, praesentem vitam aeternamque carebis". Sed cum rex mihi resisteret, tu laxabas palleum et post me

veniebas. Ego vero valde tibi molestus eram. Cumque reverteris ad
altarium, adpraehendebas palleum, sed rursum relinquebas. Dum
hunc tu tepide reteneris et ego rege viriliter resisterem, evigilavi pavore
conterritus, ignarus quid somnium indecaret.'   (HF vii.22)

In those days I had a dream, which I described to Eberulf later on in
the cathedral. I said to him: 'It seemed to me that I was in this
consecrated church celebrating the rites of the mass. After the altar,
which bore the holy offerings, had been covered with a silken cloth, I
saw King Gunthchramn come in suddenly, shouting at the top of
his voice: "Drag out the enemy of our house! Expel the murderer from
the holy altar of God!" When I heard this, I turned to you and said:
"Wretch, take hold of the altar-cloth with which the holy vessels are
covered, lest you be dragged out from here!" You held on to it, but
with a feeble grip, and without courage. I, however, with my hands
stretched out before me, setting my chest against the king's chest,
said to him: "Do not take this man by force from the holy cathedral,
or you will be in danger of your life, and the holy bishop [St Martin of
Tours] will confound you with his power. Do not perish by your own
weapon, for if you do this thing you will lose both earthly life and
the hereafter." The king resisted me and you dropped the altar-cloth
and came to stand behind me. I, however, sent you back angrily. On
returning to the altar you took hold of the altar cloth once more, but
only to leave it again. As you were holding it feebly and I stood there
resisting the king courageously, I awoke, terrified and uncertain of what
the dream might mean.'

Gregory tells his own dream, and there is no reason to believe that he
was making it up to scare Eberulf. Two gestures are repeated: the
significant holding of the altar-cloth by Eberulf, and Gregory's wholly
practical measure of pushing back the king. Here the ritual gesture of
the hapless Eberulf, who commends his fate to the power of the altar
and its offerings, becomes the center of tension: he is ordered by the
bishop to hold on ('Adpraehende palleum altaris, infelix'), but does so
weakly, without faith or resolution ('laxa eum manu et non viriliter
detenebas'); eventually he lets go ('tu laxabas palleum'), takes hold of
it once more only to abandon it again ('adpraehendebas palleum, sed
rursus relinquebas'). Eberulf is holding the cloth with dangerous dif-
fidence as Gregory wakes up ('Dum hunc tu tepide reteneris ... evigilavi'). The narrowing focus that we expect in a dream narrative is
created here by the repetition, which marks out the two centres of the

dreamer's anxiety: the bold move he is performing in pushing back the avenging Gunthchramn, and the increasing danger of the treasurer's position, represented by the gradual weakening of his hold on the altar-cloth. The obsessive organization of imagery may be recognized in the recurring gesture.

VARIETIES OF GESTURE AND MEANING

The range of gestural notation used by early medieval narrators is extremely broad and does not match the dictionary definition of 'gesture' or the common-usage understanding of the term, though it comes much closer to the former. Dictionary definitions, most often variations on the formula 'expressive movement,' make no distinction between natural symptomatic gestures and conventionally significant ones, incorporating Augustine's 'signa naturalia' and 'signa data' under a single concept.[10] They also take account of attitudes of the whole body in space (posture) and of relative position, where common usage would not count these as gestures. On the other hand, expressive sounds and involuntary expressive reactions not easily classified as movements (for example, tears and blushes) would be given at best marginal status by the dictionary. We shall come across other possibilities, such as movements that signify only because they are misunderstood, which belong to the dramatic spectrum of our narrators but fit no general definition of 'gesture' that one could imagine. The sense of the word in ordinary usage is even more distant from the range I am trying to outline here, since common usage includes non-expressive pragmatic movements such as shielding the eyes from the sun, or tossing back a lock of hair. The reason for considering such actions may be that they are felt to express unconscious meanings or emotions on occasion, and that they come to be associated with individuals (characteristic gestures) and eventually can be used to summarize an entire personality. Medieval authors, who were not very interested in the unconscious or in individual characters as such, pay little attention to this aspect of physical behaviour.[11]

The point I wish to make in this section is that the field of physical expression from which these writers draw their observations is unified and coherent, at least in so far as their gestural notes have a demonstrable common denominator. By example and analysis I will try to illustrate the common ground of their remarks, which may not be immediately apparent in many cases, and so to make clear what aspect of gesture it was that these narrators found worthy of such frequent mention.

Certain acts belong to the very paradigm of gesture, and stand in no need of further elucidation: Agilulf's kiss on Theudelinda's hand and other polite tokens of respect, as well as all the expressive movements of the hands and head. Equally obvious will be facial expressions: Theudelinda's smile and 'rubor,' the eyes raised to heaven of the martyr Quirinus ('erectis ad caelum oculis ait ... ' *HF* 1.35), and even such negative notations as the feigned placidity of the Frankish king Theuderic as he responds to an insult from his Thuringian brother-in-law 'nimiam iram vultu celans sereno' / 'concealing his great anger under a serene countenance' (*RGS* 1.9), or the treacherous cordiality of the Langobardic princess Rumetruda, who reassures a guest with smiles and hospitality only to give herself time in which to organize his murder: 'Simulat patientiam, vultum exhilarat, eumque verbis iocundioribus demulcens, ad sedendum invitat ... ' / 'She feigns patience, puts on a laughing expression and, soothing him with pleasant words, invites him to sit down ... ' (*HL* 1.20).[12]

Though our authors remark less frequently on expressive sounds and noises, they can make very dramatic use of them at times, as when Gregory of Tours describes an alcoholic bishop collapsing from a stroke as he celebrates mass; the crisis is announced by a neighing sound, a shocking detail which may also be intended as a comment on the bestiality of drunkenness: 'emissa cum hinnitu vocem, terrae conruit' / 'he cried out with a sound like a horse neighing, and then collapsed' (*HF* v.40). Barbarians, foreigners, and Arian heretics worsted in theological argument make frenzied, ferocious noises: a Slavic chieftain challenged to battle by the Saxon margrave Gero replies 'barbarico more frendens et multa convicia evomens' / 'gnashing his teeth like a barbarian and spewing out many insults' (*RGS* iii.54).[13] Tone and loudness of voice are usually indicated by such standard phrases as 'voce magna,' 'subdita et levi voce,' 'dolor in voce.' The state of mind conveyed by tone and the more subtle qualities of speech can be marked in a similar way, as when Fredegar makes the Wendish prince Samo reply 'iam saucius' / 'by now weary' (*CF* iv.68) to the threats of an overbearing Frankish envoy.

The position of the entire body considered by itself as well as relative to other bodies and things plays a very significant role in the dramatic design of early medieval narrative. I will use the term 'posture' to indicate the former, covering such basic alternatives as sitting, standing, lying down, prone, and supine, and will reserve 'position' for relative notations such as 'next to the altar' or 'to the right of the throne.' The opposition sitting/standing is extremely popular: the privilege of sitting while others stood had been interpreted since classical times as a token of despotism. This meaning is fully developed in Suetonius' anecdote of how Julius Caesar did not get up to greet the senate.[14] The courtesy of standing up to greet a guest was either performed by the emperor as a gesture of democratic humility, or omitted out of arrogance. By the fourth century AD, with the steadily increasing authoritarianism and hierarchization of the imperial government, the emperor seldom allowed others to sit in his presence, and rose for practically no one.[15] We encounter a similar interpretation in a Christian context in the story of Augustine of Canterbury's meeting with the Celtic bishops at Augustine's Oak, as told by Bede: a hermit had advised the Celts to convert to Augustine's Roman ways only if, by rising to greet them, he gave proof of a meek and holy disposition. But as a good Roman and bishop of a hierarchical church, Augustine did not rise (*HE* II.2).[16]

The dramatic possibilities of posture, and particularly of this ceremonial act of rising, are exploited to the full in a Byzantine text, the entry for *annus mundi* 6159 (667 AD) in Theophanes Confessor's *Chronographia*, a mid-ninth-century chronicle in the tradition of historiography inaugurated by Malalas. The Armenians, led by their general Saborios, have risen against Emperor Constans II, and Saborios' aide Sergios goes to Muawiyah I, Umayyad ruler of the Arabs, in search of support for the rebellion. From Constantinople, Constans' son, the future Constantine IV, sends the eunuch Andrew, his *cubicularius*, to discourage the Arabs from giving any help to the rebels. The two envoys meet in the presence of Muawiyah.

> When Andrew arrived in Damascus, he found that Sergios was already there and that Muawiyah pretended to side with the emperor. Sergios was sitting in front of Muawiyah, and when Andrew came in Sergios stood up on seeing him. Muawiyah reproved Sergios for this, and asked him: 'What are you afraid of?' Sergios replied that habit had caused him to do so. Turning to Andrew, Muawiyah asked: 'What do you want?' He replied: 'That you should give us help against the rebel.' Muawiyah said: 'You are both enemies of ours, and I shall help the one who gives me most.' Then Andrew said to him: 'Do not doubt, Caliph, that a little from the emperor is better for you than much from the rebel. You are friendly [to us]; act accordingly.' After

this Andrew was silent. Muawiyah said: 'I shall have to think about this,' and ordered the two of them to leave. He then called in Sergios by himself and told him: 'Do not bow to Andrew, or you will accomplish nothing here.'

The next day Sergios arrived before Andrew and sat in front of Muawiyah, and when Andrew came in he did not rise as the day before. Andrew glared at Sergios, insulting and threatening him terribly. He said: 'If I live, I will show you who I am.' Sergios answered: 'I will not bow to you, for you are neither man nor woman.'

As an imperial delegate, Andrew has the right to expect Sergios to rise before him. Sergios, however, wishes to express his rejection of Byzantine authority by not doing so. Muawiyah, the independent outsider who plays with both men and listens to their offers, can effectively challenge and condemn this token gesture of respect from Sergios. At any rate, the scene, which is thoroughly dramatized, revolves around the gesture's performance or omission. Later on, when Andrew's men capture Sergios at a mountain pass, the cruel outcome of the story is used to underscore the importance of the Armenian's formerly defiant demeanour.

On seeing Andrew, Sergios threw himself at his feet, begging to be spared. Andrew replied: 'You are Sergios, who boasted of your genitals before Muawiyah, and called me effeminate. Look, now your genitals will not help you at all, but will cause your death.' Having said this, he ordered that his genitals be cut off, and had him hung from a stake.

Sergios' wretched proskynesis before the eunuch refers us back to the courtesy demanded and refused at the beginning of the story, and confirms the narrative centrality of the refusal.

The fundamental alternatives of posture are used to convey purely conventional meanings more often than emotion; to throw oneself at the feet of someone else is a gesture of respect and self-abasement that may be accompanied by the implied feelings of humility and reverence, but external compliance with forms is the more common motive. The text shows a clear consciousnes of this possibility: Sergios excused his standing up for Andrew the first time by saying that he had done so out of habit. Our narrators work on the assumption that such gestures carry their meanings in themselves, quite independently of the intentions and feelings of the characters who perform them. The dilemmas of politeness are exemplified in anecdotes where conventional attitudes clash with overpowering expressive urges. Paul the Deacon's story of Alboin and Turisind may be used to illustrate this conflict, as well as the use of relative position (here left/right) in narrative. Before he can be allowed to sit at table with his father, the Langobardic prince Alboin must have received his arms from the ruler of another nation or tribe. He chooses to take them from the Gepid Turisind, whose eldest son he has recently killed in battle.

> Qui [Turisindus] eum benigne suscipiens, ad suum convivium invitavit atque ad suam dexteram, ubi Turismodus, eius quondam filius, sedere consueverat, collocavit. Inter haec dum varii apparatus epulas caperent, Turisindus iam dudum sessionem filii mente revolvens natique funus ad animum reducens praesentemque peremptorem eius loco resedere conspiciens, alta trahens suspiria, sese continere non potuit, sed tandem dolor in voce erupit: 'Amabilis', inquit, 'mihi locus iste est, sed persona quae in eo residet satis ad videndum gravis'.
>
> (HL 1.24)

> Turisind received him kindly, invited him to his table, and placed him on his right, where Turismod, his late son, had used to sit. During the meal, as they were being served various courses, Turisind, who had been thinking about his son's place at table and recalling his child's death, and who saw his murderer present there, sitting in his place, drew a deep sigh and, unable to contain himself, exclaimed with grief in his voice: 'That seat is dear to me, but the person who occupies it now is a very painful sight.'

The guest's position is interpreted for us in part by the narrator: it is the place of the dead son, who had been his father's favourite, and it is so close to the king's seat that Turisind must see Alboin whenever he raises his eyes. But it is also to the right of his own place, and the right is a favoured position, a place of honour. We do not expect the host's sorrow to turn him against his guest, whom he has himself seated 'ad suam dexteram,' and indeed it does not. The feeling betrayed by his deep sigh and the words that follow it play against his formal hospitality in a tense opposition of expressive and culturally determined gestures, resolved by the old man in the end in favour of the demands of the code.[17] The interpretation of left and right used in this scene is almost universal in human culture;[18] it had the support, for early medieval writers, of Christ's own use of it in his prophecy of judgment, when God will place the sheep to his right, the goats to his left (Matthew 25:31–3).

We must consider within the range of physical communication used in this period to dramatize an episode some elements that are hardly ever taken as gestures in real life. One such is occupation, any purposeful activity the movements of which may serve to give immediacy or to determine the dramatic shape of a scene in narrative. A clear case of the use of occupation as gesture is the decision of the king of the Heruli, reported by Paul the Deacon, to play a board game while his men join battle with the Langobards nearby: 'Rodulfus suos in pugna dirigit; ipse in castris resedens, de spe victoriae nihil ambigens, ad tabulam ludit.' / 'Rodulf sends his men out to fight. He himself remains in the camp and, having no doubt of the coming victory, plays a board game' (*HL* i.20). The king's activity expresses with some exaggeration his absolute confidence in victory, but it also spells out the blind arrogance that traditional storytelling likes to link with disaster. Though the gesture is clear enough in itself, Paul has provided a minimal gloss.

Certain problem cases are especially useful in that they indicate where the limits of the gestural range may lie, and in that way suggest where its defining criteria can be found. Among such borderline elements we find non-expressive, non-significant behaviour mistakenly interpreted as gesture. Gregory of Tours tells the story of the widow of Bishop Namatius of Clermont-Ferrand. The good lady is having a church built in the outskirts of the city; during the day, she sits there reading stories, probably from scripture, and telling the painters which episodes she wishes to have represented on the walls.

> Factum est autem quadam die, ut, sedente ea in basilica ac legente, adveniret quidam pauper ad orationem, et aspiciens eam in veste nigra, senio iam provecta, putavit esse unam de egentibus protulitque quadram panis et posuit in sinu eius et abscessit. Illa vero non dedignans munus pauperis, qui personam eius non intellexit, accepit et gratias egit reposuitque, hanc suis epulis anteponens et benedictionem ex ea singulis diebus sumens, donec expensa est.   (*HF* ii.17)

> It happened one day that, as she sat in the church reading, a pauper came in to pray. Seeing her in her black clothes, and already bent by age, he believed her to be one of the needy and taking a piece of bread, placed it on her lap and left. She, however, did not scorn the gift of the beggar, who had not understood who she was. She took it, gave thanks, and set it aside; she ate from it rather than from her other

food, and received a blessing from it for several days, until it was
eaten up.

The physical presence and attitude of the old woman, her sitting position, black widow's dress, and signs of age are brought into the scene
by the perception of the pauper, who erroneously understands her to
be begging. Probably projecting his own circumstances on to her, he
takes her to be one of his kind; he cannot have noticed her book, which
would instantly have shown him his mistake. In telling the story,
Gregory has conveyed, directly and indirectly, a picture of how this
old widow sat in church, and a possible though false interpretation of
what she was doing there. He suggests thereby the potential of a neutral
physical position to create meaning.

The materials we have been considering may seem excessively varied. While they certainly do not allow for any single psychological
criterion of definition, one important common factor brings them together as a unified and coherent range of signs: they are all bits of
interpreted or interpretable physical behaviour. No matter whether
they communicate an unmistakable natural emotion or the injunctions
of a civilized code, whether they carry these meanings deliberately, by
accident, or by mistake; they are more than mere practical motions of
the body, or are taken to be more.

The constant and often very effective use of gesture understood in
this way is a characteristic of all narrators in the early medieval period,
and becomes increasingly important in those writers who are closest
to the scenic style and less tempted or influenced by the classical
models. As historians, our authors think primarily about their material,
their facts or what they consider to be facts, and seldom about narrative
technique. That they all have recourse to expressive and ceremonial
gestures in composing the scenes of their narratives is a clear sign that
this is a deeply rooted feature of the style they have adopted or are
trying to imitate: the oral style. To focus a particular scene on the
genuflection of one of its characters, or his failure to rise before another,
is not so much a conscious stylistic decision as a formal habit, a familiar
trick learned from oral performance. We shall see later, however, that
in this case the oral background does not provide a complete explanation.

Whatever their origin, these scenic structures can be transformed by
early medieval writers with the most literary sophistication: while the
shape of the scene remains recognizably oral, the overt or implicit
glosses of the central gesture often become highly refined and individual. Paul the Deacon closes his account of the taking of Friuli by the

Avars (circa 610 AD) with a brief memoir of how his ancestor Lopichis escaped from captivity in the land of the invaders and wandered back to Italy on foot over the barren steppes. His arrival in his still-devastated home town is described as follows:

> Qui post aliquod dies Italiam ingressus, ad domum in qua ortus fuerat pervenit; quae ita deserta erat, ut non solum tectum non haberet, sed etiam rubis et sentibus plena esset. Quibus ille succisis intra eosdem parietes vastam hornum repperiens, in ea sua faretra suspendit.
>
> (*HL* iv.37)

> Coming to Italy after several days, he made his way to the house where he had been born. It stood so deserted that not only did it lack a roof, but it had grown full of thorns and brambles. When he had cut through these, he discovered inside the walls a huge ash-tree, and hung his quiver from it.

In the narrow compass of this chapter, which gives only the most general outline of Lopichis' adventure, Paul finds space for the hanging of the quiver from the tree, which is not an important action in the plot of the story. We have here the record of a family tradition, orally transmitted and of the utmost simplicity in its motifs and composition. On his journey home, the fugitive has been helped along by a myster- ious vanishing wolf and an old Slavic woman, as if he were the hero of a folktale. And yet the images of his arrival in Friuli are remarkable for the deliberate, literary quality of their symbolism. The house full of brambles into which he cuts his way, the tree that has grown inside it, and finally the hanging of the quiver from a branch of the tree are eloquent statements of recovery and appropriation; they announce the founding of a family identified with a city and a given landscape, the recognition of a *patria* and a home. In few words, they formulate the deepest meaning of epic *nostos*. We identify immediately in Lopichis' hanging up the quiver the strongly centralized gesture of oral style. But here it is introduced with a peculiar artfulness: we have to read into it a subtext that Lopichis cannot have had in mind, being unable to foresee the future of his family. He is alone in the scene, and cannot be indulging in communicative behaviour of any kind; for him, hanging the quiver can only be a matter of practical convenience, like making use of a hat-rack. The narrator gives us an ironic nudge, like Vergil when he describes Aeneas' puzzlement and pleasure as he contemplates the shield on which Vulcan has represented the future of Rome. We must take in the significance of an action performed without awareness of its deeper sense. The understanding of it must lie between narrator and reader. Here the gestural focus of the oral style is made to bear a historical consciousness and a sense of irony wholly alien to oral narrative.

ON CONVENTIONAL GESTURES

Oral literature elaborates the gestures of emotional expression, finding for them highly dramatic representations; in the orally based literary style I am describing here, it is the cultural, coded symbolism of gesture that predominates. A precise distinction between the two is naturally impossible: spontaneous signs of emotion become conventional as soon as they are imitated, or acted on the stage. There is the even more complicated matter of the incorporation of natural emotion into the regulated behaviour of a culture: is the ritual crying and tearing of the hair in traditional funeral ceremonies still 'natural'? Even when the mourners did not know the deceased, and when such gestures are prescribed for the occasion by ancient laws and by custom?[19] In analysing the narrative literature of our period, it is more productive to make distinctions between varieties of conventional gesticulation than between natural and conventional.

The early middle ages witnessed an impressive codification of public life into ceremony and ritual: our authors were familiar with court protocol, a complex system of liturgy and ecclesiastical ceremony, rituals of law, and a comprehensive personal etiquette for everyday use. The gesticulation and movement involved in these practices did not express individual emotions or interests, but formulated social ideologies.[20] They are often described in the histories of the period. Widukind gives a full account of the episcopal coronation of Otto I in August 936; he pays particular attention to the regalia and their abstract significance, glossed piece by piece by the bishop as he hands them to the ruler, but he also describes the movements of Otto and of Archbishop Hildebert of Mainz throughout the ceremony: 'Quo procedente pontifex obvius laeva sua dexteram tangit regis, suaque dextera lituum gestans, linea indutus, stola planetaque infulatus, progressusque in medium usque fani subsistit; et reversus ad populum, qui circumstabat ... "En", inquit, "adduco vobis a Deo electum ... " ' / 'The bishop came forward to meet him and touched the right hand of the king with his left hand, while in his right he carried the staff. Clad in a linen alb, wearing stole and chasuble, he advanced to the middle of the sanctuary and stood there. Turning to the people around him ... he said: "I bring you God's chosen ... " ' (*RGS* II.1). Simpler and more instructive is a tiny incident in Notker's *De Karolo rege* which reminds us instantly of the Byzantine etiquette for eating fish:

> Ab alio quoque episcopo cum benedictionem peteret et ille signato pane primum sibi perciperet deinde honestissimo Karolo porrigere voluisset, dixit ei: 'Habeas tibi totum panem illum' et sic eo confuso benedictionem illius accipere noluit.   (*DKR* I.12)

> Once Charlemagne asked another bishop for his blessing. The bishop blessed the bread, took part of it himself, and attempted to offer some to the worthy Charlemagne, who told him: 'Now keep the whole bread to yourself,' and to the bishop's embarrassment, refused to accept his benediction.

The bishop does his job in blessing the bread, but fails by ignorance of a worldly custom which prescribes that the emperor must eat first. Charlemagne's reaction in refusing to take his bishop's leftovers and in rejecting his blessing is significant by reference to contrasting codes: the emperor must disdain that piece of bread, and also show his impolite vassal that any benediction he can give has become undesirable.

There are symbolic and conventional actions, however, that do not rely on generally accepted codes for their interpretation, but are invented, like charades, on the spur of the moment, and are nevertheless understood. For this aim they make use of the most widespread symbolic associations of gesture, or of a parallelism of allusion. Notker tells the story of Charlemagne's treacherous hunchbacked son Pippin, who having conspired to take power from his father, was found out, tonsured, and exiled to the monastery of St Gall. Having caught wind of another court plot against himself, Charlemagne sends messengers to his banished son to ask his opinion on the best way to deal with the conspirators.

> Quem cum in orto cum senioribus fratribus, iunioribus ad maiora opera detentis, urticas et noxia quęque tridente extrahentem repperissent, ut usui proficua vivacius excrescere valerent, indicaverunt ei causam adventus sui. At ille ex imis praecordiis suspiria trahens, ut omnes debiles animosiores sanis esse consueverunt, in hęc verba respondit: 'Si Karolus consilium meum dignaretur, non ad tantas me deponeret iniurias. Ego nihil illi demando. Dicite illi, quid me agen-

tem inveneritis'. At illi timentes, ne sine certo aliquo responso ad
formidabilem reverterentur imperatorem, iterum atque iterum re-
quirebant ab eo, quid domino renuntiare deberent. Tunc ille stoma-
chando: 'Nihil' inquit 'aliud ei demando, nisi quod facio. Inutilia
recrementa extraho, ut holera necessaria liberius excrescere valeant'.

(*DKR* ii.12)

They found Pippin in the orchard with the older brothers, while the
younger ones were occupied with more important tasks. He was pulling
out with a rake whatever weeds and nettles he could find, so that
the useful plants might grow more vigorously. They let him know
why they had come. He, sighing from the bottom of his heart (for the
weak are always resentful of healthier people), answered as follows:
'If Charlemagne cared for my advice, he would not subject me to
such humiliations. I send him no answer. Tell him what you found
me doing.' They were afraid to go back to the formidable emperor
without a specific answer, and kept asking Pippin again and again what
reply they might give to their lord. Irritably he said: 'I have no answer
to send him, other than what I am doing. I pull out useless weeds
so that useful plants may grow more freely.'

Pippin's father understands the exile's advice immediately: he has all
the plotters executed and hands over their property to his loyal followers. The obvious parallel to nettles and useful plants, though unstated,
is strongly suggested by Pippin's own description of his activity, which
functions as a sort of parable.

A more obscure riddle of the same sort comes up in an episode told
by Widukind of Corvey about the early wars between the Franks and
the Thuringians. Theuderic, the Frankish king, who has won the war,
bribes Iring, the usually loyal vassal of the Thuringian king, to kill
Irminfrid, his defeated lord. Iring does so in the presence of Theuderic,
and then finds out to his surprise that the Frank intends to treat him
openly as a murderer and a traitor, so as to cover up his own part in
the crime.

Revocatus itaque Irminfridus prosternitur vestigiis Thiadrici; Iring
vero tamquam armiger regalis stans secus evaginato gladio prostratum
dominum trucidavit. Statimque ad eum rex: 'Tali facinore omnibus
mortalibus odiosus factus, dominum tuum interficiendo, viam habeto
apertam a nobis discedendi; sortem vel partem tuae nequitiae nolumus
habere'. 'Merito', inquit Iring, 'odiosus omnibus mortalibus factus

sum, quia tuis parui dolis; antequam tamen exeam, purgabo hoc scelus meum vindicando dominum meum'. Et ut evaginato gladio stetit, ipsum quoque Thiadricum obtruncavit, sumensque corpus domini posuit super cadaver Thiadrici, ut vinceret saltem mortuus, qui vincebatur vivus.   (*RGS* I.13)

Irminfrid was summoned back, and threw himself at the feet of Theuderic. Iring, however, who stood by with drawn sword, in the attitude of a royal arms-bearer, killed his prostrated lord. Immediately the king said to him: 'Such a crime makes you hateful to all men, for you have murdered your own lord. We leave you a free way to depart from here, for we want to have no share in your corruption.' Iring replied: 'I have made myself deservedly hateful to all mortals because I collaborated with your deceptions. Before leaving, however, I shall cleanse away my sin by avenging my lord.' As he stood there with drawn sword, he cut down Theodoric on the spot and, taking the body of his lord, he placed it over the corpse of Theodoric, so that dead he might vanquish the man by whom he had been defeated when alive.

The disposition of the corpses is glossed and interpreted by the narrator, but that does not seem necessary: being on top and lying under as attitudes of victory and defeat are constant, almost universal readings of posture. An eagerness to *decipher* movement and gesture finds expression in these privately coded actions.

GLOSS, IMAGE, DESCRIPTION

Thus far I have outlined the variety of our materials, and the examples quoted may give some idea of the importance of gestures and movement in early medieval narrative and of the multiple uses to which they are put. We now turn to the treatment of these elements in the text. How much are we told about a particular gesture? How precisely are the movements of a body portrayed?

Quite often, a gesture is named with one or two words and not described at all; it is either too commonplace to need any further specification, or its function in the particular story is clear enough that there can be no question as to its aim, significance, or possible consequences. In his tale of Brachium Fortis, Agnellus has a merchant lend money to a friend after taking an image of Christ as his witness and security. The man pays out three hundred solidi 'respiciens ad vultum

Salvatoris' / 'looking up at the face of the Saviour' (*LPR* 30). When the borrower misses his deadline, his creditor complains before the image (called Brachium Fortis precisely because of its power to coerce), saying that Christ is not doing his job properly. We are only told that 'his dictis ingemuit et recessit' / 'having said this, he sighed and left.' Such simple expressive gestures are always what we might expect given the circumstances. They serve to dramatize a speech or to give emphasis to a particular statement. Repeatedly, however, the narrators add explanatory glosses to these brief notes, even when there does not seem to be a need for them. In the same story, the two friends, debtor and creditor, meet again through the intervention of the holy image, and the loan is repaid. Agnellus writes that 'prae gaudio flebant et osculabant se invicem' / '*for joy* they wept and kissed each other,' a common type of gloss specifying the emotions expressed by the tears and kisses. Just as obvious is Fredegar's observation as he describes Queen Gundeberga's reaction to the sexual overtures of a courtier: we are told that she 'eumque dispiciens, in faciem expuit' / '*feeling contempt for him*, she spat in his face' (*CF* IV.51), where her act can hardly have had any other motive. Another type of gloss describes the impression the gesture makes on its witnesses in the story: of a deacon who goes up a ladder to fetch and expropriate a relic, Gregory of Tours tells us that he 'ita tremore concussus est, ut nec vivens putaretur ad terram reverti' / 'was shaking so badly *that they did not think he would make it back to the ground alive*' (*HF* VII.31), the 'putaretur' referring obliquely to those who watched him go up. It is not uncommon, when a gesture or movement has a hidden aim, to find it described by comparison with its ostensible purpose. The athlete Peredeo, wishing to murder two of the emperor's counsellors in revenge for having been blinded, pretends to know a secret that might interest the authorities. When the two men come to see him, he 'quasi aliquid eis secretius dicturus, propius accessit' / 'came closer, *as if wanting to tell them something in greater secrecy*' (*HL* II.30). And when a friend wishes to warn the deposed Langobardic king Perctarit that the usurper Grimoald plans to kill him, approaching him at a banquet 'quasi eum salutaturus sub mensam caput mittens' / 'bowing so that his head was below the table, *as if to salute him*' (*HL* V.2) he tells Perctarit to beware. The character's position may be connected to a certain function or station in life: a bishop playing host to Charlemagne waits upon him during the royal meal: 'Episcopus ... more famulorum propter astabat ... ' / 'The bishop ... *in the manner of a servant*, stood beside him ... ' (*DKR* I.15).

Comparative comments sometimes refer to imaginary possibilities and not to what the characters are pretending to express or actually expressing. After a violent confrontation with the bishops of his realm, the Merovingian Gunthchramn sits down to a meal 'laeto vulto et hilare faciae, quasi nihil de contempto suo fuisset effatus' / 'with happy face and laughing countenance, *as if he had said nothing about the contemptuous treatment he had suffered*' (*HF* VIII.2). Following a demonstration of brutal strength by Pippin the Short in combat with a bull and a lion, his scheming and faithless courtiers 'quasi tonitru perculsi ceciderunt in terram' / '*as if struck down by thunder*, fell to the ground' (*DKR* II.15). Perhaps the most informative type of comment specifies the result of the gesture. Thus the missionary bishop Poppo, having performed successfully in an ordeal by holding a red-hot iron before the pagan Danes, 'Manum incolumem cunctis ostendit, fidem catholicam omnibus probabilem reddit' / 'showed his unharmed hand to everyone, *and so demonstrated to all the truth of the Catholic faith*' (*RGS* III.65). It will be noticed that none of these comments concern the physical performance of the action; there is little curiosity as to how exactly Pippin's courtiers collapsed before him, or what Gunthchramn's happy expression involved. Here and there, in fact, a subjective comment is allowed to stand by itself, though it clearly refers to gestures or a bodily demeanour that are left entirely to the reader's imagination. To describe Lewis the German's impeccable behaviour at court as a child, Notker tells us that he 'collectis animis et membris compositissime collocatis equato gradu stetit ...' / '*serenely, and with his limbs set in a most elegant attitude*, he stood in the same rank [as his father] ... ' (*DKR* II.10). 'Membris compositissime collocatis' conveys no image at all; we cannot tell how the boy actually stood, though it is clear that he fulfilled every requirement of the code.

At this elementary level of gestural notation we perceive most clearly the tendency of familiar gestures and expressions to become fixed in certain phrases and formulas: ablatives with 'voce' and an adjective for tones of voice, 'pedibus eius provolutus' for prosternation in Latin, or in low-style Greek 'προσπίπτω εἰς τοὺς πόδας ' plus genitive. The evolution by which common expressive gestures cease to be performed and survive only as idiomatic expressions follows a familiar tendency that has been observed by anthropologists in various cultures.[21] We find its earliest stage in these early medieval texts: the formation of stereotypes and clichés while the corresponding gestures are still carried out in everyday life. Queen Gundeberga actually spat in the face of her intended seducer; what we have left today is the formula 'I could spit.'

The very limited descriptive treatment characteristic of this style is particularly evident in gestural punctuation. Minimal indications of movement and expression can be scattered over a scene as dramatic cues, but not to flesh out the narrative in the reader's imagination, since their visual coefficient remains always extremely low. Before a battle to be fought between Otto I and his brother Heinrich duke of Bavaria, the king confronts Agina, a vassal of his brother who has come to see him because he once swore a solemn oath to bring Heinrich to him and make peace between the brothers (*RGS* II.17). Agina greets Otto 'verbis humillimis' / 'with the humblest language'; the king, 'prospiciens' / 'looking over' as he talks with him, sees that a huge army has crossed to his side of the Rhine. 'Conversus ad Aginam' / 'Turning to Agina,' he asks him whose army it is, and the man 'satis ociose' / 'with great indifference' explains that it is Heinrich's army, and that he has failed to move his lord to reconciliation. Otto, alarmed and unable to get out of the spot, having no boats with which to cross the river, 'dolorem animi motu corporis non celabat' / 'could not conceal the anguish of his mind in the movements of his body,' and finally commends himself to God in a prayer 'ad Deum supplices expandens manus' / 'raising his hands to God in supplication.' The statement that in the motions of his body Otto did not conceal the state of his mind shows how little these notations are meant to convey an image. They make the dialogue more vivid by bringing out the emotional dynamics of the scene in the most schematic way, but they do not paint a picture.

Gestures not placed at intervals between speeches and authorial narrative but described in a single block can be represented in greater detail. However, what usually increases in that case is not information on the single motion, which continues to be indicated as summarily as in the examples just discussed, but the complexity of the series of movements, which may become very elaborate. The entire sequence often articulates one large meaning, or serves a single function, and not necessarily a larger or more important one than the brief notations we have seen: reconciliation or healing can be represented as a simple kiss or a laying on of hands, but also by involved ceremonies. The latter technique requires a breaking down of the single action into parts, and often the introduction of repeated movements. The reconciliation between Pope Paul I and Archbishop Sergius of Ravenna is portrayed by Agnellus with remarkable fullness of detail.

> Tunc iussit venire Sergium Ravennensem pontificem cum omni honore et gloria; et cum vidisset eum, sublevavit se de sella ubi sedebat, et cum prostratus humo petisset et vulto submisso, elatis manibus sub-

levatus, et irruit super collum eius, obsculans eum, et iussit deferri
sedem illius iuxta sedem suam, et locuti sunt inter se pacifica et
dulcia verba, et permisit eum redire ad sedem suam cum gaudio magno
et alacritate.   (*LPR* 157)

Then [the pope] ordered that Sergius archbishop of Ravenna should
come before him with all honour and glory. When he saw him, he rose
from the chair on which he was sitting; [Sergius] sank to the floor
in a reverence, with his face downcast, and he was raised by the
outstretched hands [of the pope, who] hung on his neck in an embrace,
kissing him, and had his chair placed next to his own. They talked
to each other with peaceful and sweet words, and the pope allowed him
to go back to his see with great joy and willingness.[22]

Bringing together nine gestural elements, if we include the 'peaceful
and sweet words,' this is clearly no private act; the personal transaction
is elevated into a public ceremony of forgiveness.[23] The single movements, however, are described with the familiar clichés of brief notation: 'vultu submisso,' 'elatis manibus.' And here is a healing performed
by St Hospicius, a recluse, as described by Gregory of Tours. The invalid, a young deafmute, is brought to Hospicius by a deacon, who first
arouses the hermit's interest in seeing the patient without directly
requesting him to attempt a cure. Finally Hospicius asks that the young
man be brought to his cell.

At ille [diaconus] nihil moratus, velociter ad metatum vadit invenitque
infirmum febre plenum, qui per nutum aures suas dare tinnitum
indecabat; adpraehensumque ducit ad sanctum Dei. At ille adpraehensa
manu caesariem, adtraxit capud illius in finestram, adsumptumque
oleum benedictione sanctificatum, tenens manu sinistram linguam
eius, ori verticique capitis infudit, dicens: 'In nomine domini mei
Iesu Christi aperiantur aures tuae, reseretque os tuum virtus illa, qui
quondam ab homine surdo et muto noxium eiecit daemonium.'
                                                              (*HF* vi.6)

The deacon went back to his inn without delay and found the invalid
in a high fever and indicating by signs of his head that there was a
ringing in his ears. Taking hold of him, he led him to the holy man
of God. He, grabbing the patient's hair with his hand, pulled his head
in through the window. Having taken oil and sanctified it with a
blessing, he held the man's tongue with his left hand and poured the

oil on his mouth and the top of his head, saying: 'In the name of
my lord Jesus Christ, may your ears be opened and your mouth un-
sealed by the same power that once cast out the demon from the
man who was deaf and dumb.'

Aside from the graphic gesture of the deafmute, which gets a single
but effective note and gloss, the scene revolves around the unctions
carried out by the healer, the description of which involves five different movements and a speech.

Full description of a given gesture or act without this kind of seg-
mentation and with a clear account of physical performance is rare
indeed, though not unknown. When it occurs, it is hard to find a reason
why it is used rather than the more common serial and analytic description. It may well be that these visually more exact representations
are traditionally tied to particular stories. A good instance of them is
the gesture performed in secret by the disguised Langobardic king Authari while he pretends to be an envoy at the Bavarian court in order
to catch a first glimpse of his betrothed Theudelinda. The princess is
asked to serve the foreign guests a cup of wine.

> Cumque rex id, ut fieri deberet, annuisset, illa, accepto vini poculo,
> ei prius qui senior esse videbatur propinavit. Deinde cum Authari,
> quem suum esse sponsum nesciebat, porrexisset, ille, postquam bibit
> ac poculum redderet, eius manu, nemine animadvertente, digito
> tetigit dexteramque suam sibi a fronte per nasum ac faciem produxit.
> Illa hoc suae nutrici rubore perfusa nuntiavit.   (HL iii.30)

> When the king assented to it that this should be done, she, taking a
> cup of wine, brought it first to the man who seemed to be eldest there.
> Then she offered it to Authari, not knowing he was her betrothed,
> and he, after drinking and handing back the cup, touched her hand with
> his finger while no one was looking and drew his right hand from
> his forehead over his nose and face. Blushing intensely, she told this
> to her nurse.

Authari's sign assumes a familiarity with the girl that would be out
of the question for a mere delegate; it seems to invite a recognition of
his countenance by his future wife. Since it corresponds to no particular
code of gesture, it cannot be interpreted exactly and retains an opacity
of its own, which may be why it is described with uncommon clarity.

The figure of Authari, however, has come down to us in incidents centred on such flamboyant, individualistic gestures, so there is reason to think that these more graphic descriptions are characteristic of his legend. On his way back to Italy from the matrimonial embassy, he surprises his Bavarian escorts with a curious demonstration of strength.

> Igitur Authari cum iam prope Italiae fines venisset secumque adhuc qui eum deducebant Baioarios haberet, erexit se quantum super equum cui praesidebat potuit et toto adnisu securiculam, qua manu gestabat, in arborem quae proximior aderat fixit eamque fixam reliquit, adiciens haec insuper verbis: 'Talem Authari feritam facere solet'. Cumque haec dixisset, tunc intellexerunt Baioarii qui cum eo comitabantur, eum ipsum regem Authari esse.   (ibid)

> Therefore, when Authari had already come close to the borders of Italy, and while his Bavarian escorts were still with him, he stood up as erect as possible on the horse he was riding and with all his strength drove the small axe he carried in his hand into the nearest tree. He left it fixed there, and spoke the following words: 'That is the kind of blow Authari strikes.' When he said this, the Bavarians who accompanied him understood that he himself was King Authari.

Here the final comment documents the function of the gesture, and it is clear that Authari made it in order to disclose his identity: nothing in the gesture itself would indicate this purpose. The act itself is remarkable enough that Paul finds a clear picture necessary. The intrinsic obscurity of Authari's action is confirmed by a later episode in his career, where practically the same gesture is used to formulate a territorial claim.

> Fama est enim, tunc eundem regem per Spoletium Beneventum pervenisse eandemque regionem cepisse et usque etiam Regiam, extremam Italiae civitatem vicinam Siciliae, perambulasse; et quia ibidem intra maris undas columna quaedam esse posita dicitur, usque ad eam equo sedens accessisse eamque de hastae suae cuspide tetigisse, dicens: 'Usque hic erunt Langobardorum fines'.   (HL iii.32)

> We are told that crossing Spoleto, he came to Benevento and conquered that region, and then travelled on until he reached Reggio, the furthermost city in Italy and closest to Sicily. There is said to be a column

there, rising amidst the waves of the sea. He reached it on horseback
and touched it with the point of his spear, saying: 'The borders of the
Langobards will reach this far.'

This is a simpler description than the first; we recognize the gesture,
if not its new meaning.[24]

The materials we have examined so far surprise us by their lack of
physical precision. Though early medieval narrators relate innumerable details and matters of fact about the action such as would have
been passed over in silence by classical authors, they show a very weak
interest in developing a visual correlative, in painting out for the reader's imagination what it would have been like to be present at the
scene. Gesture and movement are treated most often as *acts*, so that
it is only their functions, consequences, and general significance that
concern the narrator, and having indicated those and named the act
itself, he is indifferent to the way in which it was carried out. The
ablative absolute 'evaginato gladio' is used on dozens of occasions to
describe a gesture of attack or intimidation for every single time that
we read something like 'omnes ad gladiorum capulos manus iniciunt'
(*HL* 1.24).

In a style influenced by oral tradition, this limitation of the visual
interest may surprise, until we remember popular forms such as the
Märchen, with its tendency to replace description by simple naming.[25]
On this particular issue we shall obviously have to reconsider the
matter of sources and stylistic models; the labels 'oral' and 'popular'
are too broad to explain the conflicting currents in early medieval
narrative, its odd combination of dramatic immediacy and sharp economy of description.[26] Even before taking a second look at sources,
however, we can tell that our narrators were also affected by purely
literary constraints in the composition of their scenes which led them
to adopt minimal, sketchlike forms of gestural staging. Their usually
very short scenic units are crammed full of dialogue, symbolic or at
least interpretable physical actions, and significant objects. If we consider any of these scenes as a unit of meaning, it becomes evident that
the signifier is practically overwhelmed by the signified, that the surface elements of the scene carry a disproportionate load of abstract and
emotional significance. The point of the narrative is far below its surface; as long as the signifier, be it word, motion, or thing, conveys its
meaning adequately, it is sufficient and needs no further elaboration.
In this style, content preys on form and reduces the actual scene to a
fascinating but skeletal diagram. Episodes such as Theudelinda's offer
of marriage to Agilulf, or the Arian bishop's attempt to simulate a

healing, constitute end-results of this tendency: every movement is symbolic and therefore instrumental, not interesting in itself. The entire scene, in its minimal staging, points to abstract meanings which make up the real interest of the story. In the case of Theudelinda, the reversal of a standard dramatic situation, whereby it is the woman who proposes to the man, helps to translate elevation and dynastic renewal: Agilulf takes power, a duke becomes king. Gregory's account of the fraudulent healing brings out the perfidy and weakness of the heretics and the true power of the orthodox clergy with the clarity of an equation by a series of repeated and contrasting gestures and by implicit comparison with the familiar scheme of a true healing miracle.

It is also noteworthy that even when gestures and movements are described, they stand in isolation; we are told nothing about the physical appearance of the characters who perform them, about the space, large or narrow, in which they are carried out, or about the furnishings of the stage. The queen of the Langobards and her future husband are present to us only in the offer of the beaker, the kiss on the hand, her blush, smile, and correction of the gesture, his final kiss on her lips. We know nothing more about them: the colour of their hair, their eyes, their degree of physical beauty. The room in which they meet remains undescribed, a functional space. An implied servant pours her wine; a beaker is the single stage property. Paul makes no attempt to fill in the picture; gestures tell the story by themselves, reducing the possibilities of the imagined scene to a spare pattern of meaning.

I have characterized early medieval narrative as vivid and dramatic, qualities that do not seem compatible with such an absence of sensory content. This apparent paradox defines what is unique in the early medieval style; the frequent successes of our narrators in reconciling abstract schematism with the requirements of dramatic efficacy prove that they are working from a clearly conceived though probably unformulated aesthetic. Their scenes are units of dramatized meaning, schematic in the extreme and yet emotionally powerful, like the image-signs of early Christian art.[27] That this synthesis of conflicting qualities became possible and effective as a narrative language must be explained by reference to developments in public life that are characteristic of late antiquity and the early middle ages.

RITUALIZATION AND THEATRICALITY

From the fourth to the tenth century, the conduct of public life in Greek East and Latin West became increasingly codified; it hardened into complex ceremonies conceived around the major themes of government, religion, and law. This process of ritualization, to which I have referred earlier in this chapter, involved not only the rulers of state and church, and the rich and mighty among their subjects, but also the humblest citizens and even slaves. Urban populations in the late empire must have been exposed to public ceremony far more often than the inhabitants of the country, but the ubiquitous imperial bureaucracy and the lower clergy assigned to rural areas brought some sense of their various rituals to the most remote regions of the Roman world.[28]

State ceremonial was the earliest to develop. It pervades the culture of late antiquity, and its traces can be found in historiography, in panegyric orations, artistic monuments, and coinage. Beginning from the forms of an extensive court protocol, it grew into a comprehensive code of behaviour with provisions for every occasion of state and every circumstance in which the emperor was exposed to the eye of the court, the army, foreign diplomats, or the populace. There were similar though simpler ceremonies for all dignitaries of the hierarchy, political and military figures, and court officials. From the fifth century on, the code follows separate lines of evolution in East and West.[29] The growth of these ceremonies in number, complexity, and codified rigidity, and the increasing glorification of the imperial presence that attended this development, were long considered by scholars to be Oriental borrowings, tokens of Persian slavishness and despotism taken over from the Sassanids and incorporated into Roman court etiquette from the time of Diocletian. The investigations of Andreas Alföldi have shown, however, that many of these supposedly Persian traits (for example, proskynesis, the jewelled tunics and shoes of the emperors) have antecedents in the Greco-Roman tradition and can be reasonably explained as the outcome of a native Roman evolution reflected also in the development of the cult of the emperor and of authoritarian government in the third and fourth centuries.[30] By the time of Justinian, court ceremony had reached an extreme degree of formalization; the code prescribed actions, words, and transactions with symbolic and ritual objects. It involved a large number of officials and attendants, various settings or stages (in Constantinople: the palace, the basilica, the hippodrome), as well as the furnishings and material properties of these settings. A section from a book of ceremonies written during the reign of Justinian and preserved in the great tenth-century compilation by Constantine Porphyrogenitus describes the protocol followed when a Persian ambassador appeared before the emperor.[31] The passage quoted here outlines what must happen after the ambassador, having performed an involved ritual of approach, comes before the *velum* or curtain that covers the entrance to the room where the emperor sits enthroned:

> ... and when the decurion sees that the ambassador is ready, he calls 'leva,' and when the curtain has risen the ambassador throws himself to the ground outside [the threshold of the Great Consistory], on the slab of porphyry there, and prostrates himself, and stands up. After that, he walks through the door, again throws himself to the ground, and prostrates himself on the floor, and stands up. And again in the middle of the Great Consistory in the same way he prostrates himself. And there he goes and kisses the feet [of the emperor] and stands before him, and hands over the letters, and speaks [his king's] salutation of the emperor. Then the emperor asks him: 'Is our brother in health, by [the grace of] God? We rejoice in his health.' And whatever word he wishes to say, he says to the ambassador. After that the ambassador says: 'Your brother sends you presents. I beg you to accept them.'   (*De cerimoniis* I, chapter 89)

The repeated prostrations of the barbarian envoy caught the imagination of Corippus, who in his panegyric of Justin II attributes them to delegates from the Avar Cagan appearing before the newly crowned emperor.

> verum ut contracto patuerunt intima velo
> ostia, et aurati micuerunt atria tecti,
> Caesareumque caput diademate fulgere sacro
> Tergazis suspexit Avar, ter poplite flexo
> pronus adoravit, terraeque adfixus inhaesit.
> hunc Avares alii simili terrore secuti
> in facies cecidere suas, stratosque tapetas
> fronte terunt, longisque inplent spatiosa capillis
> atria et Augustam membris inmanibus aulam.
>   (*In laudem Iustini* III.255–63)

But when the curtain was raised, the inner threshold stood revealed and the halls shone with their gilded ceilings. Then the Avar Tergazis looked up at the emperor's head, radiant in the sacred crown; bending his knee three times he lay prone in adoration, and remained motionless on the ground. The other Avars, struck by the same awe, imitated him and fell to the ground on their faces, touching the floors and carpets with their foreheads. They filled the spacious rooms with

their long manes of hair, and the imperial hall with their huge
limbs.[32]

The church adopted by Constantine, and then gradually transformed
from a persecuted sect into the imperial religion, developed an extensive ritual of its own, grafting upon the Jewish-Christian liturgy of its
origins a number of ceremonies taken over from the state to express
metaphorically the supreme majesty of God and his representatives on
earth. This liturgy of mixed origin evolved considerably to adapt itself
both to the new official character of Christianity and to the large number of the faithful, increased many times over by the conversions of
the fourth and fifth centuries. The mass, which was to become the
fundamental ceremony of the middle ages, came to be an involved and
regulated action. Though it would undergo important changes in the
Carolingian period and after, already by the seventh century it was a
majestic spectacle which brought together the whole Christian community, though with a strict separation between performers and public.[33]
The *Ordo Romanus primus*, earliest of the Roman ordinals and probably written in the early eighth century, gives a detailed account of a
papal mass as celebrated then; the actions of the pope rising at the
introitus are described as follows:

⟨Et⟩ tunc pontifex elevans se dat manum dexteram archidiacono et
sinistram secundo, vel qui fuerit in ordine; et illi, osculatis manibus
ipsius, procedunt cum ipso sustentantes eum.
Tunc subdiaconus ⟨sequens⟩ cum tymiamaterio praecedit ante ipsum,
mittens incensum, et septem acolyti illius regionis cuius dies fuerit,
portantes septem cereostata accensa praecedunt ante pontificem usque
ante altare.   (45–46)

Then the pontiff, rising, gives his right hand to the archdeacon and
his left to the second deacon or whoever's turn it is. They kiss his
hands and go forward with him, supporting him.
     The subdeacon precedes him with the censer, casting the fragrance
of incense, and seven acolytes from the district of Rome in service
that day and bearing lighted candlesticks walk before the pontiff to the
altar.

The attitude of the pope, who leans or pretends to lean on his assistants
as he goes forth, is taken over from the *sustentatio* of imperial ceremony.[34] It goes without saying that the liturgy, like the rituals of court,

sets in motion a hierarchy of officials and helpers, that it requires a number of specific settings or stages and a mapping of their surface, and that it involves a great variety of vestments and symbolic utensils.[35]

A third area of ritual development, and one in which the common man could be an active participant and even protagonist, was that of the law and its transactions. The Greeks and Romans of antiquity had had conventional gestures for such procedures as betrothal, adoption, and accusation; manumission, for instance, gets its very name from the prescribed gesture. Classical literature and to some extent the Roman codes of law document this ritual component.[36] In the period which concerns us here, however, the Greco-Roman world absorbed barbarian nations with far more developed gestural and symbolic elements in their legal tradition. Jacob Grimm, in his groundbreaking study of Germanic law, remarked long ago on the tendency of the barbarians to embody legal concepts in sensory representations.[37] Though many Germanic tribes, such as the Visigoths, were drawn to the use of Roman law, others, such as the Langobards and Franks, kept the laws and institutions of their ancestors remarkably pure of Roman influence. Germanic institutions and legal customs preserved in this way were to become established in the courts of law of the middle ages throughout Western Europe. The Salic law of the Merovingians, which reflects their legal practice in the sixth century, prescribes in its much-discussed chapter 'de chrenecruda' the following actions for a man who is unable to pay wergild (compensation for murder) and who wishes to make his relatives responsible for payment:

1. Si quis hominem occiderit et, tota facultate data, non habuerit, unde ⟨conponat, ut⟩ totam legem impleat, xii iuratores donet, quod nec super terram nec subtus terram plus de facultate non habeat, quam iam donauit.

2. Et postea *sic* debet in casa sua intrare et de quatuor angulos terrae [*puluerem*] in pugno colligere ⟨debet⟩, et sic postea in duropello, hoc est in limitare, stare debet, intus in casa respiciens, et sic de sinistra manu de illa terra trans scapulas suas iactare super illum, quem proximiorem parentem habet.

3. Quod si iam pro illo et mater et frater solserunt, tunc super sororem matris aut super suos filios debet *de* illa terra iactare. ⟨Quod si ille non fuerit, de⟨bet⟩ illa terra iacta⟨re⟩⟩, id est super tres de generatione matris ⟨et super tres de generatione patris⟩, qui proximiores sunt.

4. Et sic postea in camisa discinctus ⟨et⟩ discalci⟨at⟩us, palo in manu ⟨sua⟩, sepe sallire debet, ut pro medictate, quantum de conpositione

diger est aut quantum lex addicat, *et* illi tres soluant [*de materna generatione*]; hoc et illi alii, qui de paterna generatione ueniunt, *similiter* facere debent.   (*Pactus legis Salicae* LVIII.1–4)

1. If a man commits murder and, having handed over all his property, does not have enough to pay compensation so as to satisfy completely the demands of the law, he must present twelve jurors who will swear that he has no more property, on the ground or under it, than what he has already paid.
2. After this he must go into his house and take dust from its four corners in his hand, and then standing on the *duropellum*, that is to say, on the threshold, and looking into the house, he must throw that dust with his left hand over his shoulder on whoever is his closest relative.
3. If his father and mother have already paid for him, then he must throw that dust on the three members of his mother's family and three of his father's family who are most closely related to him.
4. Afterwards, in his shirt, ungirt and barefoot, with a stick in his hand, he must leap over the hedge, so that one half of what he lacks for the compensation, or of what the law awards, is paid by the three members of his mother's family; and the other three, from his father's family, must do the same.[38]

Beyond the diverse national and ideological backgrounds of these practices, I would stress the great variety of their elements: expressive gestures codified (varieties of kiss, for example), ceremonies borrowed by one institution from another, with considerable changes in the meaning of the actions (imperial pageants used in liturgy), gestures no longer understood, but preserved in veneration of their antiquity, commemorative actions (the eucharist), properly symbolic elements (the rite of placing one's hands between those of another man to become his vassal),[39] and actions such as those described by the *Lex Salica*, which are probably magical in origin, and may therefore be considered propitiatory or effective, but not symbolic. From the last centuries of antiquity and throughout our period, these heterogeneous practices are systematized and arranged into sequences. Not the existence of many ceremonies but their codification characterizes the early middle ages.[40] The books of protocol, ordinals, and law codes of the period represent much more than an effort of compilation: they play an active role themselves in the development of public life. Codified movements and gestures attract interpretation; placed into what looks like a syntax of

action, the elements of ceremony acquire an aura of potential significance, as if their ordered sets might be read like sentences.

The linguistic analogy is tempting, and we might ask ourselves whether
the purposeful organization of these gestures and actions in ceremonial
sequences does not in itself presuppose an understanding of the parts
and of the principles used to connect them with each other, that is,
the grasp of a ceremonial language of sorts. To these considerations
might be added, still speaking from the model of a natural language,
the argument that diversity of type and origin among the elements of
a ceremony is no objection, since natural languages take over words
and idioms from each other, reinterpret the borrowed forms, and in-
corporate them into their systems. The design of late antique and early
medieval public rituals could certainly have involved such a reinterpretation of gestural, material, and verbal elements for use as signifiers
within new codes (political, religious, legal). In this case, codification
and reinterpretation would have to be understood as a single process,
or as phases of one.

Appealing as it may sound in theory, the linguistic model does not
seem to me to work. There are many possible reasons why a state, a
church, or a legal system may wish to codify its formalities, beyond
the single one that it wants to convey certain ideological messages.
Codification may be the consequence of institutional growth and increased complexity, of the compulsion to repeat awesome transactions
with exactitude that is characteristic of traditional societies, of the
need to remember how certain things are done that distinguishes both
antiquarians and illiterates, of veneration for the manners of the past.
This is not to say that there are no symbols or coded messages in the
ceremonies I have mentioned so far; obviously there are many. But
comparison with a natural language creates an excessively high ex-
pectation of coherence and functionality, qualities which we have no
reason to project into the realm of ritual.[41]

The most important indication that the linguistic analogy will not
do is that the earliest interpretations of public ceremony to appear in
our period show no common basis of understanding and share little if
anything with each other in matters of methodology. Sophronius of
Jerusalem's seventh-century commentary on the liturgy of the mass
treats every action as commemorative of the life of Christ: specific
elements keep changing their meanings, and the chronological order
of the gospel narrative is entirely lost, but at least most actions belong
to the commemorative type. When the priest carries the gospels to the
altar he imitates Christ carrying the cross, though when he later with-

draws before the celebrant he recalls John the Baptist waning that Christ may wax. His near-contemporary Maximus Confessor, however, reads the actions of the mass as symbols of various stages in the life of the soul. Not only did these exegetes decode different, though perfectly compatible, messages from the same rites, but they 'read' the material assuming totally unrelated principles of composition: where one saw pure commemorative mimesis, the other found a system of mystical symbolism. In either case, each individual action was interpreted in isolation, with the help of scriptural typology and biblical quotations. There was no sense, as there must be in using a language, that the meaning of an element is determined in great part by its context. Every movement was referred back to scripture or to patristic commentary, but its particular position in the ritual sequence was rarely taken into consideration. Maximus and Sophronius do not even agree in their selection of liturgical actions for interpretation; their 'readings' are based on very different choices of material.[42]

These two processes, codification and interpretation, affect the description of gestures in narrative in different ways. The influence of codification is clearest in rather artificial descriptions of human behaviour, where simple emotions would ordinarily be communicated by a change of facial expression, or by one of a few familiar movements. Usually such behaviour is briefly noted, with a single word or a short phrase. The more elaborate descriptions are reserved for conventional gesticulation. Some of our authors, however, and particularly Agnellus of Ravenna, represent basic emotional states as if they were public events, giving them the complex articulation of a ceremony. The evil Archbishop Theodore, 'terribili forma, orridus aspectu et omnia fallacitate plenus' / 'of dreadful appearance and terrifying countenance, and full of deceit' (LPR 117), on hearing that the clergy of Ravenna have united against him, reacts with a formal, ritualized despair: 'Tunc surrexit de sella, ubi sedebat, dedit sibi alapam in fronte, dicens: "Heu victus sum". Ab alto trahens suspiria pectore, se ipsum lamentans, cubiculum introivit.' / 'Then he rose from the chair on which he was sitting, struck himself on the forehead, and said: "Misery! I am defeated!"' Drawing sighs from deep in his breast and sorrowing for himself, he withdrew into his cell' (LPR 121). The grief of the mother, friends, and fellow citizens of a young man who dies after being cursed by the no less evil Archbishop John is transformed by Agnellus into a public ceremony of mourning. Their actions are necessary preparations for the funeral, but their main function here is to express collective sorrow.

Prostrata humo diurna mater iacebat; alii tondebat pectora, alii ora

unguibus foedabant, alii salicum vimina intextebat crates, alii tondebat
salicum ramos, qui operiebant glosochomum, alii lustrabant desuper
virentias herbas, alii evellebant ebulos, faginos, adferebant saxos,
velocius ut discurrerent rotas, alii undique praecidebant diversas salicum virgas, alii stimulo boves exagitabat, nonnulli vero gramineos
substernebant corpore flores.   (*LPR* 163)

The mother lay on the ground all day long; some beat their breasts,
others marred their cheeks with their nails, others yet were weaving
frames of wicker-work, others were clipping willow branches which
they scattered over the bier, others strewed fresh herbs upon it, others
were tearing out elders and beeches and bringing rocks so that the
wheels might move forward more swiftly, others cut willow wands
everywhere, and others drove the oxen forward with goads, while
some spread wild flowers under the corpse.

If on the one hand simple emotions show a tendency to become
rituals and to be expressed by involved codified activity, on the other
simple gestures acquire the aura of significance, the promise of hidden
meaning that impends over ceremonial forms. Many anecdotes are
structured around the interpretation of a gesture. The reading is most
often a simple psychological one, which comes up with the motive for
the gesture rather than with a deeply hidden abstraction. Each incident,
however, begins when a character asks another why he has blushed,
closed his eyes, or averted his head. The treacherous Hatho of Mainz
betrays a plot against the duke of Saxony when he explains to a gold-
smith why he has sighed while looking at a jewel commissioned by
the duke (*RGS* 1.22). Notker's Charlemagne, while having dinner at
Narbonne, watches the hurried departure of some Vikings who have
just found out that he is present in the city. As he stands by the window
looking at their ships sail away, the tears run down his face. After a
while he turns to his men and explains the reason for such tears.

... cum nullus eum compellare praesumeret, tandem aliquando ipse
bellicosissimis proceribus suis de tali gestu et lacrimatione satisfaciens:
'Scitis,' inquit 'o fideles mei, quid tantopere ploraverim? Non hoc'
ait 'timeo, quod isti nugę et nihili mihi aliquid nocere praevaleant.
Sed nimirum contristor, quod me vivente ausi sunt litus istud attingere,
et maximo dolore torqueor, quia praevideo, quanta mala posteris meis
et eorum sunt facturi subiectis.'   (*DKR* II.14)

... no one dared to question him, but finally he satisfied the curiosity of his warlike nobility about his gesture and his tears. He asked: 'Do you know, my faithful ones, why I wept so much? I do not fear that these worthless and insignificant men may harm me in any way, but I am indeed desolate that in my lifetime they should have dared to land on these shores. I am seized by the greatest sorrow when I foresee what evils they will inflict on my successors and their subjects.'

Archbishop Damian of Ravenna is long puzzled by an old man who attends his church and constantly stares at his face as he celebrates the mass. One day he invites the man to eat with him, and asks him the reason for his piercing looks. His guest humbly replies that as the bishop moves before the altar a holy and radiant presence accompanies him, particularly during the consecration, and that it is at this vision and not at the bishop that he stares (*LPR* 130). The gestures explained by these episodes are in fact not particularly significant, but in them physical behaviour has taken on the allure of meaning, of the interpretable, and the illusion is reflected in these simple narrative structures.

There have been attempts to explain the theatricality prevalent in the public life of late antiquity by connecting it with the barbarization of the Roman world, and in any case with a strong influence of popular culture on the expression of social existence.[43] We know that, at least in the laws, barbarian influence is a reality. Already in the sixth century, however, and throughout the early medieval period, this distinctive taste for collective drama, however humble its origins, had been wholly assimilated by the powerful classes called to play the leading roles in state ceremonial, liturgy, and the law. Within a short time, the pageants of the imperial palace were ruled by detailed written codes, and liturgy became another branch of religious learning. Whatever roots they may have had in popular taste, these ceremonies are aspects of the high culture of the period; it is as such that they exert their influence on narrative form, making it more receptive to conventional and symbolic movements and leading it beyond the exclusive interest in emotional expression that distinguishes most oral storytelling.

SOURCES RECONSIDERED: ORAL AND LITERARY

We must raise for a second time the question of the sources and background of the gestural component in early medieval style. I have suggested already that its origin is to be found in oral narrative and in the need of the performer to mime and act out the story he tells. But this hypothesis has serious limitations; there is much that it will not explain. The scope of the oral influence needs to be defined more narrowly, and complementary influences must be taken in consideration.

In the first place, many oral genres would make unlikely models for gestural narrative. The folk-tale and the secular legend (German *Sage*) are very limited in this regard; they seldom indicate any kind of gesticulation, and when they do, it is only by brief expressive notations, signs of happiness or grief for the most part.[44] The richest model for the narrators of our period is to be found in the oral epic and the heroic lay, cultivated in the West by the Celtic and Germanic nations.[45] Since these genres, however, have undergone literary adaptation from the moment that they were put down in writing, it is safer to judge the possible contribution of oral epic to early medieval style from texts closer to our times whose pure orality we can be sure of. In Avdo Međedović's *Wedding of Smailagić Meho*, a Serbo-Croatian heroic poem of 12,323 lines taken down from the illiterate singer's performance in 1935 by Milman Parry, the hero Meho (Mehmed), 'the grey falcon,' confronts a treacherous judge in the city of Buda; the magistrate pretends not to notice that the young man has come into his hall.

> The falcon's lips trembled. The judge was so angry that he had turned his face to the window and refused to look at the hadji's son, but was looking anywhere else. When Mehmed saw what the traitor in the hall of justice was doing, he grasped the hilt of his sword and struck it on the floor. Because of Mehmed's great strength behind the blow one would say and swear that the hall of justice was about to fall and the floor collapse on the ones below. Then he drew his sword and swung it naked in his hands. The poisoned weapon gleamed like a flash of lightning from a dark cloud. When the traitor heard the quaking and saw Meho the hadji's son with the naked sword in his hands – the hero's hair, bristling like a wolf's hair in December, had raised his plumed cap, and he gnashed his teeth in his jaws, even as a saw when men cut wood, and from his teeth living fire darted – when the traitor saw Mehmed, all the judges leapt to their feet and put their hands behind their sashes and fell at Mehmed's feet. The pens of the scribes were turned to stone, and the blood left their fingers, which stiffened even as if they were dead. And the traitor, the chief of the judges, nearly lost his mind from fear of the might of that falcon's son. The scoundrel's lips became stone, as though his head had been severed. He tried to say something but could not. His tongue stuck in his mouth. He tried to say 'aman' ['mercy'] but his jaws were paralyzed. His head and beard began to tremble.[46]

What is unusual about this passage is the length and complexity of the sequence: though the scene culminates in an abject verbal demand for mercy on the part of the judge, the narrative line up to that point is carried exclusively by the gestures and expressions of the various characters. We are reminded of those episodes in Gregory of Tours and Agnellus where the staging is entirely or predominantly gestural. Ordinarily, however, the gestures in Avdo's poem are used singly, as complements to speeches or to important developments in the plot, and do not constitute, as they do here, an alternative language. Gestures appear to have come into *Smailagić Meho* as an aspect of Avdo's 'ornamentation' of the traditional story in the course of performance. Together with other embellishments of plot and poetic phrasing, they explain the unusual, truly epic length of Avdo's version.[47] In the much shorter lays by other singers that make up the greater part of Parry's published collection, such ornamentation is limited and the few dramatic movements are quite simply described.[48] Even in Avdo's elaborate style, gestures of emotional expression, the 'signa naturalia,' are dominant, ceremonial and conventional gestures relatively rare, though not absent.

The literary epics of the early middle ages, which for the most part have their roots in oral tradition, either in their formulaic diction or because they use a plot taken from vernacular legend, show important manifestations of this gestural element, developed and refined in the course of the literary evolution of the text. Most instructive, perhaps, is a brief scene from the late-Carolingian *Waltharius* that describes a private encounter of the hero with his beloved while they are both still captives of the Huns. Waltharius, though a hostage, is nevertheless Attila's favourite young warrior. On his return from a victorious campaign, he enters the royal quarters and meets there his betrothed, a hostage like himself.

> Illic Hiltgundem solam offendit residentem
> cui post amplexus atque oscula dulcia dixit:
> 'Ocius huc potum ferto quia fessus anhelo.'
> Illa mero tallum complevit mox pretiosum
> porrexitque viro qui signans accipiebat
> virgineamque manum propria constrinxit, at illa
> astitit et vultum reticens intendit herilem.   (lines 221–7)

There he found Hiltgunt sitting alone, and after an embrace and sweet kisses said to her: 'Quick, give me something to drink, for I am worn out and panting.' She soon filled a costly cup with wine, and handed . it to the man, who crossed himself as he took it. He pressed the virgin's hand in his own, while she stood by and silently looked into her master's face.

Here too the scene develops as a complex sequence of gestures, some expressive, others ceremonial, which lead up to the young man's address to Hiltgunt asking her to flee with him. Echoes of this technique are to be found in the great French and Spanish *chansons de geste* of the central middle ages, in the choreographic death of Roland at Roncevaux, with glove outstretched to God, as well as in the tears, the backward look, and the sigh with which the Cid bids farewell to his house as he goes into banishment.[49]

Might the historians and biographers whose prose narrative we are discussing have preserved any gestural stereotypes taken from the vernacular heroic tradition? Since the work of some of them (Paul and Widukind, for example) has tribal and national legends among its sources, a heroic colouring of the narrative is almost inevitable, but we must limit the scope of our question to gesture alone. There is some evidence, neither abundant nor conclusive, of conventional heroic gestures in early medieval historiography. One instance involves a commonplace heroic gesture: a warrior raises his helmet. The narrators, however, use it in a highly specific context. The enemy are counting on the hero's absence from the battlefield; in raising his helmet he reveals his identity by a peculiar feature (grizzled hair in one case, baldness in another). The *Liber historiae Francorum* describes an encounter between Saxons and Franks on the banks of the Weser. Bertoald, duke of the Saxons, is unaware that King Chlothar of the Franks has arrived and stands before him on the other side of the river, with his head covered. The king's men tell him that Chlothar is present.

> Qui [Bertoaldus] respondit cum cacinno, dicens: 'Mentitos vos! delerare formidatis, cum Chlothario vobiscum habere dicitis, cum nos eum mortuum auditum esse habemus'. Rex quoque illuc stans, lurica indutus, galea in capite crines cum canicie variatas obvolutas. Cumque discopertus a galea apparuisset caput regis, cognovit eum Bertoaldus esse regem et ait: 'Tu hic eras, bale iumente?'   (*LHF* 41)[50]

Bertoald answered with a guffaw: 'You lie! It is fear of being wiped out that makes you say Chlothar is among you, for we have heard that he is dead.' The king stood there with his armour on, his helmet on his head, his hair variegated with many a grizzled lock. When he removed the helmet and his head could be seen, Bertoald recognized the king and said: 'So you were here, you dappled ass?'

Paul the Deacon tells of a very similar episode, where a small party of Langobards, among them Wechtari, duke of Friuli, ran into a band of plundering Slavs.

> Quem Sclavi cum tam paucis venire conspicientes, inriserunt, dicentes, patriarcham contra se cum clericis adventare. Qui cum ad pontem Natisionis fluminis, qui ibidem est ubi Sclavi residebant, propinquasset, cassidem sibi de capite auferens, vultum suum Sclavis ostendit; erat enim calvo capite. Quem dum Sclavi, quia ipse esset Wechtari, cognovissent, mox perturbati, Wechtari adesse clamitant, Deoque eos exterrente, plus de fuga quam de proelio cogitant.   (HL v.23)

> When the Slavs saw him ride up with so few men, they laughed and said the patriarch with his clerks was coming against them. As he came closer to the bridge on the river Natisio, which was occupied by the Slavs, he removed his helmet and showed the Slavs his face. He was bald-headed, and when the Slavs realized that it was Wechtari they became very upset and cried out that Wechtari was at hand. Since God drove fear into their hearts, they thought of flight rather than of battle.

The epic hero of traditional song usually reveals a more youthful and attractive countenance, but his good looks have the same paralysing effect on the enemy; these proud revelations of identity point to the style and ethos of an oral heroic model.[51]

Even so, the oral model cannot explain the variety and importance of gestural elements in early medieval narrative. The predominance of expressive over ceremonial and conventional movements and the almost exclusively complementary function of gesture in oral tradition must be seen as serious limitations. We must consider supplementary sources and a more complex historical development of the new style. The most likely hypothesis is that the gestural requirements of oral form were slowly adapted to the interests of high culture once they had been taken over by literary narrative. This process affected the organization of gestures in narrative as well as their actual number; that is to say that more complicated, nearly autonomous sequences were created, which sometimes constitute complete scenes, and also that symbolic and conventional actions were added to the repertory of the literate narrator. Many of these elements are recognizably literary, at any rate characteristic of the sphere of high or official culture, and alien to the oral-vernacular background.

We find some gestures that are directly traceable to the life and literature of antiquity. When the two grandsons of Clovis are kidnapped by their uncles Childebert and Chlothar and are about to be murdered by them, one of the children begs for his life embracing the murderer's knee: 'Quo vociferante, frater eius ad pedes Childeberthi prosternitur, adpraehensaque eius genua, agebat cum lacrimis: "Succurre, piisime pater, ne et ego peream sicut frater meus." ' / 'He [the other boy] cried out as he died; his brother threw himself at the feet of Childebert and embracing his knee implored him with tears: "Help me, dear uncle, that I may not die like my brother!" ' (HF iii.18). This attitude of supplication is familiar from classical Greek and Latin literature and Greco-Roman art, though also well documented in the literature of Christian antiquity.[52] Far more unusual is an obscene gesture described by Fredegar in an episode of the legendary vita of Theodoric: the hero is fleeing in defeat before his foe Odoacer when he runs into his mother, Lilia.

> Nam quadam vice apud Odoagrum rege et Aerolis Theudericus cum Gothis prilium concitasset, Theudericus fugiens cum suis, Ravennam ingressus est; ibique mater eius Liliam obviam veniens, increpans eum, dicens: 'Non est, ubi fugias, fili, nisi ut levi vestimenta mea, ut ingredias utero, de quo natus es'.   (CF ii.57)

> For on a certain occasion, Theodoric and the Goths were making war against King Odoacer and the Heruli and, taking flight with his men, Theodoric entered Ravenna. There his mother Lilia came out to meet him, rebuking him and saying: 'There is no place for you to escape to, my son, unless I raise my dress and you go back into the womb from which you were born.'

The gesture here is only implicit in the woman's words, but that also serves to make clear its offensive and exhortatory purpose. It appears with the same value in Plutarch and other classical authors.[53]

More important, quantitatively at least, are elements taken from hagiographic sources and the liturgy. I will give only two examples here. A recurrent gestural formula presents the sudden death of a corrupt ecclesiastic at what should be his moment of triumph: he is served some wine by the cupbearer and, having drunk or just before drinking, drops the cup or hands it back, falls dead or collapses terminally ill. Gregory of Tours places this motif at a dinner-party given by the priest Transobadus of Rodez, who is trying to have his son elected bishop of the city in contravention of the will of Dalmatius, the former bishop, who has just died. One of the guests at the banquet makes a speech against the memory of Dalmatius.

> Resedentibus autem illis, unus praesbiterorum coepit antestitem memoratum inpudicis blasphemare sermonibus et usque ad hoc erupit, ut eum delerum et fatuum nominaret. Haec eo dicente, pincerna poculum oblaturus advenit. At ille acceptum dum ori proximat, tremire coepit, laxatumque de manu calicem, super alium, qui sibi erat proximus, caput reclinans, reddidit spiritum, ablatusque ab epulo ad sepulchrum, humo contectus est.   (HF v.46)

> As they sat there, one of the priests began to speak against the aforementioned bishop, using indecent expressions, and went so far as to call him vain and a madman. As he said this, the cupbearer came bringing him a beaker. But as soon as he had taken it and raised it to his lips, he began to tremble and, letting the cup fall from his hand, lay with his head against the man who sat next to him, and breathed his last. He was taken from the banquet to the grave, and covered with earth.

There is an almost identical episode elsewhere in the same work: two evil priests who had persecuted and harassed Bishop Sidonius of Clermont-Ferrand (Sidonius Apollinaris) in his lifetime give a party at the church-house after his death. The cupbearer serves a goblet of wine to one of them and then tells him a premonitory dream he has just had, in which the priest in question is being summoned to judgment before God: 'Haec eo loquente, exterritus presbiter, elapsum de manu calicem, reddidit spiritum; ac de recubitu ablatus mortuus sepulturae mandatus est, possessurus infernum cum satellite suo.' / 'As the cupbearer spoke, the terrified priest let the cup fall from his hand, and breathed his last. He was removed dead from the seat on which he was reclining, and sent to his grave, on his way to hell, where he would join his accomplice' (HF ii.23). There is very little variation here; the motif has become a rigid formula for Gregory. Agnellus adapts it so as to make the event somewhat more natural and likely: Archbishop John of Ravenna has cursed a young man, promising that he will rejoice over his death. The youth dies, to the great sorrow of his parents and friends, and the bishop exults.

> Et dum sederet ad mensam post tribunal ecclesiae super vivarium,
> elevatis sursum manibus, respiciens ad vultum Salvatoris, dicens:
> 'Gratias tibi ago, domine Iesu Christe, et tibi, beate Apolenaris, quia
> exaudistis me. Hunc diem semper desideravi'. Et dixit pincernae suo:
> 'Misce, quia, Deo gratias, exauditus sum'. Tunc pincerna accipiens
> ex ialico dimia impleta mero porrexit pontifici. Quem ille accipiens,
> ebibit usque ad dimidium poculum, et subito in latere sinistro
> puncta percussus, celeriter calicem ministro dedit, et iussit removere
> mensam, et gaudia dapium in tristitiam versae sunt, et dedit [se] in
> lectum; septimo die post excessum iuvenis mortuus est.   (LPR 163)

> As he sat having dinner behind the sanctuary of the church, over the
> covered gallery, he said, raising both hands and looking up at the
> face of the Saviour: 'I thank you, Lord Jesus Christ, and you, saintly
> Apollinaris, for you have granted my wish. I always longed for this
> day.' And he said to his cupbearer: 'Pour the wine! For my prayers have
> been heard, thanks be to God.' Then the cupbearer, taking a goblet
> full of wine, handed it to the prelate. He took it, drank half the cup, and
> suddenly felt a stab on the left side of his body. Immediately, he gave
> the cup back to the servant and ordered the table removed, and so
> the joy of the banquet was turned into mourning. He took to his bed
> and died the seventh day after the demise of the young man.

The words of the bishop confirm the interpretation of the serving of wine as a celebration of triumph, a celebration suddenly turned into defeat *divino nutu*.[54] The stab on the side and the seven days it takes him to die give the event a minimum of medical likelihood.

A gesture unequivocally tied to the hagiographic tradition is transformed by Gregory of Tours into another cliché: a barbarian strikes at a saint with his sword, but his arm is frozen in mid-motion and the blow does not reach the holy man.[55] The historian of the Franks tells this incident of two different hermits, Maxentius of Poitiers, attacked by Frankish soldiers, and Hospicius of Nice, beset by Langobardic marauders:

> Unus autem ex his evaginato gladio, ut capud eius libraret, manus ad
> aurem erecta diriguit, gladiusque retrursum ruit. Ad ipse ad pedes
> beati viri veniam deposcens sternitur. Quod videntes reliqui, cum

timore maximo ad exercitum redierunt, timentes, ne et ipse pariter
interirent.   (*HF* ɪɪ.37)

One of the Frankish soldiers drew his sword to aim a blow at Maxentius' head, but his arm became rigid as he raised it to the level of
his ear, and his sword fell to the ground behind him. He threw himself
at the feet of the holy man, begging for mercy, and when the others
saw this they went back to their army in great fear that they might
all die.

Tunc unus, extracto gladio, ut caput eius libraret, dextera in ipso ictu
suspensa diriguit, nec eam ad se potuit revocare. Tunc gladium laxans,
terrae deiecit. Haec videntes socii eius, clamorem in caelo dederunt,
flagitantes a sancto, ut, quid agere poterent, clementer insinuaret.
                                                                (*HF* ᴠɪ.6)

Then one of the Langobards pulled out his sword to strike a blow at
his head, but his right hand was paralysed in the very act of striking,
and he was unable to bring it back to his side. Dropping the sword,
he sank to the ground. When his fellows saw this, they raised a great
outcry, begging St Hospicius to be compassionate and tell them what
they ought to do.

These two hagiographic motifs depend on objects for their effect: the
hand must drop a cup or a sword in sign of defeat. But the cup of victory
or the sword of aggression carries part of the meaning in itself, independently of the action in which it is inscribed.[56]

GESTURE IN BYZANTINE NARRATIVE

The kind of popular historiography that interests us mainly is written
by Byzantine authors in a dry, annalistic style that covers wars, con-
spiracies, and political turmoil in a few sentences, without stopping
to describe particular incidents. Scenes such as the confrontation between Sergios and Andrew the eunuch in the chronicle of Theophanes,
discussed earlier in this chapter, are rare though not entirely unknown.
However, exceptions can be found even in the works of the most literary and classicizing writers of the period.

Towards the end of Procopius' *War against the Vandals*, two scenes
staged with a wealth of dramatic gestures prove that, however classical
the author's discourse, his narrative style and sense of what must be

shown directly are very much of the sixth century.[57] In the first scene (II.26), the Byzantine general Areobindus, who has been sent to Libya by Justinian in spite of his total lack of experience in warfare, is confronted by a mutiny of the troops in Carthage, and takes refuge with his wife and sister in a monastery. The Vandal Gontharis, leader of the revolt, sends a priest to invite Areobindus to the palace, an offer which the terrified general accepts only after the most solemn oaths that he will not be harmed. First the priest is required to baptize a child and swear by the sacrament he has just imparted. Then Areobindus, wearing a cowl and holding the scriptures, goes to the palace accompanied by the priest. He lies prone on the floor before Gontharis, holding out the scriptures and a branch of olive, with the child who had been baptized for the oath standing next to him. Gontharis helps him to stand up, reassures him of his safety, dismisses priest and child, and invites him to a banquet, where he lets him have the place of honour on the couch. That same night, Areobindus is murdered in his bedroom by Gontharis' men. There is no direct speech, and the gestures are so charged with meaning that the speeches summarized in indirect form seem easily dispensable. We have here the ceremonial staging of action that is already present in much late antique narrative, though rarely in this profusion. The various rites are described in such detail to increase the pathos that arises from the victim's helplessness and the reader's awareness that Gontharis does not mean to let him go, but also to convey the heinous character of a man who is willing to disregard so many solemn oaths.

A later scene describes the murder of Gontharis by Artabanes and Artasires, the leaders of the Armenian troops, who had remained loyal to the emperor. The event takes place in the course of a banquet offered by Gontharis at the palace in Carthage, and is probably the most fully dramatized episode in Procopius' work. Not only do we get a revealing close-up of the murder itself, but the stage is set carefully in advance, first by Gontharis' seating arrangements and security measures, and then by the conspirators' plans, both of which are explained in detail before the banquet starts. In this way, we are made aware, from the beginning, of the various possibilities at play and of the limits and dangers of the situation. The representation of this murder relies less on ceremony than on ordinary expressive gestures, which brings it closer to the practice of early medieval historiography in the West.

As the banquet started, Artasires decided to carry out the task, and grasped the hilt of his sword. But Gregory restrained him, telling

> him in the Armenian language that Gontharis was still wholly himself,
> not having yet drunk a great deal of wine. Artasires groaned and
> replied: 'Man, now that I have such a good mind to act, it is not right
> that you should hold me back!'   (II.28, 15–17)

The hand on the sword-hilt, the Armenian words, the groan of regret
followed by friendly words: all these make a quiet but tense prelude
to the violence that will follow. Soon Gontharis begins to drink and
serves food to his bodyguards, who go outside to eat it, leaving only
three men to protect the host. Artasires too goes out.

> While he was outside, he secretly took off the sheath of his sword
> and, carrying it [the sword] bare under his arm, hidden by the tunic,
> he ran back in towards Gontharis, acting as if he wanted to say
> something [to him] so that the others would not hear. Seeing this,
> Artabanes became feverish with excitement, and from the great im-
> portance of their enterprise fell into a state of deep anxiety, so that
> he started to shake his head and change colour rapidly, and the
> magnitude of their attempt made him look like someone inspired.
> Peter saw this, and understood what was afoot, but did not betray
> anything to the others for, being favourable to the emperor, he was
> very pleased with what was happening. Artasires had come very close
> to the tyrant and was pushed back by one of the servants, who, as
> Artasires drew back a little, noticed the naked sword and cried out:
> 'What is this, excellent sir?' Gontharis, bringing up his hand to his right
> ear and turning his face, looked at him. As he did so, Artasires struck
> him with the sword and cut off some of his scalp, as well as his fingers.
> Peter cried out, urging Artasires to kill the most unholy of all men.
> Gontharis sprang up, but Artabanes, who saw him do so because
> he was lying near him, drew a double-edged dagger that hung down
> his thigh and was quite large, thrust it into the tyrant's left side to
> the hilt, and left it there. Gontharis did not give up, and tried to leap
> up again, but since he had received a mortal wound, he fell on the spot.
>   (II.28, 22–30)

We have here short informal speeches quoted directly, gestures, such
as those which betray Artabanes' agitation, and their interpretation by
Peter, who can tell what they mean; there also is, as we get closer to
the attack on Gontharis, an unusually sharp focus on physical action,
which has an effect similar to that of slow motion in film. Small,
negligible movements become important: Artasires, who draws back

before the servant, Gontharis raising his hand to his ear, Artabanes reaching down to his thigh to draw the dagger. The weapons, which get so much attention, have no symbolic value, unlike Areobindus' cowl and olive branch in the previous passage, but they make up for it with the special tension built around them by the fact that they are all hidden, since no weapons are allowed in the banquet-room.

Gestural staging as central to the narrative as that of the Latin West is to be found most often in religious writing, and primarily in saints' lives. This specialization reduces the repertory of gestures that are well documented in early Byzantine literature: there is a marked predominance of liturgical symbolism, and we are confronted with endless, elaborate variations on the movements of prayer, benediction, and healing.[58] Two important traits of style that are also found in Latin narrative but seem particularly pronounced in Greek lives of holy men are a posed, deliberate quality in the performance of gesture, and the tendency of the narrator to interpret the motions of his characters and comment on them whether this is necessary or not.

In Byzantine hagiography the characters strike poses with extraordinary self-consciousness; they appear to be fully aware of what their gestures mean. Movements and attitudes become hieratic and come to be used directly as a form of communication, a message to another character or a statement to the reader. A good example of this quality is the scene of prayer in the *Life of Simeon the Fool* that takes place just before the two youths, Simeon and Ioannes, leave the monastery of Abba Nikon for good. They kneel down together with the old man for the last time:

> When both had wept thus for a long time, the saintly Nikon went down on his knees with Simeon standing on his right and Ioannes on his left; he raised his hands to heaven, and said ...

The scene takes place at night, by the deserted gate of the monastery. There is no one there to appreciate the studied, symmetrical group of master and disciples; their attitudes strike us as rather public and deliberate for their setting.[59]

This hieratism of presentation or performance is not to be confused with actual immobility, an extremely significant physical attitude in Greek narrative of this period, and particularly in the lives of stylites and caged ascetics. The seventh-century *vita* of the exorcist Theodore of Sykeon describes the position adopted by the saint within the iron cage where he spent several years of his life:

> He had determined that from cockcrow on he would not shift his
> feet on the platform where he stood, and not lean for an instant against
> the iron bars of his cage until evening.   (chapter 29)

This public immobility and impassibility of the saint, expressing the
immutable serenity of the mind in contact with the eternal, is closely
related to the many portraits of hieratic, unblinking emperors in late
antique and early Byzantine art: the earthly representative of God is
not moved by circumstances or change. He takes no notice of suffering
or joy.[60]

The second trait mentioned above, the tendency not to let gesture
speak for itself, however central and manifestly symbolic it may be,
can be explained perhaps by the influence of classical models, more
available to the Byzantines than they were in the Latin West. In the
same *Life of Theodore of Sykeon*, the encounter of the saint with the
cruel consul Bonosus, who passes near Theodore's monastery and asks
to receive his benediction, is presented as follows:

> The saint went down there and received him. As he [Theodore] was
> giving him [Bonosus] his blessing, the consul stood upright without
> bending his neck. Theodore then took him by the hair of his brow
> and, pulling him forward, forced him to bow down. Thus can virtue
> make use of a holy audacity and not fear human authority, 'for the
> just man,' it is said, 'does as the lion' [Proverbs 28:1]. We, his com-
> panions, were stupefied and frightened by the brave gesture of the
> just one, for on account of the reputation that this man had of being
> as cruel as a savage beast, we believed that he would consider this
> action an insolence and conceive a mighty anger. But he took well both
> blessing and rebuke, showing his veneration for the saint, kissing his
> hands, and, having taken them between his own and pressing them
> against his breast on account of a pain from which he suffered there,
> he even asked him to pray so that he might be cured of it. The saint
> tapped lightly with his fingers on [the man's] chest and said to him:
> 'You must first pray so that the inner man in you may be corrected
> and return to health.'   (chapter 142)

The gestural conception of the scene is as thorough and effective as
anything we have seen in Latin narrative, but after Theodore has forced
Bonosus to bow his head, we are left waiting for the reaction of this
terrible man while the narrator makes pious reflections, quotes from
scripture, and lets us know how the other monks felt about the whole

thing. This temporary disregard of the incident, together with the importance given to the authorial voice while the action is suspended, bespeaks greater closeness to a classical model, the sense of historiography as oratory or sermon rather than narrative.

To see the fulfilment of early medieval style, and especially of its gestural component, in Byzantine narrative, we must look less than one century beyond the limit of our period, into the *Chronographia* of Michael Psellos. We are faced here with a paradox, since Psellos is an extremely literary, Atticizing, high-style writer who is nevertheless able to coordinate dialogue, gestures, and symbolic objects into brilliantly composed units of dramatic narrative. In his work, an original, personal voice informs these elements of traditional storytelling and takes them far beyond what tradition by itself would have been able to accomplish. This means that in the course of the previous centuries the formal lessons derived from oral narrative had produced a basic literary form, a common manner which could now be adopted and transmuted by individual writers in all freedom.[61] In the first book of the *Chronographia*, Psellos describes the meeting between Emperor Basil II and the defeated rebel and usurper Bardos Skleros, who comes to make his submission.

> The emperor sat in the imperial tent, and at a certain distance Skleros was brought in by the bodyguards and led at once towards the emperor, not on horseback but walking. Though a tall man, he was bent by age and had to be led by both hands. Seeing the man from afar, the emperor said to those who stood near him the following words, which soon became celebrated and popular: 'Here is the man I feared! He comes to me as a suppliant, and led by the hand.' Skleros, however, whether from haste or out of scorn, had taken off all other insignia of power but not removed the sandals of purple from his feet, and bearing them as a part of the imperial power he came forth to meet the emperor. The emperor, seeing this too from afar, was vexed and closed his eyes, not wishing to see him at all unless he came dressed as a mere private citizen. On the spot, Skleros took off the purple sandals before the emperor's tent, and thus he went in under its roof. XXVIII. The emperor arose immediately on seeing him. They embraced one another, and then a dialogue took place between them in which the one explained his rebellion, giving the reasons why he had chosen to revolt and had actually done so, while the other accepted this defence serenely and blamed evil fortune for what had happened. When they had to drink from the same drinking-bowl, the emperor raised

> to his own lips the cup that had been served to Skleros, and took
> a moderate draught, doing away with any suspicion and showing the
> sanctity of their agreement.   (1.27–8)

Nothing that we have seen so far matches the complexity of this sequence of gestures. It is made up of many different elements, which either are conventionally significant (the host drinking before the guest) or acquire an obvious meaning in the context of the scene (the fact that Skleros must lean on two men, a sign of age but also a privilege of royalty at one time). The sequence takes into account in its first half the movement of Skleros towards the emperor and the diminishing distance between the two; in so doing it defines the space of the scene with unaccustomed clarity. It is a proof of Psellos' clever and highly artistic manipulation of gestural narrative that the climax of the scene is made to coincide with the slightest gesture in the sequence: the emperor's deliberate closing of his eyes.[62]

All the ingredients of the early medieval manner are used here: direct speech in the emperor's pronouncement, a *bon mot* embedded in this particular incident and so to be handed down in tradition; a wealth of gestures, movements, and physical attitudes, most prominent of which is the shutting of the imperial eyes; finally, the element that justifies Basil's reaction and must be considered the focus of the scene: the sandals of purple on the usurper's feet, symbolic object *par excellence*.

GESTURE IN NARRATIVE AND IN THE VISUAL ARTS

Gestures with documented symbolic or ceremonial functions bring up the familiar problems of signifiers in all media, and most frequently that of multiple meaning. The literary scholar can turn with profit to the methods and results of art history for some clues on how to cope with these difficulties.[63] Given the weakness of the visual correlative in early medieval narrative, the arts might not seem a helpful term of comparison, but the difficulty is only apparent; the art of late antiquity and the early middle ages shows important stylistic affinities with the literary developments we are discussing, and in particular a strong tendency towards the codification and schematization of gesture.[64] The transformation of gestures from motions or poses that engage the entire body into detached, semaphoric appendages matches the hardening of narrative descriptions of movements into clichés and formulas.

Christian iconography provides instructive examples of the multiple meanings that gestures may acquire. A physically definite, easily recognizable action such as the laying on of hands, the placing of the open hand on the head of a person, may be found to have as many as five different values, including such irreconcilable ones as baptism, healing, and legal prosecution.[65] It is only by studying the context of the gesture (for example, the other figures present in the scene, distinctive props they may be carrying, even the nature of the monument on which the scene is depicted) that its meaning in a particular instance may be pinned down. Similarly the *dextrarum iunctio* or handshake described in almost the same terms by Gregory of Tours and Widukind of Corvey (by the former with 'datis inter se dextris,' by the latter as 'dextris datis et acceptis') serves in the first case to express the accord between two young people, recently married, who on their wedding night agree to remain chaste and lead secret lives of Christian renunciation (*HF* 1.47),[66] while in the second it is the greeting offered by the Frankish king Theuderic to his new allies, the Saxons, who will help him make war against the Thuringians (*RGS* 1.9). Though the two cases overlap semantically in so far as in both the handshake represents the sealing of an agreement, the distinctive sense of conjugal harmony that the gesture has in Gregory is old and well established, whereas Widukind has watered down the expression of a political alliance to a mere motion of welcome.

When the physical realization of a conventional gesture is not well defined, interpretation may rely even more heavily on context. The imperial art of late antiquity distinguishes between various gestures performed by the emperor with his upraised right hand: there are attitudes of imperial arrival or *adventus*, of public address of the troops (*adlocutio*), of largesse in public distributions of food, or tax exemptions (*liberalitas*), of clemency to defeated barbarian enemies. But there is no angle of the uplifted arm, no position of the hand that might allow us to tell one of these actions from the others, or even from Christ raising his hand in benediction.[67] As in the case of the single gesture with many values, it is the context that can tell us what we are really seeing: *adventus* is generally equestrian; *adlocutio* requires a military audience, *liberalitas* an audience of citizens and the emperor enthroned on a raised platform, the gesture of clemency a suppliant barbarian or two at the emperor's feet. However semaphoric the raising of the *invicta manus* may have become in the course of time, it did not function by itself, independently of the total scene.

A far more difficult problem arises in narrative when a stereotyped noun or phrase is used to indicate an action that can be performed in various ways. It is impossible to imagine what the character is actually doing unless the text itself adds further information to the cliché. The Greek προσκύνησις (Latin *adoratio*) and its monastic version the μετάνοια (Latin *venia*), acts of prostration before a superior, whether emperor, consul, or abbot, can be represented in the visual arts of the period as a genuflection with one knee, with two, sometimes with the forehead practically touching the floor, and also as a total prostration on the ground. Phrases such as 'μετάνοιαν βάλλειν' and 'veniam facere' in the written sources convey no image of the gesture whatsoever, but only an abstract indication of its meaning, which is all that matters (and which in the case of the monastic reverence often involves a sense of penitence).[68]

THE SPACE OF ACTION

If we are meant to visualize these scenes at all, some general sense of the space in which they happen becomes necessary. In the episodes, filled with expressive and symbolic movements, that we have surveyed in this chapter, the narrators appear to have limited the action to an implicit stage: there is as much space as one would need in order to perform such movements, and even Widukind's coronations are no more specific than that. The only indications of how early medieval narrators may have imagined the spatial setting are found in accounts of purely pragmatic action and in the visual arts. Where action can be explained entirely by a practical purpose, questions of physical and mechanical feasibility come up; motions must form a clear and possible sequence; the physical stage will have to be defined more explicitly. A feature that recurs frequently in such representations of action is extreme reduction of space, a surprising narrowness of the area allowed for gesture and movement, even in the most animated episodes.

The very paradigm of this preference for close quarters is probably Gregory of Tours' account of the priest Anastasius' struggle to get out of a coffin into which he has been locked with a decaying corpse. He has been placed there by order of Cautinus, the bishop of Clermont-Ferrand, so that he will hand over to him the deeds to his property.

> At presbiter, tamquam novus Ionas, velut *de ventre inferi* (Ionas 2, 3), ita de conclusione tumuli Domini misericordiam flagitabat. Et quia spatiosum, ut diximus, erat sarchofagum, etsi se integrum vertere non poterat, manus tamen in parte qua voluisset libere extendebat. Manabat enim ex ossibus mortui, ut ipse erat solitus referre, fetor letalis, qui non solum externa, verum etiam interna viscerum quatie-

bat. Cumque pallium aditus narium obseraret, quamdiu flatum
continere poterat, nihil pessimum sentiebat, ubi autem se quasi suf-
focari potabat, remoto paululum ab ore pallio, non modo per os
aut nares, verum etiam per ipsas, ut ita dicam, aures odorem pestiferum
hauriebat. Quid plura? Quando Divinitati, ut credo, condoluit, manum
dexteram ad spondam sarchofagi tendit, repperitque vectem, qui, de-
cidente opertorio, inter ipsum ac labium sepulchri remanserat. Quem
paulatim commovens, sensit, cooperante Dei adiutorio, lapidem
amoveri. Verum ubi ita remotum fuit, ut presbiter caput foris educeret,
maiorem quo totus egreditur aditum liberius patefecit.   (*HF* iv.12)

The priest, like a new Jonah *from the belly of death* (Jonah 2:3), was
calling upon the mercy of almighty God from the closeness of the
tomb. And since, as we said before, the grave was large, even if he could
not turn around within it, he could still reach with his hand wherever
he wanted. He used to tell later that a deadly stench emanated from
the bones of the dead man, which not only offended his nose but made
him sick to his stomach. He would cover his nostrils with his cloak
for as long as it was possible to hold his breath, and smell none of the
stench. But when he felt that he was going to suffocate and drew
the cloak from his face, he would inhale the lethal odour not only
through his mouth and nose but even, so to speak, through his ears.
To tell it briefly, God finally had compassion on him, and as he reached
out with his right hand to the edge of the tomb, he found a crowbar
that had been left between cover and rim as the lid of the sarcopha-
gus was being lowered. Moving the crowbar little by little, he felt that
with the help of God the slab was shifting. Once he had moved it
far enough that he could put his head out, it became easy to make a
larger opening and liberate his whole body.

The loss of space here is, of course, the very subject of the story and
not a matter of choice. But we may well ask ourselves why Gregory
selected this particular incident to give the most vivid and detailed
description of human movement in all his work.

A more instructive instance, because the action could have been
staged otherwise, is Paul the Deacon's story of how a very small man,
a Langobard of Turin, avenged the murder of his relative King Godepert
on Garipald, the man who had engineered the crime.

Erat quidam parvus homunculus ex propria familia Godeperti oriundus
in civitate Taurinatium. Is cum Garipaldum ducem ipso sacratissimo

paschali die ad orationem in beati Iohannis basilicam venturum sci-
ret, super sacrum baptisterii fontem conscendens laevaque manu se
ad columellum tugurii continens, unde Garipaldus transiturus erat,
evaginato ense sub amictu tenens, cum iuxta eum Garipald venisset,
ut pertransiret, ipse, elevato amictu, toto adnisu eodem ense in cervice
percussit caputque eius protinus amputavit. Super quem qui cum
Garipaldo venerant inruentes, multis eum ictuum vulneribus occide-
runt.   (HL iv.51)

There was a dwarf in the city of Turin who was a member of Godepert's family. When he found out that on Easter Sunday Duke Garipald would go to pray in the church of St John, he climbed on the font
at the baptistery and with his left hand held on to the column that
supports the roof over it, on the very spot through which Garipald
would come in, holding a drawn sword under his cloak. As Garipald
walked by next to him on his way in, the man pulled up his cloak and
struck at Garipald's head with his sword, using all his strength so
that he cut it off entirely. The men who had come with Garipald fell
upon him and killed him with numerous wounds caused by their
blows.

Space here is defined by the baptismal font, an axis from which the
two characters hardly distance themselves, since Paul has limited the
duration of the scene to the very brief moment during which Garipald
is next to the font. The murderer stands without moving on the font
itself. Though not many scenes in early medieval narrative are as easy
to visualize as these two, the taste for crowding action into minimal
spaces comes up again and again in the texts of the period.[69]

Whole chapters in the history of late antique and early medieval art
can be written in terms of the tension between a three- and a two-
dimensional representation of space, of the acceptance and rejection
of surface.[70] The conflict seems most pronounced in the narrative
branches of the visual arts; there the encroachment of schematism and
two-dimensionality that begins around 300 AD is met by repeated waves
of 'renascent' Hellenistic naturalism in the treatment of depth and
volume. What interests us here, however, as a pendant to the closeness
of the spaces suggested by narrative literature, is the early medieval
vogue of packed compositions, scenes often full of dramatic movement
and gesticulation where there is little or no space between the various
figures. This tendency can be illustrated well by carved ivories, a medium of remarkable continuity and quality of achievement in the cen-

turies that concern us. It might be objected that surfaces in ivory must by nature be small, and the compositions therefore crowded. But such pieces as the panel from the Symmachus diptych at the Victoria and Albert Museum (plate 1), carved circa 400 AD after earlier models, show figures surrounded by empty space and standing in a more or less credible relation to each other. Already here, however, the sense of depth is given more by the three-dimensional representation of the figures than by any coherent spatial relation between them. The priestess floats at an angle to the altar, instead of facing it, and her young helper has been so much reduced in size, in order to place him behind altar and priestess, that he appears to be walking by in the distance. If we compare this scene with the Barberini diptych at the Louvre (plate 2), made probably in Constantinople in the mid-sixth century, a work with classical affinities of its own, we are struck by an enormous change in taste and design. The quick movements of the emperor and his horse, caught in the act of triumphal arrival, are packed in between the attitudes of a personified Terra, recumbent under the rearing steed, and a flying Victory who occupies the angle cleared by the emperor's inclination to the right. The enthroned Christ above this scene and the group of suppliant barbarians bearing gifts at the bottom are actually present at this same moment of triumph, though the reduced scale of the barbarians turns them into a sort of frieze border to the larger scene. More significant is the cheering barbarian behind the emperor, caught between the rump of his horse and his vertical spear. The flat and artificial space, in which size is a function of rank and perspective has been totally forgotten, is nevertheless alive with movement and dramatic energy. Through the ebb and flow of classical influences, and undercut periodically by the return of a deeper space, this taste for airless, stylized compositions evolves and becomes more and more pronounced. The extraordinary Ascension at Darmstadt (plate 3), a Carolingian work of the early ninth century, may well be the high point of this anticlassical trend in representation: suppression of depth and crowding of the surface have here become principles, particularly in the superposed feet of the apostles and Mary, curiously scattered over each other and following a rhythm of their own. The patterns of hands, draperies, haloes, and upraised faces serve an almost purely expressive function bordering on the abstract; figuration has minimal importance, except in the relief given to Mary over the others by the gesture with the fold of her tunic and by her peculiar swaying stance.[71]

Plate 1

Plate 2

Plate 3

4   Things

In his influential study of the 'simple forms' of literature, published
in 1930, André Jolles sketched out a special theory of the correspon-
dence between several primary genres and specific kinds of inanimate
objects. The simple forms are, among others, the saint's legend (German *Legende*), the heroic-historical legend (*Sage*), the myth, the riddle,
the proverb, the joke. Each one of them is shaped by a particular sort
of mental activity (*Geistesbeschäftigung*). Thus, for example, the saint's
legend is defined by thinking in the exemplary mode, by thought as
imitatio, and the heroic *Sage* by thinking along lines of kinship and
dynasty. The essence of each simple form can be manifested by a thing
as well as by a text: *imitatio* is conveyed by a relic; the genealogical
interests of the *Sage* by an heirloom (weapons of heroic ancestors, the
bloody cloak of a murdered relative); the intellectual content of a myth
can be carried by a symbol or symbolic object.[1]

Much in Jolles' theory appears to have dated: the phenomenology
that allowed him to distinguish between the different *Geistesbe-
schäftigungen* is a dubious method, and what he took to be primary
forms of literature seem far less primary to us today. Some of these
genres, such as the *Sage* or the folk-tale, are considered now anything
but simple.[2] His speculations about the place of objects, however, which
received less attention than any other aspect of his book, have kept
all their interest. They remain extraordinarily suggestive, whether we
consider the relations of literature to real objects external to it, or the
functions of things within narrative texts – that is, the objects mentioned in stories and around which episodes and scenes often come to
revolve. For the student of early medieval literature, Jolles' views have

a double interest: in the first place the narratives of the period, like oral texts, place objects at the centre of the action with increasing frequency; in the second, most of Jolles' simple forms are of popular and traditional origin, and find literary expression for the first time in the early middle ages.

IN LATE ANTIQUITY

The object-focused scene or episode allows us to make no discrimination between popular and literary narrative: it is used, with characteristic formal and functional variety, at every social and stylistic level. This distinctive structure of medieval narrative already figures impressively in certain texts of late antiquity, heralding the full range of variation that will emerge between the sixth century and the tenth. Let us look at three of these early instances:

1   A Bowl of Water

At the more humble end of the spectrum we find the closest thing to pure oral form in the *Apophthegmata patrum*. A story from the anonymous collection describes the experience of three friends who seek spiritual tranquillity. One dedicates himself to making peace between men, another to the care of the sick, the third to a life of prayer and meditation in the desert. Unsatisfied with their achievement, the first two pay a visit to their friend in the desert and ask him for advice.

> After a short silence he put water in a bowl and said to them: 'Look at the water.' It was troubled. A little later he said again: 'Look once more, now that the water has settled.' And when they bent over the water they saw their faces in it, as in a mirror. He said to them: 'In the same way he who lives among men does not see his own sins because of the distractions, but when he lives alone, especially in the desert, then he can see his failings.'
>
> (Nau 'Histoires des solitaires égyptiens' no 134)

The bowl of water belongs to a small collection of objects of personal use associated with monks and hermits in apophthegmatic literature and frequently mentioned in individual anecdotes: the monk's tunic and cowl, his sandals, his handwork of rope, baskets, or nets, his jug of water and small loaf of bread. The placing of the bowl at the center of the scene in answer to the brothers' question is a gesture of the hermit himself, and equivalent to a speech or a parable. His words after the water has settled turn the bowl and the movement of the water in it into an explicit simile for the soul and its condition. The object is not symbolic in itself, but only by virtue of a verbal gloss.[3]

2   A Cross of Light

At the other end of the range we find Constantine's vision of the cross, as told by Eusebius of Caesarea in his life of the emperor.

> He said that about midday, with the sun already declining, he saw with his own eyes the trophy of a cross in the sky, made of light and lying over the sun, and an inscription attached to it which said 'Conquer by this.' Astonishment at the sight took hold of him and his entire army, which had followed him on the journey, and got to see the marvel. He said that he was at a loss as to what the vision might mean. When he had worried much and speculated about it, night fell, and as he was sleeping he saw the Christ of God with the sign that had appeared in the sky, and he [Christ] exhorted him to make an image of the sign in the sky and to use it as a defence in all encounters with his enemies. Getting up at dawn, he told the miracle to his friends.   (*Vita Constantini* I.28–30)

Here we have to do with a vision which reveals a pure symbol, referred to as 'τὸ σημεῖον' in the text. The visionary situation is standard fare in the literature of late antiquity and the early middle ages, and in Jolles' theory symbols are the objects that bear the essence of myth. What we have here, indeed, is the foundation myth of imperial Christianity. Constantine has been pondering what god he must turn to for assistance in his expedition against Maxentius. Having rejected polytheism, he turns to the One God with a prayer that he may reveal himself.[4] It is not the protagonist who draws the cross to the centre of the stage; the cross is a reply to him. The role of the emperor is fundamentally passive; he needs to make sense of this message which, unlike the bowl of water of the previous story, comes already provided with a gloss: it is interpreted for him in part by the inscription on the cross of light, and also by the words of Christ in his dream afterwards. These two glosses, however, do not define the nature of the cross, but only its power and application, so that the sign retains its mystery.

There is no suggestion of oral-traditional form; the vision is an ideological legend created by church and state, much like the pagan vision of Apollo and Victory which had been attributed to Constantine in the days before his conversion.[5] It draws, like the pagan vision, on a well-established iconographic tradition, in this case the Christian imagery of the cross. It also anticipates and encourages the further development of this traditional image and its new role as focus of an imperial policy: the sign of victory is reproduced on shields, on official coinage, in the labarum; it is transformed into splendid objects of gold and jewels; crucifixion is abolished as a punishment for criminals.[6] Eusebius' account of the vision is itself an instrument of propaganda. What characterizes it most clearly as a literary creation is the fact that it draws its interpretation of the object from an established, institutionalized tradition which it also helps to foster and develop.

3   The Divided Cloak

Compared with the former two, many episodes are more difficult to place on the social scale that runs from orality to high literature. An event as famous as Constantine's vision, the *charité* of St Martin of Tours, provides a good illustration of the possible difficulties. In the classical account by Sulpicius Severus we read that the young Pannonian soldier, not yet baptized but already saintly, performed the following act of mercy at Amiens:

> 3, 1. Quodam itaque tempore, cum iam nihil praeter arma et simplicem militiae uestem haberet, media hieme quae solito asperior inhorruerat, adeo ut plerosque uis algoris extingueret, obuium habet in porta Ambianesium ciuitatis pauperem nudum. Qui cum praetereuntes ut sui misererentur oraret omnesque miserum praeterirent, intellexit uir Deo plenus sibi illum, aliis misericordiam non praestantibus, reseruari. 2. Quid tamen ageret? Nihil praeter chlamydem, qua indutus erat, habebat: iam enim reliqua in opus simile consumpserat. Arrepto itaque ferro quo accinctus erat, mediam diuidit partemque eius pauperi tribuit, reliqua rursus induitur. Interea de circumstantibus ridere nonnulli, quia deformis esse truncatus habitu uideretur; multi tamen, quibus erat mens sanior, altius gemere, quod nihil simile fecissent, cum utique plus habentes uestire pauperem sine sua nuditate potuissent.   (*Vita Sancti Martini* 3.1–2)

Once, when he had nothing left but his armour and plain soldier's cloak, and mid-winter was harsher than usual, to the point that the cold had killed several people, he came upon a naked beggar at the city gate of Amiens. He was begging from those who went by, asking them to take compassion on him, but they all walked on heedless. Then the man filled with God understood that the others did not exercise compassion because the beggar had been reserved for him. What should he do? He had nothing except the cloak in which he was clad, having given away everything else in similar works of charity. He therefore took the sword with which he was girt, cut the cloak in two, gave one half to the pauper, and put on the other. In the meanwhile some of those who stood around laughed, for he seemed grotesque to them in his divided cloak. Many others, however, who could think more nobly, sighed deeply because they had not done like him, for they had more at hand than Martin, and would have been able to clothe the naked beggar without reducing themselves to nudity.

Like the Constantinian vision, this act is followed by a dream, in which Martin sees Christ dressed in the divided garment, and hears him proclaim the virtue of this young convert 'adhuc catechumenus' to the angels. Sulpicius Severus can claim a literary status at least as elevated as that of Eusebius, and he is a far better writer. Jacques Fontaine has pointed out a number of echoes of the pagan classics in this account of the *charité*.[7] Sulpicius' narrative stands at the origin of the long tradition of this story in literature and the visual arts, a great part of it in the realm of high, official culture.[8] The act that he describes here, however, is not invented but taken from an oral tradition about Martin; it is a manifestation of charity with familiar precedents in scripture (Matthew 25:36: 'I was naked and you clothed me') and several analogues in the *Apophthegmata*.[9] The tunic at this point has no symbolic meaning, though one was to develop later. Martin, unlike the hermit with his bowl of water, does not use it to make a statement. The act is *exemplary* and presents itself as a prototype to be imitated, a basic function which Sulpicius has stressed by describing in some detail the varying reactions of the bystanders. The centrality of the tunic is given partly by these witnesses who comment and judge, partly by the eccentric nature of Martin's act.

More clearly than the other texts, the *charité* brings home to us how object-centred episodes belong in a measure in the chapter on gestures, since they overlap constantly with physical action: the saint's tunic becomes significant only because he divides it. His gestures and activity drawing the sword and cutting through the garment are inseparable from the tunic itself as focus of the scene. We may compare the *charité* with such episodes as the dropping of the goblet by an evil priest before his death, discussed earlier as an instance of gestural stereotype. The cup has some meaning of its own: it is celebratory, triumphant, but can also appear in scripture as an image of personal fate. It must nevertheless be dropped or returned to the cupbearer suddenly to become a symbol of death and retribution. When the *mise en valeur* of the object is not effected by a single gesture or action as in these cases, it is carried out by words said about the object or written on it (the remarks of the hermit on his bowl of water; the inscription on the cross of light; Christ's words about the cross in Constantine's dream), or by dramatic action involving both words and gestures. In other words, objects as focus are not as fundamental a narrative device as direct speech or gestures; things must depend on words and actions for their role, their central position. An object-focused episode is ultimately a subtype of the verbal, gestural, or mixed narrative techniques described already, depending on the frame or context used to 'animate' the thing and bring it to the foreground. Compositionally, however, the result is a very distinctive scenic type with a still, opaque centre around which words and movements gather to elicit and create meaning.

We have found in late antiquity a characteristically oral and humble form, the apophthegm, giving this new narrative role to a thing, and on the other hand a far more ambitious literary product, the vision of Constantine, echoing this structure and in apparent readiness to absorb it. The account of the *charité* of St Martin by Sulpicius Severus proves that the assimilation of the object-centred scene into literature took place before the end of antiquity: an anecdote manifestly oral and popular in background is reproduced in the finest literary prose of the age. The early medieval centuries reveal a total integration of this scenic form into the medium of literature; the device appears in all the standard genres: history, chronicle, hagiography, political treatise. To the simple didactic and exemplary functions of the object in the late antique instances a host of new possibilities are added, particularly in the area of symbolism, in the variety of ways in which a thing can be made to point beyond itself to concepts and general values. The development of this trend is difficult to discuss as a whole: even though we are dealing with a distinctive, easily identifiable form, its manifestations are so diverse, the centring of the object and its eventual interpretation so often brought about by *ad hoc* methods that definitions, no matter how broad, are likely to leave out important variants and instructive exceptions. It is safer, therefore, to begin by looking at a number of examples taken from different authors and genres, and to discuss them individually before going on to any kind of general formulations. We shall look at nine brief anecdotes arranged roughly in chronological order.

Already in the sixth century we find a proliferation of object-centred scenes. In the work of Gregory of Tours the focal object develops new applications and eventually becomes available as a pure form of composition, independent of any significance the thing may have in itself. Like the brief dialogue in direct form, or the gesture around which an entire scene can be organized, it becomes a building block of dramatic narrative, a device of the new style. There is nothing particularly surprising about this, as Gregory is one of the most resourceful narrators of the early middle ages; our first three specimens are taken from his history of the Franks.

1   A Ewer

The first exhibit must be the episode of the *vase de Soissons*, a famous chapter in the life of Clovis, whose biography takes up book two of the *Libri historiarum*. We are dealing here with an incident from the early career of the Frankish king, before his conversion and while he was still wresting Gaul from Germanic rivals and the various kinglets left behind by Roman domination. His men have plundered a number of churches in the newly conquered territories.

Igitur de quadam eclesia urceum mirae magnitudinis ac pulchritudinis hostes abstulerant, cum reliqua eclesiastici ministerii ornamenta. Episcopus autem eclesiae illius missus ad regem dirigit, poscens, ut, si aliud de sacris vasis recipere non meretur, saltim vel urceum aeclesia sua reciperit. Haec audiens rex, ait nuntio: 'Sequere nos usque Sexonas, quae ibi cuncta que adquisita sunt dividenda erunt. Cumque mihi vas illud sors dederit, quae papa poscit, adimpleam'. Dehinc adveniens Sexonas, cunctum onus praedae in medio positum, ait rex: 'Rogo vos, o fortissimi procliatores, ut saltim mihi vas istud – hoc enim de urceo supra memorato dicebat, – 'extra partem concidere non abnuatis'. Haec regi dicente, illi quorum erat mens sanior aiunt: 'Omnia, gloriose rex, quae cernimus, tua sunt, sed et nos ipsi tuo sumus dominio subiugati. Nunc quod tibi bene placitum viditur facito; nullus enim potestati tuae resistere valet'. Cum haec ita dixis-

sent, unus levis, invidus ac facilis, cum voce magna elevatam
bipennem urceo inpulit, dicens: 'Nihil hinc accipies, nisi quae tibi
sors vera largitur'. Ad haec obstupefactis omnibus, rex iniuriam suam
patientiae lenitate coercuit, acceptumque urceum nuntio eclesiastico
reddidit, servans abditum sub pectore vulnus.   (*HF* II.27)

The troops took from a certain church a remarkably large and beautiful
ewer, together with other ornaments used in the church service. The
bishop of that church sent messengers to the king, to plead that even
if he did not get back any other of the sacred vessels, he might at
least recover the ewer of his church. Hearing this, the king said to
the messenger: 'Follow us to Soissons, for there everything that has
been taken will be shared out. If in the distribution the vessel the
bishop is asking for should fall to my share, I shall do as he requested.'
When he came to Soissons and all the plunder had been heaped
together in the middle, the king said: 'Brave warriors, I beg that you
will not refuse to grant me this vessel' – he meant the above-mentioned
ewer – 'aside from my own part of the plunder.' When he had spoken,
all those of a more rational disposition answered: 'All we see here,
glorious king, belongs to you, and we ourselves are under your rule.
Do what seems pleasing to you; none of us is able to withstand your
power.' As they were speaking, a vain, hostile and foolish warrior
raised his axe and brought it down on the ewer, crying out loudly:
'You get nothing here, except what your fair share will bring you!'
All were astonished at this reaction, but the king soothed his injured
pride with patient mildness. He took the ewer and handed it to the
bishop's emissary, keeping the wound hidden in his breast.

But Clovis does not forget. A year later, while mustering his troops,
he approaches the insolent soldier and, scolding him for the condition
of his weapons, he throws the man's axe to the ground.

At ille cum paulolum inclinatus fuisset ad collegendum, rex, elevatis
manibus, securem suam capite eius defixit. 'Sic', inquid, 'tu Sexonas
in urceo illo fecisti'.   (ibid)

When he leaned over a little to pick it up, the king raised his hands
and drove his axe into the man's skull, saying: 'This is what you
did to that ewer in Soissons!'

The ewer is a liturgical implement (taken 'cum reliqua eclesiastici ministerii ornamenta'), and Clovis' collaboration with the bishop to restore a sacred object to the church adumbrates at this point his future role as the first great Catholic monarch of barbarian Europe.[10] With his remark recalling the destruction of the ewer as he brains the offending soldier, he establishes an equation between the 'urceus' and the man's head, an analogy that comes up a few more times in early Germanic legend. The soldier is even referred to as 'the destroyer of the ewer' ('urcei percussor'). We are able to follow the story of the vessel itself in some detail; at any rate we are told more about it than about most focal objects: its origin, the bishop's plea for its restitution, its return in damaged condition to the church. But in spite of all this attention to the ewer, its interpretation remains incomplete. For one thing, the object fits only loosely into this anecdote; it could be replaced by a chalice or a reliquary. What the incident is meant to convey more than anything else is the character of Clovis as manifested in this small occasion, his long memory and fierce vindictiveness. And it is not the object that can bring out these qualities but the repeated movement, the blow on the soldier's head that duplicates that of the soldier on the ewer: 'Sic tu Sexonas in urceo illo fecisti.' In spite of some general significance derived from its religious origin and use, the ewer does not become a symbol; it remains a *motive*, an accidental reason for contention and for an act of retaliation with which it shares unequally the centre of the stage.

2   The Sword and the Scissors

Our second Gregorian specimen is taken from the life of Clovis' spouse Chrodechild in the days of her widowhood. The queen has been taking care of three of her grandchildren, the orphaned sons of Chlodomer. Her own sons Childebert and Chlothar, jealous of their nephews and eager to put these rival claimants to the throne out of the way, kidnap two of them and send a message to Chrodechild.

> Tunc Childeberthus atque Chlothacharius miserunt Archadium, cui supra meminimus, ad reginam cum forcipe evaginatoque gladio. Qui veniens, ostendit reginae utraque, dicens: 'Voluntatem tuam, o gloriosissima regina, fili tui domini nostri expetunt, quid de pueris agendum censeas, utrum incisis crinibus eos vivere iubeas, an utrumque iugulare'. At illa exterrita nuntio et nimium felle commota, praecipue cum gladium cerneret evaginatum ac forcipem, amaritudinem praeventa, ignorans in ipso dolore quid diceret, ait simpliciter: 'Satius

mihi enim est, si ad regnum non ereguntur, mortuos eos videre quam tonsus'. At ille parum admirans dolorem eius, nec scrutans, quid deinceps plenius pertractaret, venit celeriter, nuntians ac dicens: 'Favente regina opus coeptum perficite; ipsa enim vult explere consilium vestrum'.   (*HF* III.18)

Then Childebert and Chlothar sent Archadius, whom I have mentioned before, to the queen, bearing a pair of scissors and a naked sword. He came in and showed them to the queen, saying: 'Our lords your sons, glorious queen, wish to know your will and to hear what is to be done with the boys. Do you believe they should be shorn of their hair and allowed to live, or should they have their throats cut?' She, terrified by the messenger and too cruelly shaken, particularly when she saw the bare sword and the scissors, was overcome by bitterness and, not knowing in her grief what she was saying, answered simply: 'If they cannot rule the kingdom, I would prefer to see them dead rather than shorn.' The man, without considering her sorrow or waiting to see what she might say after more careful consideration, went away quickly and told them: 'Finish the task you have started. You have the queen's approval. She herself wants your design carried out.'

The children were then savagely murdered. Before turning to the sword, the scissors, and their function, we should notice that the story may have changed considerably in the passage from oral tradition to literary historiography. Gregory's description of the queen's state of mind ('terrified,' 'cruelly shaken,' 'overcome by bitterness,' and most significant, 'not knowing in her grief what she was saying') shows the intention to excuse Chrodechild, whose reputation for sainthood was quite established by this time, from the charge of having made a harsh and inhuman choice. The problem is that her reply to the messenger is much too resolute and precise for the excuse to be convincing, and I suspect that an anecdote told originally to illustrate the *feritas* and royal hauteur of the widowed queen has been converted into a pious account of the 'fatal chain of circumstances' that led to the killing of the young princes.[11]

The messenger's verbal gloss on the sword and the scissors makes the objects themselves dispensable; it is tempting to imagine an earlier version in which they were presented in silence and where the queen made her choice by pointing at one of them. Like the bowl of water and the cross of light, they are part of a dialogue. They appear on stage as a minimal coded message; unlike Clovis' ewer, they are absolutely central and do not compete with any gesture. Also, their interpretation is complete though extremely narrow: they stand for their own use, just as a spade might be used to represent the act of digging. Their juxtaposition in the hands of Archadius indicates a disjunction and an open question (either / or? Shall we do A or B?).

3   A Plate of Soup

In the episode of the sword and the scissors the meaning and possible associations of the central object have shrunk to very little; they can contract further and practically disappear in Gregory's narrative, leaving the object at the heart of the scene empty as a pure formal focus, a pretext around which the other elements of the story can be grouped. This hollowed-out object can still function as a device for gathering and releasing tension in the episode, but it has given up all didactic and propagandistic usefulness.

In the long chapter where he describes his clash with King Chilperic over the trial of Praetextatus, Gregory, who sided stubbornly with his colleague, is summoned to the royal presence.

> Cumque venissem, stabat rex iuxta tabernaculum ex ramis factum, et ad dexteram eius Berthchramnus episcopus, ad levam vero Ragnemodus stabat; et erat ante eos scamnum pane desuper plenum cum diversis fercolis.   (*HF* v.18)

> When I arrived, the king was standing next to a booth made of branches, with Bishop Bertram on his right and Ragnemod on his left. Before them there was a bench on which bread and various things to eat had been placed.

The stage has been set, and for Gregory this is quite an elaborate *mise-en-scène*; a long altercation follows between bishop and ruler, in which Gregory refuses to yield to Chilperic's accusations and threats. Taken aback by such resolute opposition, the king decides to try flattery.

> At illi quasi me demulcens, quod dolose faciens potabat me non intellegere, conversus ad iuscellum, quod coram eo erat positus, ait: 'Propter te haec iuscella paravi, in qua nihil aliud praeter volatilia et parumper ciceris continetur'. Ad haec ego, cognuscens adulationis eius, dixi: 'Noster cibus esse debet facere voluntatem Dei et non in his

diliciis dilectare, ut ea quae praecipit nullo casu praetermittamus.
Tu vero, qui alios de iustitia culpas, pollicire prius, quod legem et
canones non omittas; et tunc credimus, quod iustitiam prosequaris'.
Ille vero, porrectam dexteram, iuravit per omnipotenti Deo, quod ea
quae lex et canones edocebant nullu praetermitteret pactu. Post haec,
accepto pane, hausto etiam vino, discessi.   (ibid)

But Chilperic, as if trying to propitiate me, and believing that I did
not realize he did so deceitfully, turned towards a bowl of soup that
had been placed before him and said: 'I had this dish prepared especially
for you. It contains nothing but chicken and some peas.' Knowing
him to be a flatterer, I replied: 'Our food should be to do the will of
God, not to delight in these delicacies. We must by no means leave
undone what God has commanded. You however, who persecute others
in the name of justice, swear first that you will not overlook the
law and the canons, and then we shall believe that you seek justice.'
Then he raised his right hand and swore by almighty God that he
would not neglect for any consideration what the law and the canons
taught. After that I ate some bread, drank some wine, and departed.

Chilperic's curiously detailed description of the food, and the brief
argument to which his invitation gives rise, seem to place the 'ius-
cellum' at the dramatic centre. In itself the plate means almost nothing.
It takes on larger significance only in so far as its rejection is a refusal
of offered hospitality. Gregory is also striking the conventional priestly
attitude of 'we have not come here to fill our bellies.' But rejection of
the king's advances and a consistently ecclesiastical demeanour have
been there all along, so they cannot explain the shift of attention to
the plate of soup at this point. Assimilated to other formal resources
of narrative, the object need no longer be eloquent in itself; it requires
no interpretation, having become a factor in the composition of the
scene, an arbitrary centre which acquires and embodies, by implication,
the significance of the action that surrounds it.

Note: Gregory and Medieval Symbolism.
Certain passages in the *Libri historiarum* suggest that Gregory of Tours
may have been aware of the philosophical speculation on symbolism
that had found its most influential formulation in Augustine's *De
doctrina christiana* and *De Trinitate*.[12] In a famous passage of the
former treatise, discussing which things are things only ('res tantum')

and which are also signs of other things, Augustine had used as examples for both categories the animals and inanimate objects of scripture:

> Proprie autem nunc res appellaui, quae non ad significandum aliquid
> adhibentur, sicuti est lingum lapis pecus atque huiusmodi cetera, sed
> non illud lignum, quod in aquas amaras Moysen misisse legimus, ut
> amaritudine carerent, neque ille lapis, quem Iacob sibi ad caput
> posuerat, neque illud pecus, quod pro filio immolauit Abraham. Hae
> namque ita res sunt, ut aliarum etiam signa sint rerum.
>
> > (*De doctrina christiana* I.ii.2)

> I have exclusively called 'things' whatever does not serve to signify
> anything else, for instance wood, stone, cattle, and other such things.
> But not the wood that Moses cast into bitter waters, that they might
> give up their bitterness, nor the stone which Jacob put under his head,
> nor the ram that Abraham sacrificed instead of his son. These things
> are such, so that they may be signs for other things.

Gregory echoes these words, and particularly Augustine's range of examples, to which he adds a few of his own, in two pages of his history:
the prologue to book three, where he lists a number of biblical objects
as signs of the trinity, and his theological debate with Agila, an Arian
envoy of the Visigoths, in book five, where he uses a similar list of
things as signs of the right faith:

> 'Satius', inquio, 'faciebas, si ea te armaret fides, quam Abraham ad
> ilicem, Isac in arietem, Iacob in lapide, Moyses vidit in sente; quam
> Aaron portavit in logio, David exultavit in timphano, Salomon prae-
> dicavit in intellectu; quam omnes patriarchae, prophetae sive lex ipsa
> vel oraculis caccinit vel sacrificiis figuravit ...'   (*HF* v.43)

> 'You would be better off,' I said, 'if you were armed with the same
> faith that Abraham found in the oak, Isaac in the ram, Jacob in the
> stone, which Moses saw in the bush, Aaron wore in the ephod, David
> knew when he danced with the timbrel, and Solomon preached with
> his wisdom, the faith that all the patriarchs and prophets, and the
> law itself sang of in prophecies and prefigured symbolically in
> sacrifices ...'

Since the debate is with an Arian, the right faith referred to in this speech must be orthodox faith in the Trinity, and therefore the application of these signs is really the same in both passages. It cannot be said, however, that Gregory's possible awareness of the symbolic possibilities of things as conceived by Augustine has any effect, or is reflected in any way in Gregory's narrative practice. The soup, the ewer, the sword, and the scissors do not share a way of being significant, a single sense of how an object can convey meaning; what they have in common is primarily a compositional function, a place, however empty, in the scene.

4   A Phrygian Apple

Gregory's near-contemporary Malalas tells the following story about how the marriage of Theodosius II and Eudoxia, the auspicious beginnings of which we discussed in chapter two, came to a sorry end:

> It happened later, when at Christmas the Emperor Theodosius had gone to church, that the Magister Paulinus, who was suffering in his foot, stayed behind [in the palace] and excused himself. A poor man offered Emperor Theodosius a Phrygian apple of such exceptional size that the emperor and all his company were astounded by its largeness. The emperor, giving immediately one hundred and fifty coins to the man who had brought it, sent the apple to the Augusta Eudoxia. The augusta in turn sent it to Magister Paulinus, as he was a friend of the emperor. Paulinus, not knowing that the emperor had previously sent it to the augusta, sent it himself to the emperor as soon as he came back to the palace. On receiving it, the emperor recognized the present, but kept the secret to himself. He summoned the augusta and asked her: 'Where is the apple I sent you?' She answered: 'I ate it.' He exhorted her by her own salvation to say whether she had eaten the apple herself or given it to someone else. She swore that she had not sent it to anyone. Then the emperor had the apple brought and showed it to her. He became angry at her and suspected that, being in love with Paulinus, she had sent him the apple and now denied it. On account of this, the emperor had Paulinus eliminated. The augusta was pained and offended by this. It became known everywhere that Paulinus had perished on account of her, and he had been a handsome young man. She then asked Emperor Theodosius to allow her to go to the holy places to pray. He gave her permission, and she went from Constantinople to Jerusalem to pray.
>
> (*Chronographia* xiv)

As in the episode of the ewer, there is repetition, here not of a gesture but of an action: the fruit is offered four times, with varied nuances of intention on which Malalas does not dwell, letting the extraordinary apple pass from one character to another almost without comment. He does tell us, however, that Eudoxia sent it to Paulinus 'ὡς φίλῳ τοῦ βασιλέως' / 'as he was a friend of the emperor.' In that case we may ask ourselves why she later lied with so much determination.[13] Her attitude does not make sense, and the point of the story, if it must have one, becomes confused. As in the episode of the sword and the scissors, we may have to do here with the imperfect adaptation of a tale originating in popular gossip about an event at court, gossip current one century before Malalas wrote, into a chapter of written history. Unlike Gregory, Malalas does not seem to want to excuse or improve; he is just not very sure of the story.[14]

The apple itself, as the type of expensive curiosity that a wealthy man might buy to please a wife or mistress, would seem easy to replace by a jewel, or by any sort of exquisite food or drink. It contains, however, an element of scriptural allusion which is marked not in the description of the apple, but in the outline of the plot. An all-powerful figure leaves a couple together 'in the palace.' The woman gives the man a fruit and ruins him thereby. The omnipotent character returns to his palace, questions the woman about her responsibility in the matter, and punishes the couple. If this sketch of the story of the Fall of Man appears to explain the choice of an apple for the central object, it must be observed nevertheless that the passage does not echo the words of the Greek Genesis: where Septuagint has an indefinite 'καρπός,' Malalas introduces a specific 'μῆλον' and describes an extraordinary fruit. Nor is there any echo of scripture when Eudoxia is questioned by her husband. The reference to Adam and Eve, though undeniable, is all in the plot.[15] The apple, like Clovis' ewer but unlike the sword and scissors, has the additional significance of being a motive: when the emperor buys it he sets in motion a sequence of actions that will lead to his estrangement from the empress.

5   A Tangled Net

A second Greek anecdote comes from the *Pratum spirituale* or Λειμών of the Cilician Ioannes Moschos (d 639), a work that stands wholly in the tradition of the *Apophthegmata* and of the Eastern πατερικόν, though it is far more receptive to accounts of miracles, demons, and spectacular healings than the collections of the fourth and fifth centuries.[16] Photius describes the style of Moschos as 'leaning to the humble,' and it is certainly low by Byzantine standards.[17] The narrator, who tours Syria and Palestine gathering lore about holy men, comes to Lykos in the Thebais. There he meets Abba Isaac, a hermit who tells him the following story:

> 'Fifty-two years ago, as I was busy at my manual work, making a large mosquito-net, I erred. And I was distressed because I could not find where I had gone wrong. I spent the whole day worrying, and did not know what to do. And as I was despairing, behold, a boy came in through the window, saying: "You went astray, but give your handwork to me so that I may correct it." I said to him: "Go away from here. May this not come upon me." He answered: "But it hurts you, if you do your work poorly." I said to him: "Do not concern yourself with that." Again he said to me: "I pity you, because you are destroying your labour." Then I said to him: "Your coming here was bad, and that of those who brought you." Then he said to me: "Truly, you forced me to come, and you are mine." I asked him: "Why do you say that?" He answered: "Because for three Sundays you have taken communion and been in enmity with your neighbour."
>
> (*Pratum* chapter 161)

Abba Isaac then made peace with his neighbour and presumably returned to undisturbed net-making. The episode belongs to a traditional type of anecdote where the presence of sin or the devil is indicated by some minor mistake or accident that befalls the monk: he uses the wrong words in praying, or upsets his water-jug. The choice of a mosquito-net over more common sorts of monastic handwork such as rope-making or basket-weaving is particularly apposite. Abba Isaac has missed a knot in a very fine mesh, so that the rows in his net do not come out even when he counts the spaces. He spends the entire day counting back and forth, looking for the spot where he was distracted, and is unable to find it. As the young demon observes, the missing knot and Isaac's incapacity to find it are consequences of the sin of anger in the monk's heart. But Moschos has put a second sense into his portrayal of the toiling Isaac: '$\pi\lambda\alpha\nu\acute{\alpha}\omega$,' the verb he uses for the error in handwork, means in the passive form it takes here 'to be led astray,' 'to be made to sin,' and '$\sigma\phi\acute{\alpha}\lambda\mu\alpha$,' the corresponding noun in the text, is also a common expression for 'fault, sin.' The anxious but unavailing search for the missing knot turns into an image of the examination of conscience to which monks and hermits were expected to subject themselves continually.[18] The net and its flaw become a metaphor, just as the water-bowl of the hermit in the *Apophthegmata* is used by him as a simile of the soul. However, in that case the simile is wholly rhetorical, created by the hermit himself, who uses the bowl as a teaching aid in order to explain spiritual peace to his friends. Here the connection is objective: Abba Isaac misses a knot because he is in sin, and he is unable to find it because he is blinded by the devil. He does not use the net for a demonstration: the net reveals to him his own spiritual condition, and a demon provides the interpretive gloss to this discovery.

6   A Hidden Relic

The longest and most interesting chapter of the *Lives of the Holy Fathers of Mérida*, a text written in Spain in the seventh century, describes the struggle of the orthodox Masona, bishop of Mérida, against the Arian king Leovigild one century before. It is written in florid but awkward language which borrows its ornaments and narrative method from late antique models. Leovigild attempts to confiscate the most prized possession of the church of Mérida, the tunic of the virgin martyr St Eulalia, in order to hand it over to his heretical followers. To this end he summons Masona to Toledo and orders with threats and curses that he surrender the relic.[19] He finally gets the following reply from the Catholic bishop:

> Cui miles Dei ita imperterritus respondit: 'Iam dixi tibi semel et iterum quia minas tuas non formidabo. Sed quidquid valet mens tua perversa amplius adversum me excogitet. Ego tamen nec te pertimesco nec metu territus id quod requiris praesentabo. Sed hoc scito quia tunicam ipsam igne combussi pulveresque ex ea feci et in liquorem aquae permixtos bibi.' Et tactu manus suae contrectans stomachum suum dicebat: 'Evidenter cognosce quia in pulveres reductam bibi illam et ecce hic intus in ventre meo est. Nunquam tibi illam reddo.' Hoc autem ideo dicebat quia nullo sciente sibi eam in stomacho plicatam infra sua indumenta linteis involutam praecinxerat et ita eam Deo solo conscio gestabat. Nam sic caecavit Deus oculos ipsius regis et omnium adsistentium ei ut nullus intelligeret quemadmodum ista prosequeretur vir Dei.   (*VSPE* v.vi.20–1)

Unafraid, the soldier of God replied to him as follows: 'I have told you once and again that I do not fear your threats. But let your depraved mind plot whatever else it can against me. I neither fear you nor, driven by fear, shall hand over what you demand. Know that I have burned the tunic, made powder of it, then mixed it with water and drunk it.' And patting his stomach with his hand he added: 'Learn therefore with certainty that I drank it up after reducing it to dust of ashes, and it is here, in my belly. I will never give it to you.'' He spoke thus because, without anyone knowing, he had folded the tunic around his belly, wrapped in linen cloths, and was carrying it on him so that only God was aware of it. God so blinded the eyes of the king and all his helpers that none of them understood how the man of God had managed to do this.

The central object here, the tunic wrapped around the bishop's body under his robes, is not symbolic. This comes from its very function as a relic: to be effective it must be authentic. It need be nothing but what it is said to be. The power of a dead saint's finger comes precisely from being a genuine finger of that saint. The tunic in this scene is a powerful and prestigious object, but points to nothing beyond itself, unless to the ultimate source of all power. It is also less specific than other focal objects we have discussed in that, like Clovis' ewer, it could be replaced in the narrative by other things (any other relic that might be burned and pulverized). Essential here is its physical presence, revealed only to God and the reader, and the purpose of which is to make the bishop's words 'et ecce hic intus in ventre meo est' / 'and it is here in my belly' true. We recognize in this stratagem the theme of literalism already discussed in the chapter on speech. The object here, as elsewhere, is placed at the centre by a gesture, Masona's patting of his stomach as he speaks. As with Malalas' apple and Gregory's story of the sword and the scissors, we have a sense that the anecdote has suffered in its adaptation to literature: the literalist trick works only in part. If the bishop is going to lie anyway about burning the tunic and drinking up the ashes, there is no need for the elaborate charade that requires that he wear the tunic on his body as he replies.

7   A Cranium Beaker

Drinking vessels have appeared with some frequency in these narratives; we must now look at the most extraordinary of them all, the beaker offered by King Alboin to his wife Rosimund, which he had had made from the skull of her father. The incident, already discussed briefly in chapter two, is told in the *Historia Langobardorum* and retold

by Agnellus a half-century later with quite a few interesting changes
and additions. Paul introduces this episode as the story of how the
great king, who had led his people from Pannonia into Italy, came to
be murdered.

> Cum in convivio ultra quam oportuerat aput Veronam laetus resederet,
> cum poculo quod de capite Cunimundi regis sui soceris fecerat
> reginae ad bibendum vinum dari praecepit atque eam ut cum patre suo
> laetanter biberet invitavit. Hoc ne cui videatur inpossibile, veritatem
> in Christo loquor: ego hoc poculum vidi in quodam die festo Ratchis
> principem ut illut convivis suis ostentaret manu tenentem. Igitur
> Rosemunda ubi rem animadvertit, altum concipiens in corde dolorem,
> quem conpescere non valens, mox in mariti necem patris funus
> vindicatura exarsit, consiliumque mox cum Helmechis, qui regis
> scilpor, hoc est armiger, et conlactaneus erat, ut regem interficeret,
> iniit.   (HL ii.28)

> While he sat drinking at a banquet in Verona, longer than was good
> for him, he ordered the beaker that he had had made from the skull
> of his father-in-law, King Cunimund, to be offered to the queen to drink
> wine with, and invited her to drink joyfully with her father. This
> may sound impossible to some, but I am speaking Christ's own truth:
> I myself saw the beaker when on a feast day Prince Ratchis showed it
> to his guests, holding it in his hand. Rosimund, when she heard this
> thing, experienced a deep pain in her heart. Unable to suppress it,
> she was soon raging to avenge her father's death by the murder of her
> husband. Shortly thereafter she began to plot with Helmechis – who
> was the king's *scilpor* (that is to say his armour-bearer) and his foster-
> brother – to murder the king.

Like the Phrygian apple bought by Theodosius ii, this is an extraordinary object. It has the rarity value of any great curiosity, and Paul
feels called to authenticate it with an eyewitness's claim. The beaker
is also a kind of secular relic as well as a trophy, and this may be
another reason why it needs to be certified. Like the tunic of Eulalia,
it means nothing; its effect and significance in the scene depend exclusively on its being what it is: the head of the queen's father turned
into a utensil. Unlike the tunic, on the other hand, it does point beyond
itself, because it brings back the past, events deliberately forgotten but
which lie buried under the union of Alboin and Rosimund: the exter-
mination of her people, the Gepids, and the killing of her father. Paul's

source for this episode may have been a heroic lay, sung by the Langobards but perhaps created by the surviving Gepids in Rosimund's entourage. This particular scheme by which an object, stirring an old memory, resurrects an old feud long laid aside under an alliance or a marriage, is characteristic of the narrative structure of Germanic heroic poetry.[20] Like the *vase de Soissons*, the beaker is also significant as a motive: it is what sets off the story, and it derives its power to reactivate the feud from its connection with history, its own historicity. Like the ewer, it stands at the beginning of a personal feud. In this revenge, Clovis had established an equation between the broken ewer and the solider's head; here, the head *is* a beaker.[21] This paradoxical nature of the thing which is also a person is underscored by Alboin's pun inviting his wife to drink 'with her father'; it becomes even more apparent when we compare Paul's account with that of Agnellus. Whereas the Langobard historian refers to it only as 'hoc poculum,' for Agnellus it remains a head: 'iussit deferri caput soceri sui'; 'praecepit rex pincernae implere caput usque and summum ...' / '... he asked that the head of his father-in-law be brought'; 'the king told the cupbearer to fill the head to the brim ...' (*LPR* 96). The beaker is drawn into the story by Alboin's drunken initiative, that is by his command that it be brought, and his offer of it to Rosimund. In Agnellus' version he drinks deeply from it himself before sending it to his wife. From that point on, the thing takes over completely; detached from the action that summoned it, it liberates its own powers and takes over the centre of the scene.

8   A Golden Sceptre

Paul wrote in the late eighth century, the early years of the reign of Charlemagne; Notker put together his *De Karolo rege* a century later, in the troubled times of Charles the Fat. His narrative shows the influence of the Carolingian renaissance in language and subject matter, but also in the nostalgic look it turns back on the great emperor and his age. Throughout the first book of *De Karolo rege*, Charlemagne appears as the corrector of corrupt and misguided churchmen; the following anecdote is characteristic:

> Idem quoque episcopus, cum bellicosissimus Karolus in bello contra Hunos esset occupatus, ad custodiam gloriosissimę Hildigardę relictus est. Qui cum familiaritate illius animari cępisset, in tantam progressus est proterviam, ut virgam auream incomparabilis Karoli, quam ad statum suum fieri iussit, diebus feriatis vice baculi ferendam,

pro episcopali ferula improbus ambiret. Quę illum callide deludens, dixit non audere se eam cuilibet homini dare, sed tamen fidam se legationem eius causę apud regem fore. Veniente autem eo suggessit illa ioculariter, quę amens postulavit episcopus. Cuius peticioni iocundissime rex assensus, promisit se etiam plus facturum quam ille peteret.   (*DKR* i.17)

That same bishop was left to watch over the noble Hildegarde while Charlemagne was engaged in war against the Huns. [This is Notker's name for the Avars.] Carried away by frequent contact with the queen, he sank to such shamelessness that he aspired perversely to bear the golden sceptre which the matchless Charlemagne had had made, for solemn occasions and for use as a staff on holidays instead of the bishop's crozier. She deceived him ingeniously and said that she did not dare give the sceptre to any man, but that she would take on the charge of presenting his request to the king. When Charlemagne came back, she told him as a joke what the delirious bishop had asked for. Delighted, he assented to his petition and promised that he would do even more than he had requested.

At a general assembly gathered on his triumphal return, the emperor chastises bishops for seeking worldly prizes and neglecting their souls. Charlemagne specifies: 'Nunc vero prae cęteris mortalibus tanta ambitione corrupti sunt, ut quidam ex eis non contentus episcopatu, quem in prima Germanię sede retinet, sceptrum nostrum, quod pro significatione regiminis nostri aureum ferre solemus, pro pastorali baculo nobis ignorantibus sibi vendicare voluisset.' / 'But now [bishops] have become corrupted by ambition beyond any other human beings, so that one of them, not content with the episcopate he holds in the foremost see of Germany, has desired to take over the sceptre of gold that we bear to represent our government and, without our knowledge, to use it as a bishop's staff' (ibid). The guilty bishop confesses his fault, is forgiven, and departs.

One function of the story is to illustrate the role of the emperor in the relation between church and state; in this sense, Notker is formulating Carolingian political ideology. The sceptre around which everything revolves is entirely symbolic, but not like the hermit's bowl of water in the *Apophthegmata*, which is interpreted *ad hoc* by the hermit himself, or like the cloak of Martin of Tours, which can be understood to stand, by extension, for worldly goods in general. The meaning of the sceptre is a brand new concept, created for the ruler by his political staff in invidious emulation of the Byzantine imperial insignia; it is so new, formulated so self-consciously, that Charlemagne can proclaim it in a terse statement to the assembly: 'sceptrum nostrum, quod pro significatione regiminis nostri aureum ferre solemus' / 'the sceptre of gold that we bear to represent our government.' It is probable that the sceptre, which he had ordered to be made, was designed expressly to carry this meaning, as a piece of embodied political ideology.[22] The outline of the plot in which the object is implicated resembles in some ways Malalas' story of the Phrygian apple: the emperor goes away, leaving behind his wife and a man of his confidence; the empress proves her fidelity by denying to the man the precious object entrusted to her by her husband. In spite of this highly charged narrative context, the episode is dominated by the pre-established official meaning of the sceptre. The bishop's intention of using the splendid golden 'virga' as episcopal staff betrays a perverse plan to reinterpret it, and in so doing to modify the relation of church to state as defined by the imperial ideology.

9   A Turning Wheel

Our last specimen is Greek, and corresponds to a privileged moment in the development of Byzantine culture: the reign of Constantine Porphyrogenitus (913–59). In his treatise *De administrando imperio*, the emperor narrates the capture of Bari by Soldanos and his Saracens, and their forty-year rule over Lombardy. Emperor Lewis of the Franks and the pope, in collaboration with the Greek emperor Basil I, take the city (871 AD) and make Soldanos and his men prisoners.

> The emperor of the Romans got the city of Bari, the land, and all the prisoners, and Lewis, the king of Francia, took Soldanos and the other Saracens and led them off to the cities of Capua and Benevento. No one ever saw Soldanos laugh. Then the king said: 'If anyone can truly report to me or show me Soldanos laughing, I shall give him a great deal of money.' Later someone saw him laugh, and announced this to King Lewis. He had Soldanos summoned and asked him why he had laughed. Soldanos replied: 'I saw a cart, and its wheels were turning, and I laughed, because I too was once the head, and am now wholly brought down, but God is able to raise me up again.'
>
> (*De administrando imperio* 29)

The interpretation of the turning wheel is rooted in the literary iconography of the Wheel of Fortune, a tradition familiar to Constantine and the members of his *scriptorium* from the works of classical and late antiquity which they untiringly excerpted.[23] The anecdote shows little trace of popular origins; its central object is a creation of high, official culture. As in the story of Charlemagne's sceptre, the thing around which this incident revolves is wholly symbolic, with a very definite abstract meaning backed by centuries of expression through the image of the wheel.

The king's words make the narrative hinge on a gesture: Soldanos' laughter. This hilarity, it turns out, was occasioned by the sight of the turning wheel. The wheel thus takes on the role of motive, of necessary first element in the mechanics of plot, even though its part in the episode only emerges *a posteriori* as Soldanos later on explains to King Lewis why he had laughed.[24]

Conclusions

On the basis of these examples it is possible to draw three general conclusions about the role of focal objects in early medieval narrative:

A   These stories, and the things around which they revolve, are taken from a broad and varied range of narrative literature. The objects retain traces of this variety, particularly in the nature of their symbolic charge, in the different ways in which they point to something other than themselves, or fail to do so. Some derive all their meaning from their role in the plot, others from their causal function, others yet from an official ideology or an established iconography. Like Jolles' objects, however, they stand for the entire narrative and become the key, the vital centre of the story. This is not to say that the object contains the entire story in the manner of a summary. Some of our focal objects, like Clovis' ewer, are just the pretext that starts off the action, and appear only at the beginning. But even in that story, the king remembers the damaged vessel and reminds his enemy of it at the moment of retribution; thus the ewer comes to dominate the entire episode.

B   The gesture or action that brings the object into the story rarely has anything to do with the normal use of the thing in question. An ewer is not there to be destroyed, a sword and scissors to serve as a message, or a wheel to make someone laugh. This turning away from the ordinary or habitual functions of things is perhaps clearest in Notker's story of Charlemagne's 'virga aurea,' the plot of which turns on an intended misuse of the sceptre. Most of our stories, however, do not comment directly or indirectly on the proper use of the thing; they just ignore it and show something else.

c   The thing itself is never the point of the narrative. Its constitution and utility are not explained or illustrated by the plot, but at most assumed. This is true even in those cases where the object has no established conventional significance or where, as in the case of Alboin's beaker or the tunic of St Eulalia, its rarity might seem to call for some explanatory notes. Perhaps more important: the object is not described but simply named, with a brief, general phrase: 'a remarkably large and beautiful ewer,' 'a pair of scissors and a naked sword,' 'a Phrygian apple of exceptional size.' In the bare stage of early medieval narrative, void of furnishings and of spatial specifications, the essential stage property that is the focal object hardly becomes a physical or visual presence; a simple name, a phrase, must carry its entire weight of meaning. We remember that it is the same with gestures, named only, and not described in their physical realization.

ELOQUENT OBJECTS

Late antiquity and the early middle ages saw a proliferation of prestigious and symbolic objects. As a feature of public life, this development went hand in hand with the process of ritualization described earlier, though these objects cannot be explained away as the paraphernalia of the new rituals and ceremonies. We shall consider three main categories of such significant objects.

1   Insignia

These are at least badges of power and responsibility; they define a role in collective existence, a dignity within the hierarchy. Most insignia are based on articles of common use, particularly items of dress and jewellery. A given design, more often a special material or colour becomes restricted to a class of individuals; no one else may wear a tunic of yellow silk, sandals of purple, the fur of a certain animal. Ordinary tunics and sandals are transmuted by these materials into signs of rank, the badges of an imperial or royal court, of a bureaucracy. They may not be copied by other citizens, but are frequently reproduced in monuments and coins. Certain insignia are tied to specific rites and activities; others are worn constantly in public.[25]

Insignia, however, can be more than just badges; many have an abstract meaning, and therefore symbolic value. It is characteristic of objects of this class that they can be interpreted as symbols of concepts: the emperor's stole (*lorum*), originally an episcopal garment, indicates the sacerdotal nature of his office; his armour, when he wears it, marks his position as supreme commander of the army; the orb he holds in ceremonies represents the scope of his power.[26] This translation of the insignia into abstractions is only possible in terms of an official ideology or political theology: the insignia embody a set of refined concepts, a program formulated by the state, expressed in the official imagery of royal or imperial tradition. Translation, at any rate, is always made easy and explicit. Describing the coronation of Otto I at Aachen, Widukind has preserved the words of Archbishop Hildebert of Mainz as he hands Otto the ceremonial sword, sceptre, and staff.

> Ipse autem accedens ad altare et sumpto inde gladio cum balteo, conversus ad regem ait: 'Accipe', inquit, 'hunc gladium, quo eicias omnes Christi adversarios, barbaros et malos Christianos, auctoritate divina tibi tradita omni potestate totius imperii Francorum, ad firmissimam pacem omnium Christianorum'. Deinde sumptis armillis ac clamide induit eum: 'His cornibus', inquit, 'humitenus demissis monearis, quo zelo fidei ferveas, et in pace tuenda perdurare usque in finem debere'. Exinde sumpto sceptro baculoque: 'His signis', inquit, 'monitus paterna castigatione subiectos corripias, primumque Dei ministris, viduis ac pupillis manum misericodiae porrigas; numquamque de capite tuo oleum miserationis deficiat, ut in presenti et in futuro sempiterno premio coroneris'.   (*RGS* II.1)

> Hildebert went to the altar and, taking from it the sword and sword-belt, turned to the king and said: 'Receive this sword, with which you must expel all enemies of Christ, pagans, and bad Christians, since divine authority has granted to you full powers over the empire of the Franks, to the most firmly established peace of all Christians.' Then taking the armbands and tunic, he put them on him and said: 'Let the hem of this robe, that reaches to the ground, admonish you to burn with the zeal of faith and persist to the end in keeping the peace.' And after that, taking the sceptre and the staff, he said: 'Taught by these symbols, give paternal correction to your subjects, and before all else, extend the hand of mercy to priests of God, widows, and orphans. May the oil of compassion never be lacking from your head,

so that both in the present life and the hereafter you may be crowned
with an eternal reward.'

If there are any popular roots to the symbolism of the insignia, they
are so remote from the rationalized program of their official interpretation that they can no longer be perceived. The historical sources of
these articles and their symbolism are Greco-Roman and Persian, occasionally also Christian. They reach their greatest diversity and fullness of meaning in the Byzantine empire, which exercised a strong
influence on the ceremonial dress and the badges of office of Western
courts. In both East and West the introduction and evolution of the
insignia go back to the few decades before Diocletian, though the greatest number developed later.

In narrative, when the writer is not particularly close to court life
and official ceremony is not the point of his account, references to the
insignia are kept quite summary. Relating the accession of Tiberius II
to the Eastern throne in 578 and his victory over a plot organized against
him by the widowed Augusta Sophia, Gregory of Tours describes the
new emperor's arrival at the palace: 'Dehinc indutus purpora, diademate coronatus, throno imperiale inpositus, cum inmensis laudibus
imperium confirmavit.' / 'Afterwards, clad in purple, crowned with the
diadem, he sat on the imperial throne and was made emperor with
tremendous acclamation' (HF v.30). When Tiberius later chooses his
successor Maurice and gives him his daughter to wed, 'iussit exornare
filiam suam ornamentis imperialibus' / 'he ordered that his daughter
be adorned with the ornaments that befit an imperial princess' (HF
vi.30). After the death of Tiberius, Maurice 'indutus diademate et purpora et bisso, ad circum processit, adclamatisque sibi laudibus, largita
populo munera, in imperio confirmatur' / 'wearing the diadem, the
purple and imperial robes, proceeded to the hippodrome, where, after
being greeted with ringing acclamations, he handed out the usual gifts
of money to the people, and was made emperor' (ibid). Gregory omits
all direct interpretation of the insignia, but the emphatically repeated
references to purple and imperial ornaments at these crucial turns in
the story show that these objects are always perceived as eloquent
carriers of meaning. Their presence in itself constitutes a statement,
even when they are not the focus of the narrative, but the statement
is so familiar that Gregory can simply take it for granted and leave it
untranslated.[27]

2   Badges and Symbols of the Law

The garb of officers of the law functions most frequently like the insignia: as a marker of duties and prerogatives. Within a royal or imperial hierarchy, it belongs with the signs of delegated power. Its elements can often be traced back to objects of common use. Karl von Amira has shown that the staff or wand that marks the authority of the judge goes back, through a long evolution of form and meaning, to the staff or walking-stick of the pilgrim and wayfarer.[28] By the time it becomes a prop in the ritual of the law, it has undergone changes in design that make it useless for its original purpose and practically unrecognizable; it can now be decorated with precious materials. Like the other insignia, it is transmuted into a token of power. It does not seem possible, however, to interpret it in abstract terms; it remains badge rather than symbol.

More interesting because more distinctive are objects that were used in legal transactions (investiture, for example) and often left attached to the documents of the case. These objects are neither transmuted nor chosen from a limited list of items; they are used without alteration, just as they might be found in nature or in daily life, so that outside the legal ceremony nothing would allow us to recognize them as significant. For the various forms of investiture alone, Du Cange identifies ninety-nine material tokens or accessories, among others a strip of turf, a small branch or shoot, a knife, a ring, a cup, a church key, a glove, a handkerchief.[29] These objects are significant only in the context of the ceremony; they do not represent abstract qualities or relations, but validate legal transactions of which later, if attached to a document, they become both record and seal.[30] These legal tokens are often of Germanic origin, and their currency in early medieval civilization constitutes an aspect of the barbarization of Western institutions after the Migrations. The significance of the branch or the strip of turf may go back to unwritten tribal traditions and cannot be made explicit, though once the object is adopted in the law codes of a literate culture a new meaning for it can be invented and the token as such reinterpreted.

In narrative literature these things appear far less often than the insignia, but when they do they are immediately recognizable. Gregory of Tours describes a classical investiture: the transmission of power 'per hastam' performed by King Gunthchramn when he chooses his nephew Childebert to be his successor.

Post haec rex Gunthchramnus, data in manu regis Childeberti hasta, ait: 'Hoc est indicium, quod tibi omne regnum meum tradedi. Ex hoc nunc vade et omnes civitates meas tamquam tuas proprias sub tui iuris dominatione subice. Nihil enim, facientibus peccatis, de stirpe mea remansit nisi tu tantum, qui mei fratris es filius. Tu enim heres in omni regno meo succede, ceteris exheredibus factis'.

(*HF* vii.33)

After this, King Gunthchramn handed a spear to King Childebert and said: 'This is a token that I have delivered all my kingdom to you. Go, therefore, and put all my cities, as if they were your own, under your authority. In punishment of my sins, there remains no member of my own line except you only, who are my brother's son. Succeed me, therefore, as my heir in my whole kingdom, for all the other claimants have been disinherited.'

A more subtle reference, this time to the 'festuca' or bit of straw used symbolically in investiture and particularly in the transmission of land to vassals, can be found in Widukind.[31] The historian of the Saxons describes a confrontation between Liudulf, son of Otto i, and his uncle Heinrich of Bavaria during the siege of Mainz. Liudulf had rebelled against his father, and was holding the city against imperial troops.

Nam cum non obedirent edictis regis, motus Heinricus adversus adolescentem: 'Nichil te', inquit, 'iactitas contra dominum meum regem fecisse, et ecce omnis exercitus usurpatorem te regni invasoremque novit. Ipse ergo si accusor reus criminis, si culpabilis existo, quare non contra me legiones ducis? Signa adversum me move'; et festucam de terra sumens: 'Huius', inquit, 'pretii a me meaque potestate rapere non poteris. Quid tibi visum est sollicitare huiuscemodi rebus patrem tuum? contra summam divinitatem agis, dum domino patrique tuo repugnas. Si aliquid scis vel vales, in me furorem tuum evome, ipse enim tuam non timeo iram'. Ad haec adolescens nichil respondit, sed audito rege cum suis urbem ingressus est.   (*RGS* iii.18)

They [the prince's fellow rebels] did not obey the commands of the king, so Heinrich was angered at the youth. He said: 'You boast that you have done nothing against my lord the king, and yet the entire army knows that you are the usurper and invader of the kingdom. If I am accused of crimes, and am guilty, why don't you lead your troops to fight me? Set your standards against me.' He picked up a straw from the ground and added: 'You will not be able to take away this much from me and from my power! What has moved you to mortify your father in this manner? You are sinning against God almighty when you fight against your father and your lord. If you are worth anything, or have any wisdom, unleash all your fury against me, for I do not fear your anger.' The young man gave no answer to this, but listened to the king and went back to the city with his men.

The 'festuca' here does double service as a measure of something infinitely small ('you will not get *this* much') and as a reminder of the obedience due to the king from all those who held land and power from his hand.

3   Relics

A relic is not symbolic except in so far as it functions metonymically: the word 'corpus' when applied to a relic can refer to a very small fragment of the actual body. The body, or a part of it, comes to stand for the saint himself.[32] The relic is above all powerful, and its power manifests itself in healings, good harvests, immunity from the plague, and other specific benefits, but is conceived as a permanent benevolent influence actively protecting the territory in which the relics are found, and more particularly the city or town and the church in which they are preserved and honoured. For the relic to exercise this influence it must be authentic, so that, unlike insignia and the instruments of law and liturgy, it cannot be copied or reproduced. As early as Merovingian times, relics are provided with labels, small pieces of parchment, or inscriptions identifying the object and vouching for its authenticity, and this text becomes in time if not an intrinsic part of the relic, at least an indispensable complement. The power of the thing depends entirely on its uniqueness; there can only be one of each.[33] Heinrich Fichtenau has pointed out that if accounts of the acquisition by theft of a given relic were given readily by the congregations in possession of these stolen goods, it was primarily because they certified that the relic was genuine; those willing to counterfeit the article would not have taken the trouble of stealing it.[34]

Originally, a relic was the whole body of a saint, but very soon the division of the corpse, particularly in the case of martyrs, led to separate burial of various parts. As early as Martin of Tours, however, we see an extension by uncontrolled metonymy of the power of the relic to every article that had been used or touched by the saint, his clothes in particular. The use of relics was not limited to ecclesiastics, or to specific ceremonies, to any given purposes or applications. Anyone could pray before them, wear them next to his body, even eat or drink them (for example, a glass of water in which a piece of the cloak of the saint had been soaked). They could be used to cure cattle as well as people, to terrify barbarian invaders, as presents to settle disputes between lay and ecclesiastical lords. Their power was supernatural in origin but concrete and worldly in many of its manifestations; relics in the hands of religious communities became a weapon against oppression by seculars, a means to attract pilgrims, powerful patrons, and gifts of land and money. They had also, for the individual, the value of a status symbol; embodied power could become a commodity, a prestigious private possession. Used in this fashion, relics come close to insignia and function like them as marks of privilege and social superiority. The privately owned relic, however, begins gradually to disappear in the first century or two of the middle ages.[35]

After the requirement of authenticity, the most characteristic quality of the relic is that it is expected to function automatically: whether it is stolen, broken in small pieces, or touched by accident, it exercises its powers with the blind efficacy of a chemical. František Graus has observed that this automatism of the relic ignores and even contradicts the doctrine of grace and reveals the operation of magical thinking in the conception and worship of its power.[36] Nevertheless, the saint may occasionally fail to exert his good influence through the relic. In that case he can be publicly humiliated in various ways: ignorant people beat on the relics, calling the saint an idler and a good-for-nothing; the clergy degrade the relics by placing them on a rough cloth on the floor, by the altar, and surrounding them with ashes and thorns.[37]

The enormous importance of relics in early medieval life is reflected in narrative literature.[38] Two hagiographic genres are exclusively concerned with them: inventions record their discovery and acquisition; translations describe how they came to be in the possession of a given church or congregation, whether by theft or by more orthodox methods of appropriation.[39] Gregory of Tours, whose faith in them was absolute, gives a detailed account of the confiscation of a finger of St Sergius by Count Mummolus at Bordeaux. The duke had heard great things of the power of St Sergius, and then learned that a finger of his was in the possession of a Syrian merchant of the city. He broke into the merchant's house and eventually found the hiding place in which the relic was kept; it was handed to Mummolus in a small box.

Quam perscrutatam, Mummolus os de sancti digito repperit, quod
cultro ferire non metuit. Posito enim desuper cultro, et sic de alio
percutiebat. Cumque post multos ictos vix frangi potuissit, divisum
in tribus partibus ossiculum diversas in partes dilabitur. Credo, non
erat acceptum martyri, ut haec ille contigerit. Tunc flente vehemen-
tius Eufronio, prosternuntur omnes in orationem, depraecantes, ut Deus
dignaretur ostendere, quae ab oculis fuerant humanis ablata. Post
orationem autem repertae sunt particulae, ex quibus una Mummolus
adsumpta abscessit, sed non, ut credo, cum gratia martyris, sicut in
sequenti declaratum est.   (*HF* vii.31)

When the contents [of the box] were inspected, Mummolus found a
bone from the saint's finger, which he was not afraid to hit with
his knife. He hit it on the one side first, then on the other. The small
bone broke only after many blows; it fell into three fragments, which
were scattered in different directions. I believe the saint was not pleased
that this should fall to his lot. While Eufronius [the Syrian] wept
passionately, the others kneeled down to pray that God would deign
to let them see what he had removed from human sight. After praying in this manner, they found the small pieces; Mummolus took one
of them and left. But I think he did not have the martyr's favour, as
was shown by what happened later on.

Though Gregory says that the saint was offended, he does not indicate
that the relic lost any of its power, and does not connect the eventual
punishment of Mummolus, when it comes, with this episode. A pious
relic theft is described sympathetically by Agnellus. Archbishop Max-
imian of Ravenna is returning to his see with the body of St Andrew
the Apostle. In Constantinople the emperor tells him that he cannot
allow him to take such a great relic home with him: it must stay in
the Eastern capital: 'Non sit tibi gravis, pater, quod prima unus tenet
Roma frater, iste vero secundam teneat. Ambae sorores, et hi ambo
germani. Nolo tibi eum dare, quia et ubi sedes imperialis est, expediet
ibi corpus esse apostoli.' / 'Do not take offence, father, that since the
first Rome has one brother, the second should have the other. The two
Romes are sisters, and the two apostles are brothers. I do not wish to
give him to you because it is fitting that where the capital of the empire
is, the body of an apostle should be found' (*LPR* 76). The archbishop
gives in, but asks to be allowed to sing the liturgy at night by the
apostle's body with his clerks.

> Imperator moxque concessit. Tunc tota nocte pervigiles extiterunt, et
> post expleta omnia arripiens gladium, oratione facta, abscidit barbas
> apostoli usque ad mentum. Et ex reliquiis aliorum multorum sancto-
> rum reliquias detulit cum augusti alacritate; dehinc quoque ad propriam
> reversus est sedem.   (ibid)

> The emperor immediately granted this. They then kept a vigil through
> the night, and when they had performed all their devotions, Maxi-
> mian took a knife and, saying a prayer, shaved off the apostle's beard
> close to the chin. He also took relics of many other saints with the
> emperor's consent, and came back to his own see.[40]

Badges of office, records of legal transactions, symbols of abstract concepts, exclusive and very material channels of a saint's power, gilded
ornaments, straws, clods of earth and strips of turf, particles of a corpse:
the significant objects of the early middle ages show a bewildering
diversity of both meaning and physical composition. In narrative literature they may appear as the focus of a scene or a story (Eulalia's
tunic, Clovis' 'urceus,' the sceptre of Charlemagne), but most often
the objects in that position are quite ordinary articles of no established
significance, the centrality of which is given them by the narrative
context. On the other hand, the passages quoted in this section show
that insignia, symbols of the law, and relics appear often as accessories,
in marginal positions where they simply reflect the world of 'eloquent'
objects, the material semantics of their age.

CONVERTIBLE PROPS

The stage of early medieval narrative is, as I have pointed out already,
bare and largely undetermined. We can only know it in so far as it is
implied by the action. Furniture, decorations, the cushions and tapes-
tries characteristic of later courtly narrative are entirely absent. It appears, however, from the material covered in the previous sections,
that objects can also take on subordinate roles as useful props. Two
important features of objects in this instrumental category are that
they are not described at all and that they are part of a very limited
inventory of things that keep appearing again and again and are put to
the most diverse uses. The effect of objects presented with this economy is not unlike that of the multifunctional stage props of the modernist theatre: crates that can represent a chair, a table, or a podium;
sticks that will serve as oars, staffs, or swords. On the uncluttered

stages of the 1930s and 1940s these minimal accessories took on considerable importance; by their neutral, uninteresting shapes they pointed the spectator's attention directly to their function and meaning of the moment and prevented the distraction that can be induced by an elaborate set.[41]

Certain traditional genres show a clear principle of selection, a preference at work in the range of things they allow themselves to mention. Max Lüthi has pointed out that popular legend (German *Sage*) specializes in objects of daily use (pots, jugs, horseshoes, spools of thread) and in things that can grow, shrink, become mixed with others, or otherwise change their shape (thread, liquids, bread, magic seeds), while the folktale (German *Märchen*) tends to exclude useful, common things and presents mostly extraordinary objects that are flat, hard, and linear, often metallic, and do not change their shape or size (wands, rings, keys, animal hairs, feathers).[42] No such clear discrimination is possible in the limited inventory of props to be found in early medieval narrative, and the reason for this is quite plain: we are not dealing here with 'simple forms' or with a pure, traditional genre. The historiographic narratives we have examined constitute an unstable field in which oral models, new literary aspirations, and classical schooling exert their conflicting influences in constantly changing proportions; the relative pull of each of these factors is different for every writer. Difficult as it is to generalize about the useful objects of this literature, we may observe that certain articles appear with remarkable frequency: weapons, cups, chests. It is also noticeable that these are all articles that can be moved, handed around, manipulated. Large, stationary props (pieces of furniture, for example) are rare.

Like the crates and sticks of the modernist stage, these objects are put to the most diverse uses. Since their physical particularity is effaced by lack of description, their function in each specific context becomes the main criterion by which they are defined. We shall examine two of these objects as used by several of our authors. Let us first consider candles and candlesticks, standard accessories, though not uncommonly frequent.[43] Gregory of Tours makes the blowing out of candles a preliminary to murder. He describes the assassination of the Visigothic king Theudigisil in 549 AD:

His dum ad caenam cum amicis suis aepularet et esset valde laetus, caereis subito extinctis, in recubitu ab inimicis gladio percussus, interiit.   (*HF* III.30)

He was having dinner with his friends, and very merry. Suddenly the
candles were blown out, he was stabbed by enemies while he reclined
at table, and died.

The same gesture, expressed in a very similar ablative phrase, precedes
the killing of the drunken Sichar by his friend Chramnesind in a famous
episode: 'Et statim extinctis luminaribus, caput Sichari seca dividit.' /
'he at once blew out the candles and split Sichar's head in two' (HF
IX.19). Gregory the Great, however, uses candles to furnish the cell of
the dying nun Galla, where they become a symbol of the burning piety
of the occupant and serve to frame the nocturnal apparition of St Peter.

Nocturno autem tempore ante lectum illius duo candelabra lucere
consueuerant, quia uidelicet amica lucis non solum spiritales, sed etiam
corporales tenebras odio habebat.
4. Quae dum nocte quadam ex hac eadem iaceret infirmitate fatigata,
uidit beatum Petrum apostolum inter utraque candelabra ante suum
lectulum constitisse.   (Dialogues IV.14.3–4)

At nighttime two candles would be alight before her bed for, being a
friend of the light, she detested not only spiritual but also physical
darkness. 4. One night, while she lay there exhausted by illness, she
saw St Peter the apostle between the two candles, standing by her
narrow bed.[44]

Most remarkable perhaps is their role in an anecdote about the empress
Galla Placidia at the Church of the Holy Cross that she had built in
Ravenna. The story is told by Agnellus.

Et dicunt quidam, quod ipsa Galla Placidia augusta super quatuor
rotas rubeas marmoreas, quae sunt ante nominatas regias, iubebat
ponere cereostatos cum manualia ad mensuram, et iactabat se noctu
in medio pavimento, Deo fundere preces, et tamdiu pernoctabat in
lacrimis orans, quamdiu ipsa lumina perdurabant.   (LPR 41)

And some people tell that that same empress Galla Placidia used to
have large candles of a specific measure placed on candlesticks upon
the four round slabs of red marble that are in front of the doors
mentioned above. At night she would lie on the church floor praying
to God, and would remain in prayer there, shedding tears, for as long
as the candles themselves lasted.

As in those narratives where a focal object has equal weight with the human gesture or action that brings it into the story, here the 'lumina' are coordinated with an activity: the augusta's prayer, her posture, and her tears. Her devotions are timed but also mirrored by the burning candles.

The second object is an unusual and problematic one: a severed head. The upsetting thing about it is that it should be an object at all. In the story of Alboin and Rosimund the narrative centrality of her father's head came largely from its causal function. The episode also showed clearly that a head might appear as a simple prop: Cunimund's skull was being used as one of the most ordinary utensils in this line of narrative, a cup. But the head appears in all kinds of other roles. Even when physically absent from the stage of narrative, it can be present as a figure of speech, like a gesture that survives frozen in a phrase or an idiom. In Widukind's history, a Frankish envoy charged by the Thuringian king with a highly offensive message for his own sovereign replies: ' "Mallem," inquit, "hoc caput meum tibi tradere quam huiuscemodi verba a te audire, sciens ea multo sanguine Francorum atque Thuringorum diluenda." ' / ' "I would rather let you have my head than hear from you words such as these, for I know they will be washed away with much blood of Franks and Thuringians" ' (*RGS* i.9). And Paul the Deacon describes how two noblemen lure the usurper Alahis to a hunt, persuading him to leave his capital with promises that they will see to the destruction of Cunincpert, the rightful king: 'Egredere et vade in venationem et exerce te cum iuvenibus tuis, nos autem cum reliquis fidelibus tuis defendimus tibi hanc civitatem. Sed et ita tibi repromittimus, ut in proximo inimici tui Cunincperti caput adferamus.' / 'Go out and get some exercise with your young followers. We, with those others who are faithful to you, shall hold this city for you. And we promise once again that very soon we shall bring you the head of your enemy Cunincpert' (*HL* v.39). This promise turns out to be equivocal, a literalistic trick played on the usurper, who before his return to the city finds out that his rival is already in power there: 'Nuntius subito ad Alahis pervenit, adimplesse Aldonem et Grausonem quod ei promiserant: et caput Cunincperti attulisse, et non solum caput, sed et totum corpus, eumque adfirmans in palatio consedere.' / 'Suddenly a messenger came for Alahis, to tell him that Aldo and Grauso had carried out what they had promised him: they had brought the head of Cunincpert, and not only the head, but the whole body; and the messenger declared that Cunincpert was sitting in the royal palace' (ibid).

When a real physical presence, the head can be used as a message, to confirm or certify an execution. Paul relates the beheading of the eunuch Eleutherius, who had rebelled against the emperor: 'Qui dum a Ravenna Romam pergeret, in castro Luceolis a militibus interfectus est, caputque eius Constantinopolim imperatori delatum est.' / 'When he was on his way from Ravenna to Rome, he was killed by the soldiers at the fortress of Luceolis, and his head was sent to the emperor in Constantinople' (HL iv.34). Agnellus takes this incident from Paul and adds a touch that serves to turn the head further into a thing: 'cuius caput cunditum sacco Constantinopolim imperatori delatum est' / 'his head was put in a bag and sent to the emperor in Constantinople' (LPR 106).[45] When the head of the defeated enemy must serve as a sign of victory on the battlefield, it is not covered at all, but raised aloft impaled on a lance or pole. The Liber historiae Francorum shows the Frankish king Chlothar ii give this treatment to the head of the Saxon Bertoald, who had insulted him: 'Consurgensque rex super eum et interficit ipso Bertoaldo sustullitque caput eius in conto reversusque est ad Francos.' / 'The king went against Bertoald, killed him, and returned to the Franks bearing his head on a pole' (LHF 41). Paul the Deacon tells how Alahis, in the final battle against King Cunincpert, killed a deacon of the church of Pavia who had disguised himself in Cunincpert's arms to protect him: 'Cumque caput eius amputari praecepisset, ut, levato eo in conto, "Deo gratias" adclamarent, sublata casside, clericum se occidisse cognovit.' / 'He had the man's head cut off, that it might be stuck on a pole and raised aloft, so that all would cry out "Praised be God." But when the helmet was taken off, he realized that he had killed a churchman' (HL v.40).

Again and again, however, the head is handled as if it were the actual person. In one extreme instance of literalism a promise made to the living person is fulfilled for the head. Paul relates that Taso, the young Langobardic duke of Friuli, had asked the Byzantine patricius Gregory to become his adoptive father by ceremonially shaving his beard. Gregory accepted and then treacherously murdered Taso and his brother Caco in his stronghold at Opitergium: 'Gregorius vero patricius propter iusiurandum quod dederat caput Tasonis sibi deferri iubens, eius barbam, sicut promiserat, periurus abscidit.' / 'On account of the promise he had made, the patrician Gregory had the head of Taso brought to him, and the oath-breaker shaved Taso's beard off, as he had sworn to do' (HL iv.38). The most violent leap from reification to treatment of the head as a living person is to be found in Paul's account of the siege of Benevento by Byzantine forces. Duke Romuald is inside the city, and his tutor Sesuald, returning from a mission to Romuald's father, is captured by the enemy before he can get into Benevento. Ordered to tell his pupil that no help from the king is forthcoming, Sesuald sacrifices his life to announce the truth: that the king's forces will soon be there to end the siege and drive the invaders away: 'Cumque hoc dixisset, iussu imperatoris caput eius abscisum atque cum belli machina quam petrariam vocant in urbem proiectum est. Quod caput Romuald sibi deferri iussit idque lacrimans obsculatus est dignoque in loculo tumulari praecepit.' / 'When he had said this, his head was cut off by order of the emperor and thrown into the city by means of a war-machine called a *petraria*. Romuald had the head brought to him, kissed it tearfully, and ordered that it be buried in a place of honour' (*HL* v.8). A certificate of Sesuald's execution, and even a missile flung over the walls by a catapult, the head to the prince is his tutor in person: he kisses it and sheds tears.[46]

Finally, we must consider what is perhaps the most common function of the severed head in hagiographic narrative: it becomes a relic, often discovered by supernatural dispensation and productive of miraculous healings. Gregory of Tours relates the murder of Lupentius, abbot of St. Privatus in Javols, by the count of the city. After a few days the headless corpse is found by shepherds, but it is impossible to identify the remains. The head had been put by the murderer in a bag weighted with stones, and thrown into the river.

> Sed dum necessitates in funere pararentur et ignoraretur, quis esset e populo, praesertim cum caput truncati non inveniretur, subito adveniens aquila levavit culleum a fundere fluminis et ripae deposuit. Admirantesque qui aderant, adpraehensum culleum, dum sollicite, quid contineret, inquirunt, caput truncati repperiunt, et sic cum reliquis artubus est sepultum.
>
> (*HF* vi.37)

> The funeral was being prepared, and they did not know yet who he was, particularly since they could not find his severed head. Suddenly an eagle came, fished a bag from the bottom of the river, and left it on the bank. Those who were there, amazed, took the bag and wondered what it might contain. They found the head of the beheaded man, and so it was buried with the rest of the body.

In Paul's *Historia Langobardorum* in particular the paradox of the head, human and yet thing, utensil yet once person, recurs with obsessive frequency; it becomes for him a sort of narrative fetish.[47]

THE FORCE OF THINGS

Our collection of object-centred stories shows that considerable variation was possible in the use of this narrative device. There are a few important features common to all such stories or to most of them, particularly in their treatment of the central object:

1 Most of the 'focal objects' involved are made equivalent to speech acts or verbal moves; they become statements, questions, answers, offers or threats within the economy of the story. This acquired value is sometimes spelled out in a verbal gloss added to the inanimate thing for the sake of clarity.

2 The meaning these objects take on is never intrinsic, but derived from the narrative context. Even the sword and scissors presented to Chrodechild, which stand for their own use in everyday life, appear not as instruments but as a message, a proposition or offer to which the queen must reply.

3 The physical appearance or condition of the objects has no importance in itself and is never described.

In other respects, however, there are appreciable differences between such scenes:

1 The degree of necessity with which the object is inscribed into the episode can vary from absolute, as in the case of the sword and scissors, which cannot be replaced by anything else given the message they are used to convey, to minimal, as in that of the plate of soup, which Chilperic could have replaced with any other commodity that might serve to tempt and mollify the angry bishop.

2 The weight or importance of the object is also relative. It can dominate the scene totally, like the hermit's bowl of water, which provides by itself the point of the entire anecdote, or it can be clearly subordinated to actions or gestures of the protagonists, like Clovis' ewer, which derives most of its significance from the king's long memory and his act of retribution.

A parallel can be drawn between the process by which such objects acquire a new meaning in narrative and the concomitant development in late antiquity and the early middle ages by which ordinary things are made 'eloquent' through insertion into a pattern of ceremony or a structure of ideas (for example, a coronation ritual, the cult of the saints as both practice and belief). In the latter case, certain changes in the object itself become important precisely because they serve as marks of this semantic transformation or reinterpretation (the emperor's shoes are made of purple; the fragment of bone is placed in a reliquary of gold). Although early medieval narrators can design a scene or an episode around one of these already-interpreted objects (Charlemagne's sceptre), or around an image with a well-documented value in literary and artistic iconography (the turning wheel), most of the time their choices do not depend on a symbolism external to the narrative. Such eloquent objects as Gregory's plate of soup or Moschos' mosquito-net take their meaning exclusively from the story in which they occur.

Few of the things mentioned in these narratives occupy a central position. Many serve only as accessories, useful stage properties in scenes built around dialogue, physical action, or other objects. Given the tendency of early medieval narrators to describe as little as possible and to subordinate entire scenes to the expression of concepts and abstract relations, even these secondary objects become saturated with significance. Since they are practical, all-purpose props, part of a limited inventory of recurring objects, they soon acquire several widely divergent meanings. In certain cases one of them can appear so often and take on so many different functions in the work of a given writer that it becomes his obsessive mark, an unconscious signature of sorts.

Conclusion: Posterity of a Style

A narrative style, particularly if considered from the point of view of its most basic technical features, is not replaced at a given moment by entirely different forms and devices. Its fundamental acquisitions are most often preserved in the various styles that come after it, and transformed either by simplification or by addition of new elements. These new elements combine with the old to form narrative patterns that may seem wholly unfamiliar and unrelated to what came before. The early medieval scene, spare but packed with abstract significance, with elements that point beyond the scene itself, could not have been simplified further. Even though it introduced realistic details that had been previously ruled out by the classical model, it also reduced narrative to a series of stark and minimal units of representation. In comparison with this manner, all high and late medieval developments are bound to look extremely elaborate, the new scenes almost bewildering in the diversity and sheer number of their elements. What we want to know, however, is whether features of the earlier style can still be recognized within these new modes, in what form they have survived, and what systematic additions and deletions have taken place around them.

In trying to answer these questions, we come across an important problem of literary continuity. It arises from a perspective hardly considered in this book: that of reception. From the twelfth century on, the public of literature grows and changes considerably. Together with this transformation of the public, there is a change in the status of the various narrative genres: fiction, and in general narratives composed primarily to entertain, become immensely popular. Genres with some claim to historical truth, such as chronicles, biographies, and saints' lives, continue to be cultivated, but can no longer be seen as dominant.[1]

From our angle, this constitutes a more serious break in continuity than the rise of the vernacular literatures, which begins to take place at about the same time. Attempts to trace the survival and evolution of early medieval narrative forms into the later middle ages must be based mainly on non-fictional texts, such as can be compared directly to the work of Gregory of Tours or Paul the Deacon without introducing the unknown factor of a different genre and its constraints. Otherwise, any stylistic differences might be explained entirely by internal requirements of the genres, and have little meaning for the evolution of narrative form as such.

A historical work such as Joinville's *Vie de Saint Louis* allows us to bridge the gap in literary history created by the shifting allegiances of public taste. The book displays throughout the same subordination of narrative to information and intelligibility that we find in earlier medieval histories. Nothing is included or left out only to keep the reader amused; battles and sieges are described in detail, with dry accuracy. Another advantage of Joinville for our purpose is that his work is *à cheval* between high and late middle ages. Composed in the first decade of the fourteenth century, when Joinville was eighty or more, it goes back to experiences of the mid-thirteenth century, when the author's narrative manner and habits of style must have been formed. The *Vie* also has a certain relation to orality: it was dictated, not composed in writing, and therefore put together without the benefit of drafts and textual revisions. This of course has little to do with the orality imitated or absorbed by the early medieval historians, which does not aim at the production of a fixed text and lives in flux from performance to performance. Joinville offers an eyewitness account. The main source of his text is in any case not literary, and can be best characterized as unshaped personal experience, here taking literary form for the first time.

The *Vie* is not a masterpiece of organization. The long account of the seventh crusade which makes up the greater part of it, and in which Joinville's adventures receive greater attention than the king's own performance, is preceded, in harmony with the ostensible purpose of the book, by short sections on Louis' personal piety and his administration of justice. Both of these sections consist entirely of anecdotes chosen to illustrate the king's moral qualities as expressed in religion and legislation. Many of them must have been taken by Joinville directly from his own recollection, others from a nascent oral tradition about Louis, which may explain their striking similarity to the early medieval forms we have been studying, and particularly to Notker's

De Karolo rege. The following scene describes a clash between Joinville himself and Robert de Sorbon in the presence of the king:

35. Le saint roy fut a Corbeil a une Penthecouste, la ou il ot [bien] quatorze-vins chevaliers. Le roy descendi aprés manger ou prael, desouz la chapelle, et parloit a l'uys de la porte au conte de Bretaigne, le pere au duc qui ore est, que Dieu gart. La me vint querre mestre Robert de Cerbon, et me prist par le col de mon mantel, et me mena au roy. Et tuit li autre chevalier vindrent aprés nous. Lors demandai-je a mestre Robert: 'Mestre Robert, que me voulez vous?' Et me dist: 'Je vous veil demander se le roy se seoit en cest prael, et vous vous aliez seoir sur son banc plus haut que li, se en vous en devroit bien blasmer?' Et je li diz que oïl. 36. Et il me dit: 'Dont faites-vous bien a blasmer, quant vous estes plus noblement vestu que le roy. Car vous vous vestez de vair et de vert, ce que li roy ne fait pas'. Et je li diz: 'Mestre Robert, salve vostre grace, je ne foiz mie a blasmer se je me vest de vert et de vair, car cest abit me lessa mon pere et ma mere. Mes vous faites a blamer, car vous estes filz de vilain et de vilainne, et avez lessié l'habit vostre pere et vostre mere, et estes vestu de plus riche camelin que le roy n'est'. Et lors je pris le pan de son seurcot et du seurcot le roy, et li diz: 'Or esgardez se je diz voir'. Et lors le roy entreprist a deffendre mestre Robert de paroles, de tout son pooir.   (*Vie* 35–6)

35. On a Whitsunday, the saintly king was at Corbeil with a good two hundred and eighty knights. After dinner he came down to the court beneath the chapel and stood by the door talking with the comte de Bretagne, the father of the present duke, whom God preserve. Master Robert de Sorbon came looking for me, took me by the collar of my cloak, and led me to the king, and all the other knights followed us. I asked him: 'Master Robert, what do you want of me?' And he said: 'I want to ask you this: if the king were to sit in this court and you went and sat higher up than he on the bench, would you be at fault?' I told him yes. 36. And he said: 'Then you are very much at fault for being more finely dressed than the king. For you are clad in fur-trimmed green clothes, and the king is not.' I said to him: 'Master Robert, with your permission, I am not at all at fault if I dress in fur and green cloth, for I have the right to dress like this from my father and mother. But you are to be faulted, for you are the son of commoners and have abandoned the garb of your father and

mother, and are dressed in finer woollen cloth than the king.' Then I took a fold of his tunic and one of the king's tunic and said to him: 'See whether I speak the truth.' At that point the king began to speak in defence of Master Robert, as strongly as he could.

In the following scene, which closes the anecdote, the king tells Joinville privately that in fact he agrees with him, but felt bound to defend de Sorbon in public. The story is one of several meant to illustrate the evangelical plainness of Louis' table and wardrobe.

Nothing here seems unfamiliar, neither the cut of the scenic unit, which is brief and introduced by increasingly precise indications of time ('On a Whitsunday,' 'after dinner'), nor its contents, which are speeches in direct form, meaningful gestures, and significant things. The dialogue has a convincing 'spoken' sound, particularly Joinville's reply, which sounds a bit too lapidary to be true, but is lively and trenchant; the 'salve vostre grace' strikes the right note of polite venom. The gesture by which de Sorbon grabs Joinville's collar instantly becomes an expression of disrespect and forwardness, particularly since the argument that follows centres exclusively on rank and the symbolic tokens of respect that it imposes. De Sorbon's gesture is answered or returned at the end of the scene, after Joinville has corrected him verbally, but at this point his response to de Sorbon's challenge is hidden under an attitude of demonstration: Joinville holds the fabrics next to each other to show how they compare in quality. The garments worn by Joinville, Louis, and de Sorbon are interpreted from the beginning as badges or signs of social standing, and even translated into an equivalent system of seating arrangements in de Sorbon's question.

Two features of the scene may reveal a newer taste. In the first place, the contents seem more organized, more explicitly composed, than is usual in early medieval narrative. This is not a question of a recognizable focus or centre to the scene, for dialogue, gestures, and things have about the same relative weight; they depend too much on each other for any of them to dominate the whole. It is the simple challenge-and-response structure of the narrative that gives the elements a dramatic symmetry and makes the second half of the scene an effective reply to the first. We also notice a number of descriptive details that cannot be explained in terms of any larger purpose: the king stands chatting by the door; we are told the name of his interlocutor, who plays no role in the scene. The aim is obviously to give a fuller picture, to recall as exactly as possible the details of the occasion. Here the element of gratuitous representation is still inconsiderable. The scene is used to convey a clear ethical point, and that serves to keep Joinville's memory and imagination in check.[2]

The new directions in narrative technique appear with greater clarity in an episode early in Joinville's account of the crusade. The king has begun to recruit men for the expedition.

> 115. Endementres que je venoie, je trouvé trois homes mors sur une charrette, que un clerc avoit tuez. Et me dist-en que en les menoit au roy. Quant je oÿ ce, je envoié un mien escuier aprés, pour savoir comment ce avoit esté. Et conta mon escuier que je y envoyé, que le roy, quant il issi de sa chapelle, ala au perron pour veoir les mors, et demanda au prevot de Paris comment ce avoit esté. 116. Et le prevost li conta que les mors estoient trois de ses serjans du Chastelet, et li conta que il aloient par les rues forainnes pour desrober la gent. Et dist au roy que 'il trouverent ce clerc que vous veez ci, et li tollirent toute sa robe. Le clerc s'en ala en pure sa chemise en son hostel, et prist s'arbalestre et fist aporter a un enfant son fauchon. Quant il les vit, il les escria et leur dit que il y mourroient. Le clerc tendi s'arbalestre et traït et en feri l'un parmi le cuer, et les deux toucherent a fuie. Et le clerc prist le fauchon que l'enfant tenoit, et les ensui a la lune, qui estoit belle et clere. 117. L'un en cuida passer parmi une soif en un courtil, et le clerc fiert du fauchon, fist le prevost, et li trancha toute la jambe, en telle maniere que elle ne tient que a l'estivall, si comme vous veez. Le clerc rensui l'autre, lequel cuida descendre en une estrange meson la ou gent veilloient encore, et le clerc [le] feri du fauchon parmi la teste, si que il le fendi jusques es dens, si comme vous poez veoir, fist le prevost au roy. Sire, fist-il, le clerc moustra son fait aus voisins de la rue, et puis si s'en vint mettre en vostre prison, sire, et je le vous ameinne, si en ferez vostre volenté, et veez-le-ci. 118. 'Sire clerc, fist le roy, vous avez perdu a estre prestre par vostre proesce, et pour vostre proesce je vous retieing a mes gages, et en venrez avec moy outremer. Et ceste chose vous foiz-je encore [assavoir], pource que je vueil bien que ma gent voient que je ne les soustendrai en nulles de leurs mauvestiés'. Quant le peuple, qui la estoit assemblé, oÿ ce, il se escrierent a Nostre Seigneur et li prierent que Dieu li donnast bone vie et longue, et le ramenast a joie et a santé.   (Vie 115–8)

On my way [to Paris], I saw a cart carrying three dead men who had been killed by a clerk, and was told that they were being taken to

the king. When I heard this, I sent one of my squires to follow the
cart and find out how things had gone. And this squire I sent told me
that the king, after leaving his chapel, came down the steps to see
the dead men, and asked the provost of Paris what had happened. The
provost told him that the dead men were three of his sergeants of
the Châtelet, and that they prowled the back-streets to rob people.
He said to the king: 'They ran into the clerk you see before you, and
took all his clothes. He went back to his lodgings clad in his shirt
only, took his crossbow, and made a child carry his sword. When he
saw them again, he cried out and told them they would die. He
readied his crossbow, shot, and struck one of them through the heart;
the other two fled. Then the clerk took the sword that the child was
carrying, and ran after them under the moon, which shone full and
clear. One of the sergeants attempted to climb over a hedge into a
courtyard, and the clerk struck him with his sword,' said the provost,
'and cut off his leg, so that it is held in place only by the boot, as you
can see. Then the clerk went after the other one, who tried to take
refuge in the house of some strangers, where the people were still
up, and the clerk hit him with his sword on the head and split it down
to the teeth, as you see here,' the provost told the king. 'Then, sire,
the clerk announced what he had done to the neighbours of that street,
and came here to put himself into your prison. I have brought him
before you for you to do as you please. Here he is.' 'Master clerk,'
said the king, 'your prowess has closed off the priesthood to you,
but because of it I will have you in my pay and take you with me
overseas. And this I let you know so that my people may learn that I
shall not support them in any crimes.' When the people who were
gathered there heard this, they called out to God our Lord and prayed
for him to give the king a long and happy life, and bring him back
to France in joy and good health.

The complexity of the composition would seem excessive if it were
not for Joinville's easy and unemphatic manner, which allows him to
manipulate points of view and narrative frames effortlessly and with
a total lack of self-consciousness. He is careful to motivate his telling
of this incident by starting out from his own point of view: he saw the
bodies before the king did. The first (or outermost) frame, which is left
wholly undeveloped, is the report of Joinville's squire to his master.
Within it, two carefully staged moments compete for our attention:
the conference outside the king's chapel, which begins as a report of
the provost to the king and ends with a confrontation of Louis and the

clerk before a crowd, and the midnight massacre of the three sergeants by the clerk, as described by the provost. Dialogue and gestures are introduced with skill: the words of the provost to the king glide easily from indirect speech to direct; his gestures as he points out the various wounds and introduces the clerk are implicit in his speech: 'as you can see,' 'as you see here,' 'Here he is.'

There is also a great deal of pure description, particularly in the night chase as narrated by the provost. The conversation before the chapel is located simply at the 'perron,' and we assume that the corpses are lying before Louis in the cart in which Joinville first saw them. This scene, however, serves throughout as a filter for the clerk's adventures, and the provost does not spare us the dramatic details. After being held up, the clerk returns home in an undergarment; a child goes with him carrying his sword; there is a radiant moon, which makes it easy to keep his assailants in sight. We are told the exact circumstances in which each of the sergeants is killed, what weapon the clerk used, and what sort of wound he inflicted.

A new conception of the aims of narrative emerges from Joinville's practice. The episodes he represents with so much talent by means of this complex set of frames have ceased to illustrate a larger, non-representable reality; they have undergone a weakening or blurring of significance. At the same time, and coming closer in that to a journalistic conception of his task as historian and narrator, Joinville feels responsible for all the facts and for every aspect of their occurrence that might stir the curiosity of his audience, even if it means little or nothing in itself. With the growth of dramatic complexity that is evident in this last scene comes a loss of abstract focus. The point of the story can no longer be defined: is it meant to give another instance of Louis' clemency and sense of justice, or to impress us with the uncommon ferocity and valour of the clerk? Even if we were to decide for one of these options, taking the other as subordinate or secondary, such vivid touches as the return home of the clerk in his shirt or the boy carrying his sword for him in the moonlight cannot be accounted for in terms of one or the other. They are there because of their own dramatic force, and perhaps also because they happened.

There is abundant evidence that the fictional genres of the high and late middle ages assimilated and transformed early medieval narrative structures in much the same way as historiography did. I shall only point out a few cases. Dialogue, in direct and indirect form, becomes a pervasive feature of narrative and is rendered in a great variety of styles, from the long expository speeches of allegories such as the *Roman de la Rose* and *Piers Plowman* to the trenchant and mannered brevity of the Icelandic sagas. I have already noted that the *Chanson de Roland* and the *Poema del Cid* have scenes centred on significant gesture.[3] The object-focused scene has an equally important evolution. Taking examples only from Middle High German literature, we can point to the decisive role of the ring and girdle in the confrontation between Kriemhild and Brünhild before the minster in the *Nibelungenlied* (*âventiure* 14, stanzas 847–50 of the B–text). The narrative logic whereby crucial questions of identity are settled by an object is at work in the scene in Gottfried von Strassburg's *Tristan und Isold* where the heroine identifies her teacher and friend as the killer of her uncle by fitting a fragment of steel taken from her uncle's death-wound to the broken edge of Tantris' sword (*Tristan*, lines 10050–10112), and in the remarkable episode in Wolfram's *Parzival* where the hero is hypnotized by three drops of blood on the snow, in which he recognizes the complexion of his absent wife (*Parzival* VI, paragraphs 281.10–283.24).

One particular scene from a less important German work provides perhaps the best example of the survival of the earlier style in a work of fiction. The work in question, *Rother*, is a 'minstrel epic' (German *Spielmannsepos*) written sometime in the mid-twelfth century. Rother, a king with his capital in Bari, sends an embassy to Constantinople to ask for the hand of Emperor Constantine's daughter. Not only is his suit refused, but his envoys are imprisoned for their temerity. The hero then decides to go himself to the eastern capital, pretending to be an exiled enemy of Rother. As the courtly and generous warrior Dietrich, he becomes extremely popular in the imperial court. Finally, through the agency of the princess's serving-maid Herlint, he is able to meet Constantine's daughter and reveal his true identity to her. Before we look more closely at the scene in which this revelation takes place, I must point out that if *Rother* makes a particularly good illustration of the survival of an earlier narrative manner, it is because of its multiple connections to early medieval tradition. The hero is named after Rothari, a Langobardic king of the seventh century, and his story resembles in many ways that of Authari, another Langobardic ruler, whose incognito wooing of a Bavarian princess has been discussed in chapter three. The general formula for such stratagems in royal courtship (German *Brautwerbung*), though extremely popular in German literature from 1150, has deep roots in early medieval narrative, where it has shaped the accounts of Clovis' wooing of Chrodechild in Fredegar and in the *Liber historiae Francorum*.[4] Finally, as a minstrel epic, *Rother* seems to be only one short stage beyond its own earlier tradition in oral performance.[5]

The princess hears so much about the splendid Dietrich that she can no longer control her curiosity. She sends Herlint to him with a request that he visit her in secret. Dietrich-Rother pretends to refuse regretfully, out of regard for his host and for the princess, and sends Herlint back to her mistress with gifts of gold and silver shoes. However, he keeps one shoe from each pair, and very soon the maid is back, bringing another invitation and asking for the missing shoes. To distract the courtiers from the comings and goings of the hero, Rother's men perform spectacular athletic feats. The princess awaits the visitor standing at her window, welcomes him, and asks him to put the golden shoes on her feet.

> 'Ich han dich gerne, herre,
> durch dine vromicheit gesen;
> daz ne is durch anderis nicht geschen.
> Desse schon lossam,
> die saltu mir zien an'.
> 'Vile gerne', sprach Dietherich,
> nu irs geruchit an mich.'
> Der herre zo den uoten gesaz,
> vil schone sin geberre was.
> Vffe sin bein saze sie den uoz;
> iz ne wart nie urowe baz geschot.   (*Rother*, lines 2191–2200)

> 'I have seen you with pleasure, my lord, because of your merit and
> for no other reason; you will put these fine shoes on my feet.' 'Gladly,'
> said Dietrich, 'since you wish me to do so.' The lord sat at her feet,
> and his conduct was impeccable. She set her foot on his lap. No woman
> was ever better shod.

A long dialogue follows, in the course of which Rother leads the princess to confess that if she could choose among all the heroes in the world, she would take King Rother, her former suitor, for her husband. He then insinuates that, far from being an enemy of Rother, he is his emissary, and she, very excited, asks him to reveal his true identity.

> 'Nu ne virhel mich der rede nicht;
> swaz mir hute wirt gesagit,

daz ist imer wole virdagit
biz an den iungistin tac.'
Der herre zo der urowen sprach:
'Nu lazich alle mine dinc
an godes genade ande din.
Ja stent dine voze
in Rotheris schoze.'   (lines 2255–63)

'Hide nothing from me in your speech. Whatever is told me today, I
shall keep it secret until judgment day.' The lord spoke to the lady:
'Now I place the success of my whole enterprise on God's mercy and
on yours. Your feet are resting on Rother's lap.'

After a first reaction of alarm on her part, the princess and Rother come
to an understanding. His words confirm the fact that he has been
holding her foot on his lap for the duration of the dialogue (lines 2203–
64). The shoe itself has an archaic sexual meaning, but as a gift it is
an established part of the legal ceremony of betrothal.[6] Here the public
nature of that ceremony is left out by having the scene take place in
the princess's private rooms, so that the shoes as symbol stand at best
halfway between erotic and legal meanings. We can see how, at this
point in the tradition, earlier layers of symbolic significance are fading
away; the shoes are becoming a mere instrument in the courtship
stratagem. Together with the intimate posture of the hero and the
princess, they remain nevertheless the conceptual focus of the scene.
Their centrality is weakened, however, because in the scene itself the
act of putting them on her feet, which coincides with the disclosure
of his identity, is split in two by over fifty lines of conversation. Here
too, the shift away from early medieval style consists in good part in
the expansion and greater complexity of the scenic unit.

Notes

1 On the *Iohannis* see Blänsdorf 'Aeneadas rursus cupiunt,' and Ehlers 'Epische Kunst.'
2 The scant information on the career of Corippus is summarized by Averil Cameron in her edition of *In laudem Iustini* 1–2, and in Stache *Kommentar* 1–3. See also Averil Cameron 'The Career of Corippus Again.'
3 According to Dagron, 'Aux origines de la civilisation byzantine,' Greek replaced Latin in Byzantium as soon as it became identified with Orthodoxy and adapted to the legal and bureaucratic uses of Latin. See also Toynbee *Constantine Porphyrogenitus* 552–74, and Baldwin 'Latin in Byzantium.'
4 The work to which I refer here is found primarily in specialized studies, but some general statements are available; see, for example, Peter Brown *The Making of Late Antiquity*, and Marrou *Décadence romaine*. See also the critical discussions in Murray 'Peter Brown and the Shadow of Constantine' and Fontaine 'Le culte des saints.'
5 See Peter Brown *Religion and Society* 9–21, and *The Cult of the Saints*. Byzantine and medieval art have long been established fields in art history, but there too a change of direction is perceptible; see Kitzinger *Byzantine Art in the Making*, and Grabar *Les voies de la création*.
6 The most influential statements of this approach to the early middle ages as *Nachleben der Antike* are found in Curtius *Europäische Literatur*, particularly in excursus five and six, 'Spätantike Literaturwissenschaft' and 'Altchristliche und mittelalterliche Literaturwissenschaft,' 435–42 and 443–61 resp. The best-known English survey of the intellectual life of Europe in the early middle ages, Laistner *Thought and Letters*, is strongly influenced by the *Nachleben* approach. A radical shift in per-

spective characterizes See, et al *Europäisches Frühmittelalter*, which presents a very different picture of the age by focusing on new developments, and in particular on the rise of the vernacular literatures, but unfortunately has as little to say about narrative prose as the earlier and more traditional surveys.

7 See Auerbach *Literatursprache und Publikum*, particularly the essays 'Sermo humilis,' 25–53, with its appendix 'Gloria passionis,' 54–63, and 'Lateinische Prosa des frühen Mittelalters,' 65–133; also MacMullen 'A Note on *sermo humilis,*' and Mohrmann 'Quelques traits caractéristiques,' and 'Le problème de la continuité.'

8 On Sidonius as imitator of the classics see Gualandri *Furtiva lectio* 75–104. See also the recent analysis of Boethius' *Consolatio* and its classical sources in Chadwick *Boethius; The Consolations* 223–53.

9 See Diaz y Diaz 'La trasmisión de los textos antiguos' 174, and Fontaine *Isidore de Seville*. Fontaine's analysis of Isidore's encyclopaedic activity as a liberation of knowledge by fragmentation is especially valuable: 'Le refus d'une composition véritable était vertu en un temps ou la civilisation occidentale était en plein devenir' (885). See also Marrou 'Isidore de Seville.'

10 'quid quoque Sedulius vel quid canit ipse Iuvencus, / Alcimus et Clemens, Prosper, Paulinus, Arator, / quid Fortunatus, vel quid Lactantius edunt, / quae Maro Virgilius, Statius, Lucanus et auctor; / artis grammaticae vel quid scripsere magistri ... ' / '[You will find there ...] the poems of Sedulius and Juvencus, those of Alcimus Avitus, Prudentius, Prosper, Paulinus, and Arator, as well as what Fortunatus and Lactantius have sung, the works of Vergil, Statius, and Lucan, and what the masters of the art of grammar once wrote ... ' ('Versus de patribus regibus et sanctis Euboricensis ecclesiae,' lines 1550–3, in Alcuin *The Bishops, Kings, and Saints of York*). On this aspect of the early medieval canon see also Glauche *Schullektüre* 5–16.

11 On education in Visigothic Spain and Anglo-Saxon England see Riché *Education et culture* 291–310, 339–50, 401–9, 353–70, 419–49; also Fontaine 'Fins et moyens de l'enseignement;' Bullough 'The Educational Tradition in England,' and T.J. Brown 'An Historical Introduction to the Use of Classical Authors.'

12 Momigliano 'L'età del traspasso.'

13 On Visigothic use of late antique models see Fontaine 'Die westgotische lateinische Literatur,' Messmer *Hispania-Idee* 87–137, and Riché *Ecoles et enseignement* 22–5 and 80–7.

14 On the relation between legend and history, a classic statement is Heusler

Die altgermanische Dichtung 162–3. A critical response to Heusler can be found in Mohr 'Geschichtserlebnis.' Hainer 'Das epische Element,' esp 30–1 and 53, is an early attempt to show legendary patterns at work in early medieval historiography, but it suffers from an excessively broad conception of the epic element, which ends by including almost every kind of fictional influence on historical narrative. An instructive case-study on the relation of heroic legend to historiography is Andersson 'Cassiodorus and the Gothic Legend.'

15 Simson *Sacred Fortress* 23–40.

16 Vinay *Alto medioevo latino* 323.

17 On Charles the Bald and his relations with the clergy, see Wallace-Hadrill *The Frankish Church* 241–57.

18 Alföldi 'Insignien und Tracht,' and Pertusi 'Insigne del potere sovrano.' See also Bullough '*Imagines regum*' passim.

19 See below, 41–2.

20 Kubler *The Shape of Time* 129.

21 Bede was capable of extraordinarily subtle and effective gestural staging, as shown, for instance, by Wetherbee 'Some Implications of Bede's Latin Style.' But, however excellent, this kind of dramatic narrative is the exception and not the rule in the *HE*.

22 These contacts are splendidly documented in Berschin *Griechisch-lateinisches Mittelalter*. See also Pickering 'The Western Image of Byzantium.'

23 The exceptions are Procopius (below, 158–61), Psellos (163–4), and Constantine Porphyrogenitus (194–5).

CHAPTER ONE

1 Bolaffi *Sallustio e la sua fortuna* 241–51, Sorrento 'Tito Livio dal Medio Evo al Rinascimento,' Guido Billanovich *Lamperto di Hersfeld e Tito Livio*, and Giuseppe Billanovich 'Dal Livio di Raterio'; see also Mordek 'Livius und Einhard,' who denies direct knowledge and use of Livy by the Carolingian author and argues against excessively generous estimates of classical influence in the early middle ages.

2 Wiseman *Clio's Cosmetics* 27–53.

3 See the analysis of a scene from Tacitus' *Annals* in Auerbach *Mimesis* 40–6. On 48–9 Auerbach employs an informal definition of the scenic unit very close to the one I am using here, and points out that such scenes are exceptional in classical historiography.

4 Burck *Die Erzählungskunst* 197–209; also Walsh *Livy* 181–90.

5 Dionysus of Halicarnassus tells the same story at much greater length in his *Roman Antiquities* IV. 28–40; see the comparative analysis in Ogilvie *A Commentary* 184–94.

6 Fuhrmann 'Narrative Techniken.'

7 The account by Dionysius of Halicarnassus contains some important variations. There are two full scenes, one at the Forum and one on the Street of Crime. In the former there are two speeches in direct form: one by Servius, who asks Tarquin how he dares put on royal insignia, and the usurper's fairly short, arrogant reply. The ensuing struggle, however, is centred on the throne, as in Livy. At the Street of Crime there is a short exchange between Tullia and her driver. She slaps him with her shoe and tells him to drive on after he points out to her that her dead father is lying on the path. Dionysius' account is more thoroughly dramatized than Livy's, even if altogether less successful.

8 See Dill *Roman Society in Gaul* 296–307. A far more cautious and less conclusive view of the subject is given by Wallace-Hadrill 'The Blood-feud of the Franks.'

9 On this formula, which he calls 'le prophète chez le roi,' see Fontaine 'Une clé littéraire.'

10 Smalley 'Sallust in the Middle Ages.'

11 Procopius *De bello Gothico* I.ix.11–21 tells a very similar story: Belisarius is about to give up on the siege of Naples when a soldier in his army, an Isaurian, decides out of pure curiosity to explore the aqueduct that supplies the city with water, and discovers that it would be possible to get into Naples through the aqueduct. The story may well be a standard motif in the literature of warfare and strategy.

12 Barthes 'Structure du fait divers.'

13 Manitius *Geschichte* I, 218, argues that Gregory had direct knowledge of Sallust; more recently Reynolds *Texts and Transmission*, 345, states that Sallustian influence got off to a comparatively slow start in the Carolingian period. Reynolds' view seems to be based exclusively on the manuscript tradition.

14 On Sallust's influence on Widukind see Beumann *Widukind von Korvei* 94–100.

15 Auerbach *Mimesis* 81–97.

16 Auerbach *Mimesis* 97: 'Mit Gregors Sprache hingegen liegt es so, daß sie die Tatbestände nur sehr unvollkommen zu ordnen vermag; einen Ereigniszusammenhang der nicht sehr einfach ist, vermag er nicht über-sichtlich darzustellen. Seine Sprache ordnet schlecht oder überhaupt nicht.'

17 See for example Roberts 'Gregory of Tours and the Monk of St. Gall';

Roberts even proposes a comparison with the informal prose of children's speech (183–5).

18 Monod 'Les aventures de Sichaire,' and Fustel de Coulanges 'De l'analyse des textes historiques.'

19 Momigliano 'L'età del traspasso,' 102–9 and 'The Lonely Historian Ammianus Marcellinus,' and Vogt 'Ammianus Marcellinus.'

20 Rosen *Studien zur Darstellungskunst* 194.

21 Vogt 'Ammianus Marcellinus' 810–11.

22 See Kech *Hagiographie als christliche Unterhaltungsliteratur*, and Fuhrmann 'Die Mönchsgeschichten des Hieronymus' 41–58. Fuhrmann shows numerous similarities between the life of Hilarion and pagan biography, but also points of contact with such literary transformations of the oral tradition of early monasticism and eremitism as Athanasius' *Vita Antonii*, the *Historia monachorum in Aegypto*, and Palladius' *Historia Lausiaca*. He has deliberately excluded any consideration of oral tradition (cf his exchange with Jacques Fontaine on the subject in the discussion that follows his paper, pp 90–9).

23 See Gustavo Vinay's highly critical 'Epilogo' to *La Bibbia nell'alto medioevo*, and Lehmann 'Der Einfluss der Bibel.'

24 *Apophthegmata patrum* cols 77–9. Cf Bousset *Apophthegmata* 76–7: 'Und eben weil wir hier eine gänzlich unliterarische Schicht vor uns haben, sind die Apophthegmata ein so vorzügliches Paradigma der Art und des Wesens mündlicher Überlieferung.'

25 Mintz *Legends of the Hasidim* 314. In spite of its very contemporary setting, the story has remarkably close analogues in two miracles told by Gregory of Tours and discussed below, 157–8.

26 *Harmless Poisons* 9. Mrabet has described how he composes and sets down his stories in the autobiographical *Look & Move On* 89–97, though he says little about style. Paul Bowles, his editor and translator into English, gives a brief account of the taping and transcription of these narratives in his introduction to Charhadi *A Life Full of Holes* 9–13.

27 A reference to the war of liberation of 1948 (personal communication from Jerome R. Mintz).

28 Brian Stock's thesis in *The Implications of Literacy* that a decisive and irreversible transition from oral to literate thinking took place in the course of the eleventh and twelfth centuries seems to me unproved and unlikely. Much of the evidence provided by the author for a redefinition of orality, which according to him begins to function within a framework of literacy and textuality at that time, can also be found in abundance in late antiquity and the early middle ages: Arianism and iconoclasm were based on 'textual communities' as firmly as the Milanese Pataria.

Stock's analysis, which is focused on the most refined expressions of medieval literacy (mainly theology and philosophy) can hardly be used to make a case about the fate of oral culture.

29 Finnegan *Oral Poetry* 58–72.
30 See Labov and Waletzky 'Narrative Analysis,' Gülich 'Konventionelle Muster,' and Hrdličková 'Japanese Professional Storytellers.'
31 Hrdličková 'Japanese Professional Storytellers' and Toelken 'The "Pretty Languages" of Yellowman' provide excellent illustrations of those aspects of oral prose narrative that only exist in performance: the expressive range of the storyteller's voice, his gestures, timing, and building up of a rapport with the audience.
32 Hofmann 'Die Einstellung der isländischen Sagaverfasser' argues for a historical division of labour among the medieval Icelandic genres in consequence of which skaldic poetry was defined as a vehicle for commentary and self-expression, while Eddic poetry and, even more exclusively, prose were expected to provide 'objective' narrative. The antiquity and formal excellence of skaldic poetry are therefore the cause that 'die Erzähler sich der Prosa zuwandten und die Kunst der Wirklichkeitsillusionierung entdeckten' (16).
33 On the Old Testament, see Gerhardsson *Memory and Manuscript* passim. Gerhardsson's book shows clearly that in the tradition of religious texts, only some of which are narrative, the line between strict repetition and improvisation is less fluctuating than for secular texts and their performance. Alter *The Art of Biblical Narrative* suffers, in spite of excellent individual readings, from the assumption that oral-traditional schematism and literary subtlety in the adaptation and variation of individual patterns are wholly incompatible factors (eg 47–52). Not only is literary subtlety to be expected wherever, as in the Bible, oral schemes have long been incorporated into a literary language, but variation and adaptation are an essential part of actual performance in first-hand oral material. For the New Testament, and especially on Mark, see Kelber *The Oral and the Written Gospel* 44–89. The controversy as to the oral or written origins of the Icelandic sagas has an immense literature, but not much has been written on the subject of scenic structure and its possible oral background. Fundamental on this topic is Clover 'Scene in Saga Composition.' See also Clover 'The Long Prose Form,' which discusses the specific problems of oral tradition in prose, a subject largely ignored by scholarship so far.
34 Guenée *Histoire et culture historique* 78–85.
35 Andersson 'The Textual Evidence' focuses on the problem of distinguishing between such empty formulas and genuine references to oral tradition.

36 On the possible influence of the ancient novel on Jerome's *Vitae patrum*, see Bauer 'Novellistisches bei Hieronymus.'

CHAPTER TWO

1 This is doubtless a sweeping statement. It expresses a mere conjecture based on recent studies of early literatures, which have shown that directly quoted dialogue comes frequently from oral tradition. The case of Herodotus is particularly well studied; the classical analysis is Aly *Volksmärchen, Sage und Novelle*. See also, more recently, the detailed but less conclusive discussion in Hohti *The Interrelation of Speech and Action*, especially 139–40. Lang *Herodotean Narrative* 18–36 and 142–9 builds squarely on the assumption of an oral-traditional background, but her analyses emphasize the role of speeches in the construction of episodes, rather than the actual representation of speech.

2 Barthes *La chambre claire* 73–95.

3 See White 'The Value of Narrativity' on these early medieval efforts to create continuity by means of chronologies and framing devices. Goffart *The Narrators of Barbarian History*, the most detailed and penetrating study to date of early medieval histories as macronarratives, has much to say on the subject of narrative discontinuity. A weakness of Goffart's discussion, however, is that he offers different explanations for this feature as it appears in the works of different writers. Thus, the aim of discontinuity in Gregory of Tours' *History* is to indicate the irrationality of worldly affairs: 'these were base strivings after worthless goals and had to be portrayed in their senselessness' (206). On the other hand, the jagged, fragmented narrative of Paul the Deacon's Roman and Lombard histories hides elaborate patterns and symmetries meant to bring out the meaning and direction of the course of events being described, which Paul saw as anything but irrational. 'The taxing aspect of Paul's work is what least strikes the eye, namely, the imposition of coherent interpretations upon the jumbled records of the past' (428). But it seems likely that, to an important degree, discontinuity in both Gregory's and Paul's histories can be accounted for in purely technical terms as a consequence of the gradual fading out of the authorial voice, which had earlier been used to connect one episode to another, and one scene to the next.

4 On Agnellus as a performer of sorts, see Vinay *Alto medioevo latino* 319–22, and Fasoli 'Rileggendo il "Liber pontificalis." '

5 On Gregory's use of direct speech and dialogue, see Hellmann 'Studien zur mittelalterlichen Geschichtschreibung. i.' 16–21, and Brunhölzl *Geschichte der lateinischen Literatur*. i. 139.

6 Very little work has been done on the stylistics of direct speech in early medieval historiography. The best discussion known to me is Thürlemann *Der historische Diskurs* 74–84 and 100–11.

7 In Agnellus' retelling of the story, Alboin's words are given directly and the passage takes the form of a brief dialogue: 'Quo porrecto, ait rex: "Bibe per totum". Illa mox ut accepit, gemuit, sed fronte serena dixit: "Iussa domini mei alacriter expleam." ' / 'Offering her the cup, the king said: "Drink it all." As she took it she sobbed, but with a calm countenance she replied: "I shall obey the commands of my lord with alacrity" ' (*LPR* 96).

8 On the lost heroic lay of Alboin und Rosimund, see Gschwantler 'Die Heldensage von Alboin und Rosimund.' Gschwantler sees in Paul's version a Langobardic reinterpretation of a Gepid lay of Rosimund created by the survivors of the queen's Gepid retinue. The hypothesis of a lost lay of Rosimund does not seem to me absolutely necessary to explain Paul's narrative. The invitation to drink and the murder in the bedroom, which have led generations of *Sagenforscher* to posit the lost lay, have a great deal in common with Judith 12–14. Paul could easily have derived the two most dramatic moments in the story from the Vulgate Judith, and added them to the narrative of the death of Alboin, which is a genuine Langobardic tradition documented in several earlier sources. Goffart *The Narrators of Barbarian History* 425–9 expresses doubt about Paul's reputation as a collector and preserver of authentic Langobardic legends: the stories he tells fit too well into the design of his books and his general interpretation of Langobardic history for us to see them as pristine, unedited *Volkssagen*. Goffart gives great importance to the story of the murder of Alboin, which according to him constitutes the turning point and catastrophe in Paul's account of the national past, as the king's death made a bloodless occupation of Italy by the Lombards impossible (388–94).

9 Analogues in Procopius *De bello Vandalico* i.iv.1–11, and Theophanes *Chronographia* anno mundi 6194.

10 On the episode as a whole, see Scheibelreiter 'Justinian und Belisar,' which describes the adaptation of Byzantine rumour and history to a Frankish point of view and to various folk motifs.

11 Hainer 'Das epische Element' 41 describes both passages as 'epic' in spite of the significant differences between them.

12 On Gregory's awareness of stylistic levels see Beumann 'Gregor von Tours und der Sermo Rusticus.'

13 On Gregory the Great's own references to his oral sources, see the remarks

of A. de Vogüé in the introduction to his new edition of the work, *Dialogues* 1.43–4 and 124–6, as well as the cautious observations of Le Goff *'Vita* et *"pre-exemplum"* ' 111–14.

14 *Pappa* is, of course, Italian. Cf Meyer-Lübke *Romanisches etymologisches Wörterbuch* and Prati *Vocabolario etimologico italiano* sv *pappare*, and Du Cange *Glossarium* sv *papare*. None of them refers to Agnellus, although he provides very early evidence for the word.

15 Hofmann *Lateinische Umgangsprache* 58–64.

16 For a comparable use of ecclesiastical rhetoric by a very secular speaker, see 96–8 and note 20 below.

17 Tessier 'La conversion de Clovis,' especially 152–4.

18 The description of St Apollinaris in this speech, leading the sheep entrusted to him over the pleasant meadows of Christ, matches the great sixth-century mosaic in the apse of San Apollinare in Classe too exactly for a coincidence to be possible. The rebellious priests are clearly addressing the image of the founder of the church of Ravenna, and asking him for support in their struggle.

19 Vinay *San Gregorio di Tours* 101–44.

20 Buchner, in his edition of Gregory's history, *Historiarum libri decem* 1.344, note 1, points out that Fredegund here is speaking very much like Gregory himself in his prologue to book five: 'Quid agetis? Quid quaeritis? Quid non habundatis? In domibus dilitiae supercrescunt, in prumtuariis vinum, triticum oleumque redundat, in thesauris aurum atque argentum coacervatur. Unum vobis deest, quod, pacem non habentes, Dei gratiam indegetis.' / 'What are you doing? What are you seeking? What is it that you do not have in abundance? Your houses overflow with comforts; in your cellars there is more wine, grain, and oil than you have need for; in your treasuries gold and silver are accumulated. Only one thing do you lack: not having peace, you are without divine grace.' Buchner goes too far when he remarks that in Fredegund's exhortation it is really Gregory we hear, but this opinion turns up again in Thürlemann *Der historische Diskurs* 49–50.

21 It is remarkable, nevertheless, that in spite of the pious and repentant tone of the speech, Fredegund transforms the tears of paupers, the lamentations of widows, and the sighs of orphans, sentimental commonplaces of clerical rhetoric, into instruments of murder. I owe this observation to my friend Ralph Hexter. It is also worth noticing that even at this point the queen appears engaged in an act of destruction: she is burning the tax-requests and encouraging her husband to do the same.

22 Thürlemann *Der historische Diskurs* 80–1.

23 See above, 65–8.

24 See Stafford *Queens, Concubines, and Dowagers*, especially chapter 1, 'Sources and Images,' 1–31.

25 Ševčenko 'Levels of Style.'

26 Browning 'The "Low Level" Saint's Life'; Mango 'A Byzantine Hagiographer at Work.'

27 On the accompanying gestures, see Rydén *Bemerkungen zum Leben des heiligen Narren Symeon* 103–4.

28 Rydén *Das Leben des heiligen Narren Symeon* 26–7, Mango 'A Byzantine Hagiographer at Work' 27–30.

29 On the various strands of oral tradition in Byzantine literature, and the transitions from oral to literary, see Patlagean 'Discours écrit, discours parlé.'

30 On Malalas as writer and historian, see Hunger *Die hochsprachliche profane Literatur der Byzantiner* ı.319–26.

31 Recent scholarship agrees in seeing the story of Athenais' marriage and rise to power as based on a legend; see Holum *Theodosian Empresses* 112–30, and Alan Cameron 'The Empress and the Poet' 270–9.

32 Both the episode and the empress's actual words to her brothers are influenced by the biblical account of Joseph's reunion with his brothers in Egypt. When he finally makes himself known to them, he speaks as follows: 'I am Joseph your brother, whom you sold into Egypt. 5. Now, do not grieve and do not think it evil in yourselves that you sold me here, for God sent me here ahead of you to save lives.' 8. 'It is not you who sent me here, but God, and He has made me as a father to Pharaoh, and the master of all his estate, and the ruler of all Egypt.' (Septuagint; Genesis 45:4–5 and 8). Clearly, the reasoning is the same in both speeches, though the newly christianized empress still talks of her 'ἀγαθὴ τύχη' rather than of God.

33 Byzantine popular historiography often had highly literate and socially prominent readers, and was not composed primarily with a lower-class public in mind, as shown by Beck 'Zur byzantinischen "Mönchschronik." ' The term 'popular' needs to be used in a broader sense here, to indicate that these histories and chronicles were accessible to a larger audience than equivalent narratives in the middle and high styles, even though their authors and many of their readers would have been able to follow the more demanding high-style texts.

CHAPTER THREE

1 See Mor 'Simbologia e simboli,' especially 17–18.

2 The importance of this attitude is also brought out by Paul in his story
of the betrothal of Authari and Theudelinda (discussed and partly quoted
on 138–40 below), where Authari's ambassadors ask the Bavarian king
to let his daughter serve them a cup of wine: ' "Quia talem filiae vestrae
personam cernimus, ut eam merito nostram reginam fieri optemus, si
placet vestrae potestati, de eius manu, sicut nobis postea factura est, vini
poculum sumere praeoptamus." ' / ' "Since we see that the appearance
of your daughter is such that we may rightly choose her to be our queen,
we would like, if it pleases your mightiness, to be served a cup of wine
by her hand, as she will do so in the future." ' (*HL* iii.30).

3 The gesture has many meanings and a long iconographic history. As an
element of the legal rite of adoption, it appears in Roman art; cf Ryberg,
Rites of the State Religion 133, plate xlvii, fig 72a. Medieval art uses it
more often as a ceremonial gesture of presentation before the emperor or
before God; cf the gesture with which Peter and Paul present St Cosmas
and St Damian before the throne of Christ in the sixth-century mosaic at
SS Cosma e Damiano in Rome, or that with which St Demetrios embraces the prefect Leontios and Bishop Ioannes in the early seventh-century
mosaic at Hagios Demetrios in Thessaloniki. Christ himself also appears
performing the gesture, as in the sixth-century icon of Christ and Abbot
Menas in the Louvre. In the story of Lauricius, St Lawrence is presenting
the *cubicularius* to God and to the Emperor Honorius as the builder and
donor of his church. A different meaning is documented in Du Cange
Glossarium sv *brachium*: 'brachium in collo ponere, in signum susceptae
servitutis.'

4 On the sticking out of the tongue, see Richter 'Charakterzeichnung und
Regie,' especially 67.

5 On Notker and the Greeks see Zöllner *Die politische Stellung der Völker*
151–2. The ideological and political background of this rivalry is analysed by Franz Dölger in 'Europas Gestaltung im Spiegel der fränkisch-
byzantinischen Auseinandersetzung.'

6 See Schneider 'Die Geschichte vom gewendeten Fisch' for later versions
of this story.

7 Gregory's dislike and distrust of Chilperic are clearly expressed in the
suggestion that the new canons are not authentic. In any case, he appears to have quoted them inaccurately, substituting 'homicidio' for the
original 'furto' (see Krusch's comment on p 223, note 1 of the *MGH*
edition).

8 De Bruyne 'L'imposition des mains.'

9 This sort of story about an ill-fated attempt to fool a saint has many
analogues in the historical literature and hagiography of the period; cf

LPR 144, where a man pretends to be dead so that his friends can get alms for his burial from Archbishop Sergius of Ravenna, and actually dies on the spot.

10 Augustine *De doctrina christiana* ii.i.2 and ii.3. Notice, however, that Augustine draws the line between natural and conventional somewhat differently from modern semiotics: for him a sign produced by instinct can be 'conventional,' and the crowing of the cock to announce that it has found some food belongs to the 'signa data.' What distinguishes these from the metonymic, involuntary 'signa naturalia' is a 'voluntas significandi.' See also, on Augustine's theory of signs, Ayres *Language, Logic and Reason* 61–81, and, on the meaning of gestures in particular, Peil *Die Gebärde bei Chretien, Hartmann und Wolfram* 297–303 ('Exkurs: Zur Bedeutung der Gebärde').

11 Habicht *Die Gebärde* 9 outlines the dangers of an excessively narrow definition of gesture.

12 Another vengeful heroine, Agnellus' Rosimund, receives the cup made from her father's skull with false serenity ('fronte serena'); see above, 230, note 7. These brief notations can take on extraordinary importance. See Goffart *The Narrators of Barbarian History* 312–3 on the significance of a smile attributed by Stephen of Ripon to King Oswy of Northumbria during the synod of Whitby (*Vita Wilfridi* 10) and left out by Bede in his account of that event (*HE* iii.25).

13 Cf *HF* v.43: the Arian Visigoth Agila, who argues with Gregory 'nescio quid quasi insanus frendens' / 'grinding his teeth like a madman [and saying] I don't know what,' and *HF* v.44, where Chilperic himself, corrected in his theology, 'frendens siluit' / 'ground his teeth and was silent.'

14 Suetonius *De vita caesarum*; Divus Iulius 78.

15 See Alföldi 'Die Ausgestaltung des monarchischen Zeremoniells,' especially 42–3.

16 Writing under the influence of the classical models available in eighth-century Northumbria, Bede does not make the bishop's failure to rise the focus of a scene: 'Fecerunt, ut dixerat. Factumque est, ut uenientibus illis sederet Augustinus in sella. Quod illi uidentes mox in iram conuersi sunt, eumque notantes superbiae, cunctis, quae dicebat, contradicere laborabant.' / 'They did as the hermit had told them, and it happened that when they came in Augustine [remained] sitting on a chair. When they saw this, they immediately became very angry and charged him with pride, making efforts to contradict whatever he said.' He does, however, present the earlier dialogue between the Celts in *oratio recta*.

17 See Eis 'Zum Turisindlied,' Wagner 'Alboin bei Thurisind,' and particularly

Gschwantler 'Versöhnung als Thema einer heroischen Sage,' especially 243–52, where the situation at table is interpreted, rather speculatively, by means of a Germanic ritual of adoption.

18 The evidence is assembled in Needham, ed *Right and Left*, which includes material from a great variety of cultures, predominantly non-Western.

19 Kriss-Rettenbeck 'Probleme der volkskundlichen Gebärdenforschung,' especially 18–22, has excellent remarks on the cultural and acquired character of many such 'psychophysically conditioned' gestures.

20 Cf below, 141–50, where the point is made that although they did formulate social ideologies, they did not operate as a language of gesture.

21 See Röhrich 'Gebärdensprache und Sprachgebärde,' especially 25–36.

22 Bertolini 'Sergio arcivescovo di Ravenna' 48 translates this passage as if all the actions described in it had been carried out by the new pope. It is not possible to tell with certainty from the text which of the two men lies prone before the other, but it seems to me extremely unlikely that the newly elected pontiff, who was not responsible for Sergius' arrest and incarceration, would have humiliated himself in this manner. It is, however, possible that Agnellus, animated by his strong local patriotism, would have chosen to represent Roman power 'vultu submisso.' Agnellus identifies the pope incorrectly as Stephen II, who was in fact Paul's predecessor and Bishop Sergius' enemy.

23 The ceremony is in fact the public side of a sordid private arrangement between the new pope and Archbishop Sergius, who promises his liberator that he will let him take any treasure of the church of Ravenna that he may choose in exchange for his liberty. Later on Pope Paul plunders the Ravennate church treasury, and has cartloads of precious objects carried away.

24 See Grimm *Deutsche Rechtsalterthümer* vol 1, pp 96–104, where this last episode is used with many others to illustrate measurement and setting of limits by touch. Note that already in the earlier case Authari had made his gesture as he and his Bavarian escorts were coming 'iam prope Italiae fines'! The notion of a territorial claim might be present vestigially in that story too.

25 Lüthi *Das europäische Volksmärchen* 25: 'Die scharfe Kontur kommt in Märchen schon dadurch zustande daß es die einzelnen Dinge nicht schildert, sondern nur nennt. Handlungsfreudig, wie es ist, führt es seine Figuren von Punkt zu Punkt, ohne irgendwo schildernd zu verweilen.' Lüthi later (26) refers to this formal tendency of the *Märchen* as a 'Technik der bloßen Benennung.'

26 Cf below, 150–8.

27 Grabar *Christian Iconography* 8 (on the paintings of the catacombs and

sarcophagi): 'This art is an easygoing one, indifferent to detail, to the individual expression of the figure, to the precise traits of a face. One finds uncompleted architecture, and surprising negligence in Biblical images of a narrative character. But these paintings of the catacombs are not meant to represent events – they only suggest them. It is enough to indicate one or two salient features, in order to designate a specific person, event, or object. These few traits do not define the images at all, but the informed viewer is invited to make use of the summary indications to divine the subject. In other words, the paintings are schematic – that is, they are image-signs, which appeal above all to the intellect and which imply more than they actually show. Since the value of a sign is commensurate with its brevity, there are no limits to its use except those imposed by the necessity of remaining understandable.'

28 On ritualization in late antiquity, see MacMullen 'Some Pictures in Ammianus Marcellinus'; for Byzantium see the general observations in Kazhdan and Constable *People and Power in Byzantium* 59–65. MacCormack *Art and Ceremony in Late Antiquity* provides a detailed analysis of the evidence in panegyrics, monuments, and coinage about the meaning of occasions of state such as *adventus* and *consecratio*. On provincial acquaintance with court ceremonial, see van Dam *Leadership and Community* 122–5.

29 See MacCormack *Art and Ceremony* 222–66.

30 On this 'Persian topos' see Alföldi 'Die Ausgestaltung des monarchischen Zeremoniells' 9–25.

31 On this section of the *Book of Ceremonies* see Bury 'The Ceremonial Book of Constantine Porphyrogennetos' 212–13.

32 See Averil Cameron, ed, Corippus *In laudem Iustini* 191, and Stache *Kommentar* 442–5.

33 Jungmann *Missarum Sollemnia* vol 1, p 97: 'Freilich erfaßt das Leben nicht mehr die ganze versammelte Gemeinde in der alten Stärke und Unmittelbarkeit. Das Volk respondiert anscheinend nicht mehr und ist auch nicht mehr beteiligt am Gesang, der zur Kunstübung einer Gruppe geworden ist ... '

34 Jungmann *Missarum Sollemnia* vol 1, p 91; see also Klauser 'Der Ursprung der bischöflichen Insignien.' On the date of *Ordo Romanus primus* see Vogel *Introduction aux sources de l'histoire du culte* 131.

35 On papal ceremony in the early middle ages and the stational liturgy in particular, see van Dijk 'The Urban and Papal Rites,' and Llewellyn *Rome in the Dark Ages* 124–7.

36 Sittl *Die Gebärden der Griechen und Römer* 129–46.

37 *Deutsche Rechtsalterthümer* vol 1, p 56; speaking of the peculiarities of
   early Germanic law concerning measurements and limits, Grimm
   writes: 'Ihr Grundcharakter ist Auffaßung des Rechtlichen durch das
   Sinnliche, Weihung dessen, was festgesetzt werden soll, durch etwas
   Unfestes, dem Zufall nie ganz zu Entziehendes.' See also Schmidt-Wiegand
   'Gebärden.'
38 Kaufmann 'Chrenecruda.' See also Schmidt-Wiegand 'Chrenecruda.
   Rechtswort und Formalakt,' which uses Anglo-Saxon charms as evidence
   that the throwing of dust goes back to a magical action in the pagan
   cult of the Earth.
39 Le Goff 'Les gestes symboliques dans la vie sociale.'
40 See, for instance, the observations of Ourliac and de Malafosse *Droit
   romain et ancien droit* vol 1, p 54: 'L'évolution des contrats en Gaule,
   contrairement à ce qu'ont affirmé d'illustres maîtres (COLLINET), marque
   non le triomphe du consensualisme, mais le triomphe de l'écriture, et
   a cet égard les pratiques de l'Occident paraissent suivre celles de l'Orient."
   On a comparable tendency in the liturgy, see Klauser *Kleine abendländische Liturgiegeschichte* 59–63.
41 An impressive attempt to establish this analogy of language and ritual
   by means of a detailed comparison is Schmidt-Wiegand
   'Gebärdensprache im mittelalterlichen Recht.' But the weight of the
   evidence seems to indicate that in most cases the analogy can only be very
   loose. If we consider, for instance, the informational function of language,
   ceremony and ritual turn out to be comparable with a language that
   conveys no information at all and serves only to formulate what everyone
   already knows (eg the function of an inscription on a monument). See
   in this regard the observations of Tambiah 'A Performative Approach to
   Ritual,' especially 130–42.
42 Cf Sophronius of Jerusalem *Commentarius liturgicus* and Maximus
   Confessor *Mystagogia*. There are important commemorative elements in
   Maximus' interpretation. However, they represent a very different reading
   from that of Sophronius. In the *introitus*, Maximus sees a reference to
   the Incarnation when the celebrant comes into the church, and one to
   Christ's Ascension and return to his heavenly throne when the celebrant
   moves on towards the sanctuary. Also, in his work the commemorative
   elements are held in a broader framework of mystical symbolism. A
   church is an image of the soul, and the world is an image of man, so the
   priest's entrance must be understood as the purification of the human
   soul by the coming of Christ into the world (cf *Mystagogia* chapters
   5–8). Suntrup *Die Bedeutung der liturgischen Gebärden* takes as its

starting point Amalarius of Metz' ninth-century allegorical interpretation of the liturgy, the success of which created a consensus about the meaning of religious ceremony that had not existed before.

43 Cf the concluding remarks of Ramsay MacMullen 'Some Pictures in Ammianus Marcellinus' 455: 'These cultural developments, much as they connect and mingle with each other, have nothing to do with 'classical' culture. They represent the upthrust of non-Greek and non-Roman elements through an upper surface worn thin.'

44 See Boggs 'Gebärde.' Storytellers in traditional societies, however, may use an elaborate repertory of gestures in performance; cf the ethnographic evidence collected in Calame-Griaule 'Pour une étude des gestes narratifs' and 'La gestuelle des conteurs.'

45 See See 'Was ist Heldendichtung?' and the classical statement on Germanic heroic poetry: Heusler *Die altgermanische Dichtung* 150–74. On Celtic epic and saga see Melia 'Parallel Versions.'

46 Međtedović *The Wedding of Smailagić Meho* 143.

47 On the development of the epic from the short heroic lay by 'swelling,' see Heusler *Lied und Epos.*

48 Serbo-Croatian poems of more average length provide only short notes on gestures of emotional expression, couched in poetic stereotypes; cf a weeping family from 'The Captivity of Dulić Ibrahim' as recited by Salih Ugljanin, in Lord, ed and trans *Serbo-Croatian Heroic Songs* vol 1, p 102: 'When the old woman heard these words, she wailed bitterly and cried out: "Alas, my son Dulić the standard-bearer!" She toppled forward and her spirit departed from her; the old woman fainted there in the chamber. And his sister Fata also began to cry out. They began to cry out like poor orphans; they swayed back and forth like swallows; and they wept tears like bereaved mothers.'

49 Cf *laisses* 174–6 of the *Chanson de Roland* and lines 1–7 of the *Poema del Cid.* In the first *laisse* Roland lies down under a pine, places sword and 'olifant' under his body, turns his face towards the heathens, confesses his sins beating his breast, and offers his gauntlet to the Lord in atonement for his sins. The other two *laisses* repeat this with slight modifications: for example, he turns his face towards Spain. The Cid leaves his home weeping and turns his head to look at it once more. He lets his eyes roam over open doors and desolate halls, sighs deeply, and speaks to God, accusing his enemies.

50 Bertoald's 'bale iumente' is not easy to interpret; my translation is based on the reading proposed in Eis 'Das Turisindlied' 174–6.

51 The gesture is ascribed to William the Conqueror at the battle of Hastings by William of Poitiers *Histoire de Guillaume le Conquérant* ii.18 (pp

190–1), by Guy of Amiens *Carmen de Hastingae proelio* lines 447–8, and by the Bayeux tapestry; cf Gibbs-Smith, ed. *The Bayeux Tapestry* plates 39 and 53. The epic background of the tapestry has been established by Dodwell 'The Bayeux Tapestry and the French Secular Epic.' See also William of Malmesbury's description of King Edmund's behaviour on the field at Sherstone, *Gesta regum anglorum* ii.180.

52 Cf Sittl *Die Gebärden der Griechen und Römer* 163–4 and 282–3. In Greek this is the action expressed by the verb γουνάζεσθαι, cf *Odyssey* XXII, lines 310–12 (one of the suitors embraces Odysseus' knee); see also Burkert *Structure and History*, illustrations on 46–7 and note 42 on 164. In Latin see Ammianus Marcellinus, XIV.11,33: 'quam multi splendido loco nati eadem rerum domina coniuuente Viriathi genua sunt amplexi et Spartaci!'

53 Sittl *Die Gebärden der Griechen und Römer* 104.

54 The meaning of the cup in this particular motif is hard to interpret. The gospel gives a few instances of the use of a cup to represent personal destiny, the most famous in Jesus' words in Gethsemane (Matthew 26:39; Mark 14:36; Luke 22:42), but the evidence is insufficient and the Vulgate does not use the word 'poculum' in these passages. Could there be a connection with the phrase 'poculum mortis' which occurs, in Latin and Old English, in Anglo-Saxon literature and remains itself something of a mystery? See Brown '*Poculum Mortis* in Old English,' and Magennis 'The Cup as Symbol and Metaphor.'

55 This general type of miracle, paralysis as punishment, is discussed in Festugière 'Lieux communs littéraires et themes de folk-lore,' especially 146–8. Cf the Hasidic story quoted above on 54.

56 In the work of Gregory of Tours the tendency of the gestural formula to harden into an unchanging cliché extends to all descriptions of physical action and affects representations of considerable complexity. We come upon very specific gestural sequences repeated with minimal alterations to suit different and unrelated contexts: for example, an unsuspecting person is invited to plunge his arm into a chest of treasure and pull out whatever he wants; as he bends over the chest he is murdered or an attempt is made to kill him. The formula fits both the murder of Chloderic by the envoys of Clovis (*HF* II.39) and the attempted murder of Rigunth by her mother (*HF* IX.34). The pattern was first pointed out by Halphen 'Grégoire de Tours, historien de Clovis.' Thürlemann *Der historische Diskurs* 36–7, note 2, quotes a strikingly similar folktale parallel that is also discussed in Geninasca 'Conte populaire et identité du cannibalisme' 225.

57 On Procopius and his literary standards see Hunger *Die hochsprachliche*

profane Literatur der Byzantiner vol 1, pp 291–300, and Averil Cameron *Procopius and the Sixth Century* 19–46.

58 See Severus 'Gebet,' especially cols 1228–34, and Wessel 'Gesten,' especially col 772.

59 This is still in the more literary half of Simeon's biography (see above, 102–3).

60 On immobility see MacMullen 'Some Pictures in Ammianus Marcellinus' 439, and van Dam *Leadership and Community* 61–2. The late antique topos of immobility ('he did not budge') and its extraordinarily complex background, which is military and spiritual, Stoic and Christian, Vergilian and biblical, are explored thoroughly in Fontaine 'Un cliché.'

61 Not, of course, that there is anything like a 'transitional' quality to these texts, which are fully literary and very remote from the oral roots of the style. Psellos (as also Gregory of Tours!) represents the outcome of an evolution, not the process of adaptation and assimilation itself. In Psellos the oral quality has been swallowed up entirely by the man of letters; it reappears in his work entirely transformed.

62 See Brok 'Majestätsfrevel durch Missbrauch des Purpurs.' On the combination of theatre and political calculation in these symbolic dramas of political power, see the evidence gathered by Gadolin *A Theory of History and Society* 114–15 and passim.

63 This is not a new idea. Lommatzsch *System der Gebärden* used miniatures and manuscript illuminations to complement the literary evidence, though the value of his work is compromised seriously by its naively ethnographic aim and the author's constant identification of art with real life. More recently Maguire *Art and Eloquence in Byzantium* has drawn impressively detailed correspondences between rhetoric and pictorial techniques.

64 Brilliant *Gesture and Rank in Roman Art* 163–211, and Garnier *Le langage de l'image au moyen âge* 43–66.

65 See de Bruyne 'L'imposition des mains,' and Korol 'Handauflegung.' An additional sense, the reconciliation of a heretic with the church, is documented in Duchesne's edition of the *Liber pontificalis* vol 1, p 167, note 3.

66 Kötting '*Dextrarum iunctio*.' The action was already used to represent marital concord in Roman sarcophagi of the Antonine period; cf Brilliant *Gesture and Rank in Roman Art* 157–9.

67 Some possible distinctions are outlined in L'Orange '*Sol invictus imperator*' 86–94.

68 On proskynesis, the most recent and fullest iconographic study is Gabel-

mann *Antike Audienz- und Tribunalszenen* 86–104. See also Cutler
Transfigurations 53–110, and the remarks of Festugière *Les moines
d'Orient* III²:110 note 253. Important ethnographic materials for comparison are analysed in Firth 'Gestures and Postures of Respect.'
69 Van Dam *Leadership and Community* chapter 11 (pp 230–55) provides
an original and penetrating discussion of the organization of space
within St Martin's church at Tours as reflected in the narratives of Gregory
of Tours. Gautier Dalché 'La représentation de l'espace' is concerned
exclusively with geographic space.
70 See on the first stages of this loss of the third dimension Kitzinger
Byzantine Art in the Making 45–65. A general discussion is found in
Bunim *Space in Medieval Painting* 38–61.
71 Volbach *Elfenbeinarbeiten der Spätantike* plates 26, 29, 106, and pp
47–8, 51, and 134; Gaborit-Chopin *Ivoires du moyen âge* 50–2.

CHAPTER FOUR

1 Jolles *Einfache Formen* 32–3, 61, 90, 124–5, and passim.
2 See Petsch 'Die Lehre von den "Einfachen Formen," ' Mohr 'Einfache
Formen,' and Ranke 'Einfache Formen.' None of them has anything to
say for or against Jolles' theory of the relation of things to literary
genres.
3 A similar object combines comparable didactic use with a wholly different
meaning in one of the most famous works of early Christian literature,
the *Passio Perpetuae*. The martyr's own statement begins with the following dialogue in prison between her and her father, who attempts
to make her abjure her faith: ' "Cum adhuc" inquit "cum prosecutoribus
essemus et me pater verbis evertere cupiret et deicere pro sua affectione
perseveraret: 'Pater,' inquam, 'vides verbi gratia vas hoc iacens, urceo-
lum sive aliud?' Et dixit: 'Video'. Et ego dixi ei: 'Numquid alio nomine
vocari potest quam quod est?' Et ait: 'Non'. 'Sic et ego aliud me dicere
non possum nisi quod sum, Christiana.' " ' / ' "While we were still under
arrest," she said, "my father tried to lead me astray with words, and
attempted insistently to overturn my resolve because of his affection for
me. I said to him: 'Father, do you see for instance that vessel there, a
water-bowl or something of the sort?' And he said: 'I see it.' I asked him:
'Can it be called by any other name than what it is?' He answered: 'No.'
'So I too cannot call myself anything other than what I am: a Christian' " '
(*Passio sanctarum Perpetuae et Felicitatis* chapter 3).
4 On the interpretation of this vision see Alföldi 'Hoc signo victor eris,'

and the critical summary in Vogt 'Constantinus der Große,' especially cols
318–25. On the aims of Eusebius in the *Vita Constantini* see Barnes
Eusebius and Constantine 261–71.

5 Rodgers 'Constantine's Pagan Vision.'

6 Cechelli *Il trionfo della croce*. On early medieval iconography of the
cross in the visual arts, see Henderson *Early Medieval* 201–38.

7 *Vie de Saint Martin* vol 2 (Commentaire [jusqu'a *Vita* 19]): 473–509,
especially 478, 484–5.

8 Leclercq 'Chape de Saint Martin.'

9 'Histoires des solitaires égyptiens' no 358, and Nisterus 4 in the alphabetic
collection (*PG* 65, col 308). See also *Vie de Saint Martin* vol 1 (introduction, texte et traduction): 185–8, and Fontaine 'King Sisebut's *Vita Desiderii*' 115.

10 It probably also shows Clovis beginning to move away from the more
'democratic' attitudes of a warlord towards true monarchy; this development is dramatized by the distribution of plunder, a moment of assumed
equality, and is the reason for the attack on the ewer. Cf Kurth *Clovis*
vol 1, pp 241–4, and Tessier *Le baptême de Clovis* 84.

11 These contradictions can be explained as the outcome of two irreconcilable
legendary types: Chrodechild as saint, a view of her strongly developed
by Gregory's time, and her image as a vindictive Germanic princess who
could pressure her sons and her Frankish vassals to take revenge on her
Burgundian relatives (cf *HF* iii.6; *CF* iii.19; *LHF* 12 [on which see above,
90–1] where the same elements appear in conflict in one speech attributed to Chrodechild).

12 Chydenius 'The Theory of Medieval Symbolism.'

13 Could this part of the story be influenced by the folktale situation in
which a heroine sees herself forced to keep silent, or to deny a charge
she knows is true? This predicament comes up frequently as a blind
motif in popular storytelling; cf Lüthi *Das Volksmärchen als Dichtung*
80–1.

14 Holum *Theodosian Empresses* 176–94.

15 The sense of erotic choice that goes back to the story of the judgment of
Paris is also present here; it has other manifestations in Byzantine
literature, and in all of them the fruit is called specifically 'μῆλον.' See
Littlewood, 'The Symbolism of the Apple,' especially 46–8.

16 On Moschos' literary elaboration of oral-traditional material, see Maisano
'Tradizione orale e sviluppi narrativi.'

17 *Bibliotheca* 199: 'The style of the language sinks to a lower and more
elementary level than that of the previous work.' The work referred to,
Bibliotheca 198, is a collection of *apophthegmata patrum* which seems

very similar if not identical to the anonymous collection published by Nau as 'Histoires des solitaires égyptiens.'

18 Though the Greek fathers gave enormous importance to the examination of conscience, there is hardly any explicit reference to it in monastic literature before the fifth century; cf Guy 'Examen de conscience.'

19 The episode follows the scenic formula called by Fontaine 'le prophète chez le roi' (see above chapter one, note 9). On the political significance of this confrontation between Masona and Leovigild, see Collins 'Mérida and Toledo: 550–85.'

20 See above chapter two, note 8. It is possible that this scene in the story of Alboin and Rosimund is simply *modelled* on Germanic legends, that is, that it makes use of this scheme without having a heroic lay as its direct source. Cf for instance the story of Ingeld (*Beowulf* lines 2020–68), where the tribal feud interrupted by the marriage of the hero erupts again with greater violence when one of his men sees a warrior in his wife's retinue sporting a sword that had been taken from his own people in the past. On the putative lay of Rosimund and its origin see Gschwantler 'Die Heldensage von Alboin und Rosimund.'

21 The equation seems to be international and very ancient; it is represented in the etymology of numerous names for the cranium; cf Walde, *Lateinisches etymologisches Wörterbuch* sv *caput*; von Wartburg *Französisches etymologisches Wörterbuch* sv *těsta*; compare also with more recent compounds such as German *Gehirnschale* and English *brainpan*. See also Löfstedt *Syntactica II* 352, and Benveniste *Problèmes* 295–6. On the use of crania as drinking vessels, see Andree 'Menschenschädel als Trinkgefässe.' See also Goffart *The Narrators of Barbarian History* 392, note 198.

22 Focke 'Szepter und Krummstab,' especially 373, and Kleinschmidt *Untersuchungen* 138–46.

23 The image goes back to *The Consolation of Philosophy* ii.2, 9, but it is not rendered in visual terms until the eleventh century; see Pickering *Literatur und darstellende Kunst* 112–45, and Kitzinger 'World Map and Fortune's Wheel,' especially 361–9.

24 The anecdote may have been inspired by Procopius *De bello Vandalico* ii.vii.14–17, where friends of the Vandal king Gelimer interpret his immoderate laughter as he surrenders to Belisarius.

25 See Wessel, Piltz, Nicolescu 'Insignien,' and Schramm *Herrschaftszeichen und Staatssymbolik*; see also Bak 'Medieval Symbology of the State.' Nelson 'Symbols in Context' discusses the giving of meaning to 'things' by insertion in ritual, insisting on the relevance of material and economic aspects of the objects and substances in question to the symbolic

functions they take on: the oil used in rulers' inauguration rituals, for example, gets to have different meanings in Byzantium and the West because of its availability in the Eastern Mediterranean and scarcity in Northwestern Europe.

26 Alföldi 'Insignien und Tracht,' and Pertusi 'Insigne del potere sovrano'; see also Elze 'Insegne del potere sovrano,' and Grabar 'Zur Geschichte von Sphaira, Globus und Reichsapfel.'

27 Averil Cameron 'The Byzantine Sources of Gregory of Tours' argues persuasively that this passage in *HF* is derived from a Byzantine chronicle; this would explain to some degree Gregory's unwonted emphasis on the insignia.

28 Amira *Der Stab in der germanischen Rechtssymbolik.*

29 Du Cange *Glossarium* sv *investitura.*

30 Ourliac and de Malafosse *Droit romain et ancien droit* vol 1, pp 58–9.

31 Ogris 'festuca.'

32 Gregory the Great, however, still makes an explicit distinction between bodies and other relics; cf *Dialogues* ii.38, where the deacon Peter asks why the martyrs 'non tanta per sua corpora, quanta beneficia per reliquias ostendant' / 'do not perform as many miracles through their bodies as through relics.'

33 This is the *theory* of the relic, so to speak. The proliferation of fragments of the cross and of forgeries later on should not obscure the fact that authenticity was always desired and claimed. On authentication, see Leclercq 'Reliques et reliquaires,' especially cols 2338–46, and also Heinzelmann *Translationsberichte* 83–8.

34 Fichtenau 'Zum Reliquienwesen,' especially 77. On relic theft in general see Geary *Furta Sacra.*

35 See Brown 'Relics and Social Status' and *The Cult of the Saints* 30–6.

36 Graus *Volk, Herrscher und Heiliger* 182.

37 Geary 'L'humiliation des saints.'

38 Saxer *Morts martyres reliques* 230–79 is excellent on the narrative expressions of the relic cult in the earliest period.

39 See Heinzelmann *Translationsberichte.*

40 On the political meaning of this act, see Sot 'Arguments hagiographiques' 100–1.

41 Cf Hrdličková 'Japanese Professional Storytellers' 174–6, on the multi-purpose props of the storyteller's trade.

42 Lüthi *Das europäische Volksmärchen* 26–9, and 'Märchen und Sage,' especially 35–6.

43 Leclercq 'Chandelier,' and Bouras 'Lighting Devices.'

44 On the symbolic relation of the candles to the 'ardent' spirit of Galla,

see de Vogüé's remark in his edition, Grégoire le Grand *Dialogues* vol 3, p 56, note 2.

45 The incident is narrated and explained in Guillou *Régionalisme et indépendance* 205–6.

46 Cf the account in Constantine Porphyrogenitus *De administrando imperio* chapter 29, where the head, however, does not play a role.

47 The paradox is much more acute with an unattached head than with a corpse, still too similar to the living person to be put to use, transformed into a missile or a goblet. The dread and wonder this image inspires is not medieval, but timeless; we hear it again in the last page of Marguerite Yourcenar's recent essay on Yukio Mishima, *Mishima ou la vision du vide*, where she describes a photograph of the heads of the novelist and one of his followers after their ritual suicide in 1970 at the headquarters of the Japanese army: 'Deux têtes sur le tapis sans doute acrylique du bureau du général, placées l'une à côté de l'autre comme des quilles, se touchant presque. ... Les jugements de valeur, qu'ils soient moraux, politiques ou esthétiques sont en leur présence, momentanément du moins, réduits au silence. La notion qui s'impose est plus déroutante et plus simple: parmi les myriades de choses qui sont, et qui ont été, ces deux têtes ont été; elles sont. ... Deux objets, débris déjà quasi inorganiques de structures détruites, et qui, eux aussi, ne seront plus une fois passés par le feu, que résidus minéraux et cendres; pas meme sujets de méditation, parce que les données nous manquent pour méditer sur eux' (124–5).

CONCLUSION

1 On the internal, non-generic implications of this evolution, see the provocative remarks of Shepherd 'The Emancipation of Story.'

2 As so often in the *Vie*, the point Joinville ends up making does not seem to be what he set out to prove. The simplicity of the king's attire becomes a mere side issue. Led astray by the temptation to make his own reply the focus of the scene, Joinville turns the episode into a dogmatic defence of hereditary rank and its symbols.

3 Cf above, 152–3, and 238, note 49. In the case of Roland, a symbolic object, the gauntlet which he hands back to God, is implicated in the gesture. In the same way, when the Cid turns around for a last look at his house, he gives the poet a chance to mention the empty falcon-stands, an eloquent symbol of desolation, banishment, and joy turned into sorrow.

4 Frings *Brautwerbung*.

5 Fromm 'Die Erzählkunst des *Rother*-Epikers.'
6 Gregory of Tours *Liber vitae patrum* xx.i (De Sancto Leobardo reclauso): 'Denique dato sponsae anulo, porregit osculo, praebet calciamentum, caelebrat sponsaliae diem festum.' / 'Having given his fiancée the ring, he kisses her, provides her with shoes, and celebrates the betrothal on a feast day.'

Bibliography

ABBREVIATIONS

DACL	*Dictionnaire d'archeologie chrétienne et de liturgie.* Ed F. Cabrol, H. Leclercq, and H.I. Marrou. 15 vols. Paris: Letouzey & Ané, 1907–51
MGH	*Monumenta Germaniae historica*
LNG	*Leges nationum Germanicarum*
SSRG	*Scriptores rerum Germanicarum ad usum scholarum*
SSRL	*Scriptores rerum Langobardicarum et Italicarum saec.* VI–IX
SSRM	*Scriptores rerum Merovingicarum*
Settimane	*Settimane di studio del centro italiano di studi sull'alto medioevo*

PRIMARY SOURCES

Latin

Agnellus
    Agnelli qui et Andreas liber pontificalis ecclesiae Ravennatis. Ed O. Holder-Egger. MGH, SSRL. Hannover: Hahn 1878; rpt 1964
Alcuin
    Alcuin. The Bishops, Kings and Saints of York. Ed Peter Godman. Oxford: Clarendon Press 1982
Ammianus
    Ammianus Marcellinus. *Res Gestae.* Ed W. Seyfarth. 2 vols. Leipzig: Teubner 1978
Augustine
    Sancti Augustini confessionum libri xiii. Ed Lucas Verheijen OSA. Corpus christianorum; series latina 27. Turnhout: Brepols 1981

Sancti Aurelii Augustini de doctrina christiana libri iv. Ed Joseph Martin. Corpus christianorum; series latina 32. Turnhout: Brepols 1962
Bede
Venerabilis Baedae historia ecclesiastica gentis Anglorum. Ed Charles Plummer. Oxford: Clarendon Press 1896; rpt 1969
Boethius
Boethius consolationis Philosophiae libri v. Ed Karl Buchner. 2nd ed. Heidelberg: Carl Winter 1960
Corippus
Flavii Cresconii Corippi Iohannidos seu de bellis Libycis libri viii. Ed J. Diggle and F.R.D. Goodyear. Cambridge: Cambridge University Press 1970
Flavius Cresconius Corippus. *In laudem Iustini Augusti minoris libri iv*. Ed and trans Averil Cameron. London: Athlone Press 1976
Fredegar
Chronicarum quae dicuntur Fredegarii scholastici libri iv. Ed Bruno Krusch. *MGH, SSRM*, vol 2. Hannover: Hahn 1888; rpt 1956
Gregory the Great
Grégoire le Grand. *Dialogues*. Ed and commentary Adalbert de Vogüé; trans Paul Antin. Sources chrétiennes 251, 260, 265. Paris: Editions du Cerf 1978–80
Gregory of Tours
Gregorii episcopi Turonensis libri historiarum x. Ed Bruno Krusch and Wilhelm Levison. *MGH, SSRM*, vol 1.1. Hannover: Hahn 1951
Gregorii episcopi Turonensis historiarum libri decem. Ed Rudolf Buchner. 2 vols. Berlin: Rutten & Loening, nd (This edition is not quoted, but only used for some of its notes.)
Liber vitae patrum in *Gregorii episcopi Turonensis miracula et opera minora*. Ed Bruno Krusch. *MGH, SSRM*, vol 1.2. Hannover: Hahn 1885; rpt 1969
Guy of Amiens
Guy of Amiens. *Carmen de Hastingae proelio*. Ed C. Morton and H. Muntz. Oxford: Clarendon Press 1972
Jerome
Hieronymi vita Hilarionis. Ed A.A.R. Bastiaensen. In *Vita di Martino; vita di Ilarione; In memoria di Paola*. Introduction by Christine Mohrmann; ed A.A.R. Bastiaensen and Jan W. Smit; trans Luca Canali and Claudio Moreschini. Milano: Fondazione Lorenzo Valla: Mondadori 1975
Lex Salica
Pactus legis Salicae. Ed Karl August Eckhardt. *MGH, LNG*, vol 4.1. Hannover: Hahn 1962.

249   Bibliography

Liber historiae Francorum
   Liber historiae Francorum. Ed Bruno Krusch. *MGH, SSRM*, vol 2. Hannover:
   Hahn 1888; rpt 1956
Liber pontificalis
   Le Liber pontificalis. Ed L. Duchesne. Bibliothèque des écoles françaises
   d'Athènes et de Rome: ser 2. v 3. 2 vols. Paris: E. Thorin 1886–92; rpt
   E. de Boccard 1955
Livy
   Titi Livi ab urbe condita. Tomus I. Libri I–V. Ed R.M. Ogilvie. Oxford:
   Clarendon Press 1974
   Titi Livi ab urbe condita. Tomus II. Libri VI–X. Ed C.F. Walters and R.S.
   Conway. Oxford: Clarendon Press 1919; rpt 1970
Notker
   Notker der Stammler. *Taten Kaiser Karls des Grossen*. Ed Hans F. Haefele.
   MGH, Scriptores rerum Germanicarum, nova series xii. Berlin: Weidmann
   1962
Ordo Romanus primus
   Ordo Romanus primus in *Les Ordines Romani du haut moyen âge. Vol.
   2. Les Textes (Ordines I–XIII)*. Ed Michel Andrieu. Louvain: 'Spicilegium
   sacrum Lovaniense' 1948
Orosius
   Pauli Orosii historiarum adversum paganos libri vii. Ed C. Zangemeister.
   Corpus scriptorum ecclesiasticorum Latinorum, vol 5. Vienna: Gerold
   1882
Passio Perpetuae
   Passio sanctarum Perpetuae et Felicitatis. Ed J.M.J. van Beek. Nijmegen:
   Dekker & v.d. Vegt 1936
Sallust
   C. Sallusti Crispi Catilina. Iugurtha. Fragmenta ampliora. Ed A. Kurfess.
   3rd ed. Leipzig: Teubner 1957
Stephen of Ripon
   Vita Wilfridi I. episcopi Eboracensis auctore Stephano. *MGH, SSRM*, vol
   6. Hannover and Leipzig: Hahn 1913
Suetonius
   C. Suetoni Tranquilli de vita caesarum libri viii. Ed M. Ihm. Stuttgart:
   Teubner 1978
Sulpicius Severus
   Sulpice Sévère. *Vie de Saint Martin*. Ed, trans, and commentary Jacques
   Fontaine. Sources chrétiennes 133–5. Paris: Editions du Cerf 1967–9
   Dialogi in *Sulpici Severi libri qui supersunt*. Ed Karl Helm. Corpus scrip-
   torum ecclesiasticorum Latinorum, vol 1. Vienna: Gerold 1866

Vergil
  P. Vergili Maronis Aeneidos libri xii. Ed Remigio Sabbadini, rev A. Castig-
  lioni. Torino: Paravia 1944; rpt 1970
Vitas sanctorum patrum Emeretensium
  The Vitas sanctorum patrum Emeretensium. Ed, trans, and commentary
  Joseph N. Garvin. Washington: Catholic University of America Press 1946
Vulgate
  Biblia sacra iuxta vulgatam versionem. Ed Robert Weber OSB. Stuttgart:
  Deutsche Bibelgesellschaft 1983
  Translation [Douay version]: *The Holy Bible Translated from the Latin
  Vulgate.* Baltimore: John Murphy 1914
Waltharius
  Waltharius of Gaeraldus. Ed A.K. Bate. Reading University Medieval and
  Renaissance Texts. Reading: Department of Classics, University of Read-
  ing 1978
Widukind
  Die Sachsengeschichte des Widukind von Korvei. Ed Paul Hirsch and H.E.
  Lohmann. 5th ed. *MGH, SSRG.* Hannover: Hahn 1935; rpt 1977
William of Malmesbury
  Willelmi Malmesbiriensis monachi de gestis regum Anglorum libri quinque.
  Ed William Stubbs. Vol. 1. Rolls Series 90. London: Her Majesty's Station-
  ery Office 1887; rpt 1964
William of Poitiers
  Guillaume de Poitiers. *Histoire de Guillaume le Conquérant.* Ed Raymonde
  Foreville. Les Classiques de l'histoire de France au moyen âge. Paris:
  Société d'édition 'Les Belles Lettres' 1952

    Greek

apophthegmata patrum; alphabetic
  Apophthegmata patrum in *Patrologiae cursus completus;* series graeca
  prior, vol 65, cols 71–440. Paris: J.P. Migne 1864
apophthegmata patrum; anonymous
  'Histoires des solitaires égyptiens'. Ed F. Nau. *Revue de l'orient chrétien*
  12–14 (1907–9) and 17–18 (1912–13)
Constantine Porphyrogenitus
  Constantine Porphyrogenitus. *De administrando imperio.* Ed Gy. Moravcsik,
  trans R.J.H. Jenkins. New, revised ed. Washington DC: Dumbarton Oaks
  Center for Byzantine Studies 1967
  *Constantini Pophyrogeniti imperatoris de cerimoniis aulae byzantinae
  libri duo.* Ed J.J. Reiske. 2 vols. Bonn: Weber 1829

Dionysius of Halicarnassus
   Dionysi Halicarnasensis antiquitatum Romanarum quae supersunt.
   Ed C. Jacoby. 4 vols. Leipzig: Teubner 1885–1905
Eusebius of Caesarea
   Über das Leben des Kaisers Konstantin. Ed Friedhelm Winkelmann.
   Eusebius Werke vol 1.1. Berlin: Akademie Verlag 1975
Homer
   Homeri opera. Ed Thomas W. Allen. 2nd ed. 5 vols. Oxford: Clarendon
   Press 1913; rpt 1966
Leontios of Neapolis
   Das Leben des heiligen Narren Symeon von Leontios von Neapolis.
   Ed Lennart Ryden. Stockholm: Almqvist & Wiksell 1963
Malalas
   Ioannis Malalae chronographia. Ed L. Dindorf. Bonn: Weber 1831
Maximus Confessor
   S. Maximi confessoris mystagogia in *Patrologiae cursus completus;* series
   graeca prior, vol 91; cols 657–718. Paris: J.P. Migne 1865
Moschos
   Bloemlezing uit het Pratum spirituale van Johannes Moschos. Ed D.C.
   Hesseling. Aetatis imperatoriae scriptores Graeci et Latini adnotationibus
   instructi, vol 2. Utrecht: G.J.A. Ruys 1916
Photius
   Photius. *Bibliothèque.* Ed and trans René Henry. 8 vols. Paris: 'Les Belles
   Lettres' 1959–77
Procopius
   Procopii Caesariensis opera omnia. Ed J. Haury, rev G. Wirth. 4 vols.
   Leipzig: Teubner 1962–4
Psellos
   Michel Psellos. *Chronographie, ou histoire d'un siècle de Byzance.*
   (976–1077). Ed Emile Renauld. 2 vols. Paris: 'Les Belles Lettres' 1926–8
Septuagint
   Septuaginta, id est vetus testamentum graece iuxta lxx interpretes. Ed
   Alfred Rahlfs. 2 vols. Stuttgart: Privilegierte Württembergische Bibelanstalt
   1935
Sophronius of Jerusalem
   Sophronii patriarchae Hierosolymitani commentarius liturgicus in *Patrol-
   ogiae cursus completus;* series graeca prior, vol 87[3], cols 3981–4002. Paris:
   J.P. Migne 1865
[Life of] Theodore of Sykeon
   Vie de Théodore de Sykéôn. Ed A.J. Festugière OP. 2 vols. Subsidia hagio-
   graphica 48. Bruxelles: Société des Bollandistes 1970

Theophanes Confessor
  Theophanis chronographia. Ed C. de Boor. 2 vols. Leipzig: Teubner 1883–5

  Vernacular

Beowulf
  Beowulf and The Fight at Finnsburg. Ed Fr. Klaeber. 3rd ed with first and
  second supplements. Lexington, Mass: D.C. Heath and Company 1922;
  rpt 1950
Chaucer
  The Works of Geoffrey Chaucer. Ed F.N. Robinson. 2nd ed. Boston:
  Houghton Mifflin 1957
Cid
  Poema de Mio Cid. Ed and commentary Ian Michael. 2nd ed. Madrid:
  Castalia 1978
Edda
  Edda: Die Lieder des Codex Regius nebst verwandten Denkmälern. Ed
  Gustav Neckel and Hans Kuhn. 4th ed. Heidelberg: Carl Winter 1962
Gottfried von Strassburg
  Gottfried von Strassburg. *Tristan und Isold.* Ed Friedrich Ranke. 15th ed.
  Dublin/Zürich: Weidmann 1970
Joinville
  La Vie de Saint Louis. Le témoignage de Jehan, seigneur de Joinville. Ed
  Noel L. Corbett. Sherbrooke, Québec: Naaman 1977
Nibelungenlied
  Das Nibelungenlied. Ed Karl Bartsch. 20th ed, ed Helmut de Boor. Wies-
  baden: Brockhaus 1972
Roland
  The Song of Roland: An Analytical Edition. Ed and trans Gerald J. Brault.
  2 vols. University Park/London: Pennsylvania State University Press
  1978
Rother
  Rother. Ed Jan de Vries. 2nd, unrevised ed. Heidelberg: Carl Winter 1974
Wolfram von Eschenbach
  Wolfram von Eschenbach. *Parzival.* Ed Albert Leitzmann. 7th ed, rev Wilhelm
  Deinert. Altdeutsche Textbibliothek 12–14. Tübingen: Niemeyer 1961–5

  SECONDARY LITERATURE

Alföldi, Andreas. 'Die Ausgestaltung des monarchischen Zeremoniells am
  römischen Kaiserhofe.' *Mitteilungen des deutschen archaeologischen In-*

stituts: Römische Abteilung 49 (1934) 3–118; rpt in Andreas Alföldi. *Die monarchische Repräsentation im römischen Kaiserreiche.* Darmstadt: Wissenschaftliche Buchgesellschaft 1970; pp 3–118
– 'Insignien und Tracht der römischen Kaiser.' *Mitteilungen des deutschen archaeologischen Instituts; Römische Abteilung* 50 (1935) 1–171; rpt in Andreas Alföldi. *Die monarchische Repräsentation im römischen Kaiserreiche.* Darmstadt: Wissenschaftliche Buchgesellschaft 1970; pp 121–276
– 'Hoc signo victor eris. Beiträge zur Geschichte der Bekehrung Konstantins des Großen.' *Pisciculi. Studien zur Religion und Kultur des Altertums Franz Joseph Dölger zum sechzigsten Geburtstag dargeboten von Freunden, Verehrern und Schülern.* Ed Th. Klauser and A. Rücker. *Antike und Christentum.* Ergänzungsband 1. Münster: Verlag Aschendorff 1939; pp 1–18
Alter, Robert. *The Art of Biblical Narrative.* New York: Basic Books / Harper 1981
Aly, Wolf. *Volksmärchen, Sage und Novelle bei Herodot und seinen Zeitgenossen.* 2nd revised ed. Göttingen: Vandenhoeck and Ruprecht 1969
Amira, Karl von. *Der Stab in der germanischen Rechtssymbolik. Abhandlungen der Königlich Bayerischen Akademie der Wissenschaften; Philosophisch-philologisch und historische Klasse.* Vol 25, Abhandlung 1. München: Verlag der Königlich Bayerischen Akademie der Wissenschaften 1909
Andersson, Theodore M. 'Cassiodorus and the Gothic Legend of Ermanaric.' *Euphorion* 57 (1963) 28–43
– 'The Textual Evidence for an Oral Family Saga.' *Arkiv för nordisk Filologi* 81 (1966) 1–23
Andree, Richard. 'Menschenschädel als Trinkgefässe.' *Zeitschrift des Vereins für Volkskunde* 22 (1912) 1–33
Auerbach, Erich. *Mimesis. Dargestellte Wirklichkeit in der abendländischen Literatur.* Bern: Francke 1946
– *Literatursprache und Publikum in der lateinischen Spätantike und im Mittelalter.* Bern: Francke 1958
Ayres, R.H. *Language, Logic and Reason in the Church Fathers.* Hildesheim and New York: Georg Olms Verlag 1979
Bak, J.M. 'Medieval Symbology of the State; Percy E. Schramm's Contribution.' *Viator* 4 (1973) 33–63
Baldwin, Barry. 'Latin in Byzantium.' *From Late Antiquity to Early Byzantium.* Proceedings of the Byzantinological Symposium in the 16th International Eirene Conference. Ed Vladimír Vavřínek. Prague: Academia 1985; pp 237–41
Barnes, T.D. *Eusebius and Constantine.* Cambridge, Mass: Harvard University Press 1981

254   Bibliography

Barthes, Roland. 'Structure du fait divers.' *Médiations* 5 (1962) 27–36; rpt in
Roland Barthes. *Essais critiques*. Paris: Seuil 1964; pp 188–97
– *La chambre claire. Note sur la photographie*. Paris: Gallimard Seuil 1980
Bauer, J.B. 'Novellistisches bei Hieronymus Vita Pauli 3.' *Wiener Studien*
74 (1961) 130–7
Beck, Hans-Georg. 'Zur byzantinischen "Mönchschronik." ' *Speculum
historiale. Geschichte im Spiegel von Geschichtsschreibung und
Geschichtsdeutung*. Ed Clemens Bauer, Laetitia Boehm, and Max Müller.
Freiburg / München: Verlag Karl Alber 1965; pp 188–97
Benveniste, Emile. *Problemes de linguistique générale*. Paris: Gallimard
1966
Berschin, Walter. *Griechisch-lateinisches Mittelalter. Von Hieronymus zu
Nikolaus von Kues*. Bern: Francke 1980
Bertolini, Ottorino. 'Sergio arcivescovo di Ravenna (744–769) e i papi del suo
tempo.' *Studi Romagnoli* 1 (1950) 43–88
Beumann, Helmut. *Widukind von Korvei. Untersuchungen zur
Geschichtsschreibung und Ideengeschichte des 10. Jahrhunderts*. Weimar:
Hermann Bohlaus Nachfolger 1950
– 'Gregor von Tours und der Sermo Rusticus.' *Spiegel der Geschichte.
Festgabe für Max Braubach zum 10. April 1964*. Ed Konrad Repgen and
Stephan Skalweit. Münster West.: Verlag Aschendorff [1964]; pp 69–98
Billanovich, Giuseppe. 'Dal Livio di Raterio (Laur. 63, 19) al Livio di Petrarca
(B.M. Harl. 2493).' *Italia medievale e umanistica* 2 (1959) 103–78
Billanovich, Guido. *Lamperto di Hersfeld e Tito Livio*. Padua: Casa editrice
Dott. Antonio Milani 1945
Blänsdorf, Jürgen. 'Aeneadas rursus cupiunt resonare Camenae. Vergils epische
Form in der Johannis des Corippus.' *Monumentum Chiloniense; Studien
zur augusteischen Zeit. Kieler Festschrift für Erich Burck zum 70.
Geburtstag*. Ed Eckard Lefèvre. Amsterdam: A. Hakkert 1975; pp 524–45
Boggs, R.S. 'Gebärde.' *Handwörterbuch des deutschen Märchens*. Ed L.
Mackensen. Berlin: De Gruyter 1934–40; vol 2, pp 318–22
Bolaffi, Ezio. *Sallustio e la sua fortuna nei secoli*. Roma: Perrella 1949
Bouras, Laskarina. 'Lighting Devices.' *Dictionary of the Middle Ages*. Vol 7,
'Italian Renaissance – Mabinogi.' Ed Joseph R. Strayer. New York: Scribner
1986; pp 574–9
Bousset, Wilhelm. *Apophthegmata. Studien zur Geschichte des ältesten
Mönchtums*. Ed Theodor Hermann and Gustav Krüger. Tübingen: J.C.B.
Mohr 1923
Brilliant, Richard. *Gesture and Rank in Roman Art. Memoirs of the Con-
necticut Academy of Arts and Sciences* 14 (1963)

Brok, M.F.A. 'Majestätsfrevel durch Missbrauch des Purpurs (Ammianus Marcellinus 16, 8, 8).' *Latomus* 41 (1982) 356–61

Brown, Carleton. '*Poculum Mortis* in Old English.' *Speculum* 15 (1940) 356–61

Brown, Peter. *Religion and Society in the Age of Saint Augustine.* London: Faber and Faber 1972

– 'Relics and Social Status in the Age of Gregory of Tours.' Stenton Lecture 1976. University of Reading 1977

– *The Making of Late Antiquity.* Cambridge, Mass: Harvard University Press 1978

– *The Cult of the Saints: Its Rise and Function in Latin Christianity.* Chicago: University of Chicago Press 1981

Brown, T.J. 'An Historical Introduction to the Use of Classical Latin Authors in the British Isles from the Fifth to the Eleventh Century.' *La cultura antica nell'occidente latino dal VII all'XI secolo. Settimane* XXII. Spoleto 1975; pp 237–93

Browning, Robert. 'The "Low Level" Saint's Life in the Early Byzantine World.' *The Byzantine Saint.* University of Birmingham Fourteenth Spring Symposium of Byzantine Studies. Ed Sergei Hackel. London: Fellowship of St Alban and St Sergius 1981; pp 117–27

Brunhölzl, Franz. *Geschichte der lateinischen Literatur des Mittelalters. Erster Band. Von Cassiodor bis zum Ausklang der karolingischen Erneuerung.* München: Wilhelm Fink Verlag 1975

Bruyne, Luc de. See de Bruyne, Luc.

Bullough, D.A. 'The Educational Tradition in England from Alfred to Aelfric.' *La scuola nell'occidente latino dell'alto medioevo. Settimane* XIX. Spoleto 1972; pp 453–94

– ' "Imagines Regum" and Their Significance in the Early Medieval West.' *Studies in Memory of David Talbot Rice.* Ed Giles Robertson and George Henderson. Edinburgh: Edinburgh University Press 1975; pp 223–76

Bunim, M.S. *Space in Medieval Painting and the Forerunners of Perspective.* New York: Columbia University Press 1940

Burck, Erich. *Die Erzählungskunst bei T. Livius.* Berlin: Weidmann 1934

Burkert, Walter. *Structure and History in Greek Mythology and Ritual.* Berkeley: University of California Press 1979

Bury, J.B. 'The Ceremonial Book of Constantine Porphyrogennetos.' *English Historical Review* 86 (1907) 209–27 and 417–39

Calame-Griaule, Geneviève. 'Pour une étude des gestes narratifs.' *Langage et cultures africaines.* Ed Geneviève Calame-Griaule. Paris: Maspero 1977; pp 195–215

– 'La gestuelle des conteurs: état d'une recherche.' *Oralità; cultura, letteratura, discorso.* Atti del Convegno Internazionale (Urbino 21–25 luglio 1980). Ed Bruno Gentili and Giuseppe Paioni. Rome: Edizioni dell'Ateneo 1985; pp 301–11

Cameron, Alan. 'The Empress and the Poet: Paganism and Politics at the Court of Theodosius II.' *Yale Classical Studies* 27 (1982) 217–89

Cameron, Averil. 'The Byzantine Sources of Gregory of Tours.' *Journal of Theological Studies* 26 (1975) 421–6

– 'The Career of Corippus Again.' *Classical Quarterly* 30 (1980) 534–9

– *Procopius and the Sixth Century.* London: Duckworth 1985

Cechelli, Carlo. *Il trionfo della croce; la croce e i santi segni prima e dopo Constantino.* Roma: Edizione Paoline 1954

Chadwick, H. *Boethius. The Consolations of Music, Logic, Theology, and Philosophy.* Oxford: Clarendon Press 1981

Charhadi, Driss ben Hamed. *A Life Full of Holes.* Trans Paul Bowles. New York: Grove Press 1964

Chydenius, Johan. 'The Theory of Medieval Symbolism.' *Societas scientiarum Fennica; Commentationes humanarum litterarum* 27 (1961) 1–42

Clover, Carol J. 'Scene in Saga Composition.' *Arkiv för nordisk Filologi* 89 (1974) 57–83

– 'The Long Prose Form.' *Arkiv för nordisk Filologi* 101 (1986) 10–39

Collins, Roger. 'Mérida and Toledo: 550–585.' *Visigothic Spain.* Ed Edward James. Oxford: Clarendon Press 1980; pp 189–219

Constable, Giles. See Kazhdan, Alexander.

Curtius, Ernst Robert. *Europäische Literatur und lateinisches Mittelalter.* Bern: Francke 1948

Cutler, Anthony. *Transfigurations: Studies in the Dynamics of Byzantine Iconography.* Pennsylvania State University 1975

Dagron, Gilbert. 'Aux origines de la civilisation byzantine: langue de culture et langue d'Etat.' *Revue historique* 241 (1969) 23–56

de Bruyne, Luc. 'L'imposition des mains dans l'art chrétien ancien. Contribution iconologique à l'histoire du geste.' *Rivista di archeologia cristiana* 20 (1943) 113–278

Diaz y Diaz, Manuel C. 'La trasmisión de los textos antiguos en la península ibérica en los siglos VII–XI.' *La cultura antica nell'occidente latino dal VII all'XI secolo. Settimane* XXII. Spoleto 1975; pp 133–75

Dill, Samuel. *Roman Society in Gaul in the Merovingian Age.* London: Macmillan 1926

Dodwell, C.R. 'The Bayeux Tapestry and the French Secular Epic.' *Burlington Magazine* 108: 764 (November 1966) 549–60

Dölger, Franz. 'Europas Gestaltung im Spiegel der fränkisch-byzantinischen

Auseinandersetzung des 9. Jahrhunderts.' *Der Vertrag von Verdun. Neun Aufsätze zur Begründung der europäischen Völker-und Staatenwelt.* Ed Th. Mayer. Leipzig: Koehler and Amelang 1943; pp 203–73; rpt in Franz Dölger. *Byzanz und die europäische Staatenwelt.* München: Buch-Kunst Verlag Ettal 1953; pp 282–369

Du Cange, Ch. Du Fresne dom. *Glossarium mediae et infimae latinitatis.* 10 vols. Paris: Librairie des sciences et des arts 1937–8

Ehlers, Wilhelm. 'Epische Kunst in Coripps Johannis.' *Philologus* 124 (1980) 109–35

Eis, Gerhard. 'Zum Turisindlied.' *Zeitschrift für deutsches Altertum* 79 (1942) 167–77

Elze, Reinhard. 'Insegne del potere sovrano e delegato in occidente.' *Simboli e simbologia nell'alto medioevo. Settimane* xxiii. Spoleto 1976; pp 569–93

Fasoli, Gina. 'Rileggendo il "Liber Pontificalis" de Agnello Ravennate.' *La storiografia altomedievale. Settimane* xvii. Spoleto 1970; pp 457–95

Festugière, A.J. 'Lieux communs littéraires et themes de folk-lore dans l'Hagiographie primitive.' *Wiener Studien* 73 (1960) 123–52

– *Les moines d'Orient III². Cyrille de Scythopolis, Vie de Saint Sabas.* Paris: Editions du Cerf 1962

Fichtenau, Heinrich. 'Zum Reliquienwesen im früheren Mittelalter.' *Mitteilungen des Instituts für österreichischen Geschichtsforschung* 60 (1952) 60–89

Finnegan, Ruth. *Oral Poetry: Its Nature, Significance and Social Context.* Cambridge: Cambridge University Press 1977

Firth, Raymond. 'Postures and Gestures of Respect.' *Echanges et communications. Melanges offerts à Claude Lévi-Strauss à l'occasion de son 60ème anniversaire.* Ed Jean Pouillon and Pierre Maranda. Vol 1. The Hague: Mouton 1970; pp 188–209

Focke, Friedrich. 'Szepter und Krummstab. Eine symbolgeschichtliche Untersuchung.' *Festgabe für Alois Fuchs zum 70. Geburtstage.* Ed W. Tack. Paderborn: Verlag Ferdinand Schöningh 1950; pp 337–87

Fontaine, Jacques. *Isidore de Seville et la culture classique en Espagne visigothique.* 2 vols. Paris: Etudes Augustiniennes 1959

– 'Une clé littéraire de la *Vita Martini* de Sulpice Sévère: la typologie prophétique.' *Mélanges offerts a Mademoiselle Christine Mohrmann.* Utrecht/Anvers: Spectrum 1963; pp 84–95

– 'Die westgotische lateinische Literatur. Probleme und Perspektiven.' *Antike und Abendland* 12 (1966) 64–87

– 'Fins et moyens de l'enseignement ecclésiastique dans l'Espagne wisigothique.' *La scuola nell'occidente latino dell'alto medioevo. Settimane* xix. Spoleto 1972; pp 145–202

- 'King Sisebut's *Vita Desiderii* and the Political Function of Visigothic Hagiography.' *Visigothic Spain*. Ed Edward James. Oxford: Clarendon Press 1980; pp 93–129
- 'Un cliché de la spiritualité antique tardive: *stetit immobilis*.' *Romanitas - Christianitas. Untersuchungen zur Geschichte und Literatur der römischen Kaiserzeit. Johannes Straub zum 70. Geburtstag am 18. Oktober 1982 gewidmet.* Ed Gerhard Wirth, Karl-Heinz Schwarte, Johannes Heinrichs. Berlin / New York: Walter de Gruyter 1982; pp 528–52
- 'Le culte des saints et ses implications sociologiques. Réflexions sur un récent essai de Peter Brown.' *Analecta Bollandiana* 100 (1982) 17–41

Frings, Theodor. *Brautwerbung. Verhandlungen der sächsischen Akademie der Wissenschaften zu Leipzig; Philologisch-historische Klasse* 96 (1944–8)

Fromm, Hans. 'Die Erzählkunst des *Rother*-Epikers.' *Euphorion* 54 (1960) 347–79

Fuhrmann, Manfred. 'Die Mönchsgeschichten des Hieronymus. Formexperimente in erzählender Literatur.' *Christianisme et formes littéraires de l'antiquité tardive en occident.* Ed Manfred Fuhrmann. Fondation Hardt; Entretiens sur l'antiquité classique. Vol 23. Vandoeuvres-Genève: Fondation Hardt 1977; pp 41–89; discussion pp 90–9

- 'Narrative Techniken im Dienste der Geschichtsschreibung (Livius, Buch 21–22) – Eine Skizze.' *Livius: Werk und Rezeption. Festschrift für Erich Burck zum 80. Geburtstag.* Ed Eckard Lefèvre and Eckart Olshausen. München: Verlag C.H. Beck 1983; pp 19–29

Fustel de Coulanges, N.D. 'De l'analyse des textes historiques.' *Revue des questions historiques* 41 (1887) 5–35

Gabelmann, Hanns. *Antike Audienz- und Tribunalszenen.* Darmstadt: Wissenschaftliche Buchgesellschaft 1984

Gaborit-Chopin, D. *Ivoires du moyen âge.* Fribourg: Office du Livre 1978

Gadolin, Anitra. *A Theory of History and Society, with Special Reference to the Chronographia of Michael Psellos; 11th-Century Byzantium.* Stockholm: Almqvist & Wiksell 1970

Garnier, François. *Le langage de l'image au moyen âge. Signification et symbolique.* Paris: Le Leopard d'Or 1982

Gautier Dalché, Patrick. 'La réprésentation de l'espace dans les *Libri miraculorum* de Grégoire de Tours.' *Le moyen âge* 88 (1982) 397–420

Geary, Patrick. *Furta Sacra: Thefts of Relics in the Central Middle Ages.* Princeton: Princeton University Press 1978

- 'L'humiliation des saints.' *Annales. Economies-sociétés-civilisations* 34 (1979) 27–42

Geninasca, Jacques. 'Conte populaire et identité du cannibalisme.' *Nouvelle revue de psychanalyse* 6 (1972) 212–30

Gerhardsson, Birger. *Memory and Manuscript: Oral Tradition in Rabbinic Judaism and Early Christianity*. Uppsala: Almqvist & Wiksell 1961

Gibbs-Smith, Charles H. *The Bayeux Tapestry*. London: Phaidon 1973

Glauche, Günter. *Schullektüre im Mittelalter. Entstehung und Wandlungen des Lektürekanons bis 1200 nach den Quellen dargestellt.* Münchener Beiträge zur Mediävistik und Renaissance-Forschung 5. München: bei der Arbeo Gesellschaft 1970

Goffart, Walter. *The Narrators of Barbarian History [A.D. 550–800]: Jordanes, Gregory of Tours, Bede, and Paul the Deacon*. Princeton: Princeton University Press 1988

Grabar, André. 'Zur Geschichte von Sphaira, Globus und Reichsapfel.' *Historische Zeitschrift* 191 (1960) 536–48; rpt in André Grabar. *L'art de la fin de l'antiquité et du moyen âge*. Vol 1. Paris: Collège de France 1968; pp 103–11

– *Christian Iconography: A Study of Its Origins*. Princeton: Princeton University Press 1968

– *Les voies de la création en iconographie chrétienne*. Paris: Flammarion 1979

Graus, František. *Volk, Herrscher und Heiliger im Reich der Merowinger. Studien zur Hagiographie der Merowingerzeit*. Prag: Tschechoslowakische Akademie der Wissenschaften 1965

Grimm, Jakob. *Deutsche Rechtsalterthümer*. Vol 1. Leipzig: Dieterich 1899

Gschwantler, Otto.'Versöhnung als Thema einer heroischen Sage (Die Alboin-Thurisind Sage und eine archaische Form der Buße: an. *vera í sonar stað*).' *Beiträge zur Geschichte der deutschen Sprache und Literatur* (Tübingen) 97 (1975) 230–62

– 'Die Heldensage von Alboin und Rosimund.' *Festgabe für Otto Höfler zum 75. Geburtstag*. Ed Helmut Birkhan. *Philologia Germanica* 3 (1976) 214–54

Gualandri, Isabella. *Furtiva lectio. Studi su Sidonio Apollinare*. Milano: Cisalpino-Goliardica 1979

Guenée, Bernard. *Histoire et culture historique dans l'Occident médiéval*. Paris: Aubier-Montaigne 1980

Guillou, André. *Régionalisme et indépendance dans l'empire byzantin au VIIe siècle. L'exemple de l'exarchat et de la pentapole d'Italie*. Roma: Istituto storico italiano per il medio evo 1969

Gülich, Elisabeth. 'Konventionelle Muster und kommunikative Funktionen von Alltagserzählungen.' *Erzählen im Alltag*. Ed Konrad Ehlich. Frankfurt am Main: Suhrkamp 1980; pp 335–84

Guy, Jean-Claude. 'Examen de conscience; chez les pères de l'Eglise.' *Dic-*

tionnaire de spiritualité, ascetique et mystique, doctrine et histoire. Vol 4. Ed A. Rayez and Ch. Baumgartner. Paris: Beauchesne 1961; cols 1801–7

Habicht, Werner. *Die Gebärde in englischen Dichtungen des Mittelalters. Bayerische Akademie der Wissenschaften; Philosophisch-historische Klasse. Abhandlungen; Neue Folge 46.* München: Verlag der bayerischen Akademie der Wissenschaften 1959

Hainer, Carl. *Das epische Element bei den Geschichtschreibern des früheren Mittelalters.* Dissertation, Giessen. Giessen: Otto Kindt 1914

Halphen, Louis. 'Grégoire de Tours, historien de Clovis.' *Mélanges d'histoire du moyen âge offerts a Monsieur Ferdinand Lot par ses amis et ses élèves.* Paris: Champion 1925; pp 235–44; rpt in Louis Halphen. *A travers l'histoire du moyen âge.* Paris: Presses universitaires de France 1950; pp 31–8

Heinzelmann, Martin. *Translationsberichte und andere Quellen des Reliquienkultes. Typologie des sources du moyen âge occidental* 33. Turnhout: Brepols 1979

Hellman, Siegmund. 'Studien zur mittelalterlichen Geschichtschreibung. I. Gregor von Tours.' *Historische Zeitschrift* 107 (1911) 1–43

Henderson, George. *Early Medieval.* Harmondsworth: Penguin 1972

Heusler, Andreas. *Lied und Epos in germanischer Sagendichtung.* Dortmund: Ruhfus 1905

– *Die altgermanische Dichtung.* 2nd revised ed. Potsdam: Athenaion 1941

Hofmann, Dietrich. 'Die Einstellung der isländischen Sagaverfasser und ihre Vorgänger zur mündlichen Tradition.' *Oral Tradition-Literary Tradition. A Symposium.* Ed Hans Bekker-Nielsen, Peter Foote, Andreas Haarder, and Hans Frede Nielsen. Odense: Odense University Press 1977; pp 9–27

Hofmann, J.B. *Lateinische Umgangsprache.* 3rd ed. Heidelberg: Carl Winter 1951

Hohti, Paavo. *The Interrelation of Speech and Action in the Histories of Herodotus. Societas scientiarum Fennica; Commentationes humanarum litterarum* 57. Helsinki: Societas scientiarum Fennica 1976

Holum, Kenneth G. *Theodosian Empresses: Women and Imperial Dominion in Late Antiquity.* Berkeley: University of California Press 1982

Hrdličková, V. 'Japanese Professional Storytellers.' *Genre* 2:3 (September 1969) 179–210; rpt in *Folklore Genres.* Ed Dan Ben-Amos. Austin: University of Texas Press 1976; pp 171–90

Hunger, Herbert. *Die hochsprachliche profane Literatur der Byzantiner. Erster Band. Philosophie-Rhetorik-Epistolographie-Geschichtsschreibung-Geographie.* München: C.H. Beck'sche Verlagsbuchhandlung 1978

Jolles, André. *Einfache Formen.* Halle (Saale): Max Niemeyer Verlag 1930; rpt Tübingen 1974

Jungmann, J.A. *Missarum Sollemnia. Eine genetische Erklärung der römischen Messe.* 3rd ed. Freiburg: Verlag Herder 1952

Kaufmann, E. 'Chrenecruda.' *Handwörterbuch zur deutschen Rechtsgeschichte.* Vol 1. Ed A. Erler and E. Kaufmann. Berlin: E. Schmidt Verlag 1971; cols 611–13

Kazhdan, Alexander, and Giles Constable. *People and Power in Byzantium: An Introduction to Modern Byzantine Studies.* Washington, DC: Dumbarton Oaks Center for Byzantine Studies 1982

Kech, H. *Hagiographie als christliche Unterhaltungsliteratur. Studien zum Phänomen des Erbaulichen anhand der Mönchsviten des hl. Hieronymus.* Göppinger Arbeiten zur Germanistik 55. Göppingen: Kümmerle 1977

Kelber, Werner. *The Oral and the Written Gospel.* Philadelphia: Fortress Press 1983

Kitzinger, Ernst. 'World Map and Fortune's Wheel: A Medieval Mosaic Floor in Turin.' *Proceedings of the American Philosophical Society* 117 (1973) 344–73

– *Byzantine Art in the Making: Main Lines of Stylistic Development in Mediterranean Art, 3rd–7th Century.* London: Faber and Faber 1977

Klauser, Theodor. 'Der Ursprung der bischöflichen Insignien und Ehrenrechten.' *Bonner akademische Reden* 1. Krefeld: Scherpe Verlag 1948

– *Kleine abendländische Liturgiegeschichte. Bericht und Besinnung.* Bonn: Peter Hanstein Verlag 1965

Kleinschmidt, Harald. *Untersuchungen über das englische Königtum im 10. Jahrhundert.* Göttinger Bausteine zur Geschichtswissenschaft 49. Göttingen: Musterschmidt 1979

Korol, Dieter. 'Handauflegung II (ikonographisch).' *Reallexikon für Antike und Christentum* XIII. Ed Theodor Klauser et al. Stuttgart: Hiersemann 1984; cols 493–519

Kötting, B. 'Dextrarum iunctio.' *Reallexikon für Antike und Christentum.* Vol 1. Ed Th. Klauser. Stuttgart: Hiersemann 1957; cols 881–8

Kriss-Rettenbeck, Lenz. 'Probleme der volkskundlichen Gebärdenforschung.' *Bayerisches Jahrbuch für Volkskunde* 1964/5, 14–46

Kubler, George. *The Shape of Time: Remarks on the History of Things.* New Haven: Yale University Press 1962

Kurth, Godefroid. *Clovis.* 2 vols. 2nd revised ed. Paris: Petaux 1901

Labov, William, and Joshua Waletzky. 'Narrative Analysis: Oral Versions of Personal Experience.' *Essays on the Verbal and Visual Arts; Proceedings of the 1966 Annual Spring Meeting of the American Ethnological Society.* Ed June Helm. Seattle and London: University of Washington Press 1967; pp 12–44

Laistner, M.W.L. *Thought and Letters in Western Europe A.D. 500–900.* 2nd ed. London: Methuen 1957

Lang, Mabel L. *Herodotean Narrative and Discourse.* Cambridge, Mass: Harvard University Press 1984

Leclercq, Henri. 'Chandelier.' *DACL*; vol 3, cols 210–15
– 'Chape de Saint Martin.' *DACL*; vol 3, cols 381–90
– 'Reliques et reliquaires.' *DACL*; vol 14, cols 2294–2359

Le Goff, Jacques. 'Les gestes symboliques dans la vie sociale: les gestes de la vassalité.' *Simboli e simbologia nell'alto medioevo. Settimane* XXIII. Spoleto 1976; pp 678–777
– '*Vita* et "*pre-exemplum*" dans le 2e. livre des *Dialogues* de Grégoire le Grand.' *Hagiographie, cultures et sociétés IVe–XIIe siècles.* Paris: Etudes Augustiniennes 1981; pp 105–17

Lehmann, Paul. 'Der Einfluss der Bibel auf frühmittelalterliche Geschichtsschreiber.' *La Bibbia nell'alto medioevo. Settimane* X. Spoleto 1963; pp 129–40

Littlewood, A.R. 'The Symbolism of the Apple in Byzantine Literature.' *Jahrbuch der österreichischen Byzantinistik* 23 (1974) 35–59

Llewellyn, Peter. *Rome in the Dark Ages.* London: Faber and Faber 1970

Löfstedt, Einar. *Syntactica. Studien und Beiträge zur historischen Syntax des Lateins. II. Syntaktisch-stilistische Gesichtspunkte und Probleme.* Lund: Gleerup 1933

Lommatzsch, Erhard. *System der Gebärden, dargestellt auf Grund der mittelalterlichen Literatur Frankreichs.* Dissertation, Berlin. Berlin: Georg Reimer 1910 (only introduction and chapter 1 published)

L'Orange, H.P. '*Sol invictus imperator.* Ein Beitrag zur Apotheose.' *Symbolae Osloenses* 14 (1935) 86–114

Lord, Albert B., ed and trans. *Serbo-Croatian Heroic Songs Collected by Milman Parry.* Vol 1. Cambridge, Mass: Harvard University Press 1954

Lüthi, Max. 'Märchen und Sage.' In his *Volksmärchen und Volkssage; zwei Grundformen erzählender Dichtung.* Bern: Francke 1961; pp 23–48
– *Das europäische Volksmärchen.* 4th ed. München: Francke 1974
– *Das Volksmärchen als Dichtung. Ästhetik und Anthropologie.* Düsseldorf: Diederichs 1975

MacCormack, Sabine. *Art and Ceremony in Late Antiquity.* Berkeley: University of California Press 1981

MacMullen, Ramsay. 'Some Pictures in Ammianus Marcellinus.' *Art Bulletin* 46 (1964) 435–55
– 'A Note on *Sermo Humilis.*' *Journal of Theological Studies* ns 17 (1966) 108–12

Magennis, Hugh. 'The Cup as Symbol and Metaphor in Old English Literature.' *Speculum* 60 (1985) 517–36

Maguire, Henry. *Art and Eloquence in Byzantium*. Princeton: Princeton University Press 1981

Maisano, Riccardo. 'Tradizione orale e sviluppi narrativi nel *Prato* di Giovanni Mosco.' *Bollettino della badia greca di Grottaferrata* ns 38 (1984) 3–17

Malafosse, J. de. See Ourliac, Paul.

Mango, Cyril. 'A Byzantine Hagiographer at Work: Leontios of Neapolis.' *Byzanz und der Westen. Studien zur Kunst des europäischen Mittelalters*. Ed Irmgard Hutter. Preface by Herbert Hunger. Österreichische Akademie der Wissenschaften; Philosophisch-Historische Klasse. Sitzungsberichte 432; pp 25–41

Manitius, Max. *Geschichte der lateinischen Literatur des Mittelalters. Erster Teil. Von Justinian bis zur Mitte des zehnten Jahrhunderts*. München: C.H. Beck'sche Verlagsbuchhandlung 1911

Marrou, Henri-Irénée. 'Isidore de Seville et les origines de la culture médiévale.' *Revue historique* 235 (January – March 1966) 39–46

– *Décadence romaine ou antiquité tardive? IIIe–VIe siècle*. Paris: Seuil 1977

Melia, Daniel F. 'Parallel Versions of "The Boyhood Deeds of Cuchulainn." ' *Oral Literature: Seven Essays*. Ed J.J. Duggan. Edinburgh: Scottish Academic Press 1975; pp 25–37

Messmer, H. *Hispania-Idee und Gotenmythos*. Zurich: Fretz & Wasmuth 1960

Međedović, Avdo. *The Wedding of Smailagić Meho. Serbo-Croatian Heroic Songs Collected by Milman Parry*. Vol 3. Ed and trans Albert B. Lord. Cambridge, Mass: Harvard University Press 1974

Meyer-Lübke, Wilhelm. *Romanisches etymologisches Wörterbuch*. 3rd ed. Heidelberg: Carl Winter 1935

Mintz, Jerome R. *Legends of the Hasidim: An Introduction to Hasidic Culture and Oral Tradition in the New World*. Chicago: University of Chicago Press 1968

Mohr, Wolfgang. 'Einfache Formen.' *Reallexikon der deutschen Literaturgeschichte*. Vol 1. 2nd ed. Ed W. Kohlschmidt and W. Mohr. Berlin: De Gruyter 1958; pp 321–8

– 'Geschichtserlebnis im altgermanischen Heldenliede.' *Zur germanisch-deutschen Heldensage. Sechzehn Aufsätze zum neuen Stand der Forschung*. Ed Karl Hauck. Bad Homburg vor der Höhe: Hermann Gentner 1961; pp 82–101

Mohrmann, Christine. 'Quelques traits caractéristiques du latin des chrétiens.' *Miscellanea Giovanni Mercati*. Vol 1. *Studi e testi* 121 (1956) 937–66; rpt in Christine Mohrmann. *Etudes sur le latin des chrétiens*. Vol 1. Roma: Edizione di storia e letteratura 1958; pp 21–50

– 'Le problème de la continuité de la langue littéraire.' *Il passagio*

dall'antichitá al medioevo in occidente. Settimane IX. Spoleto 1962; pp
329–49

Momigliano, Arnaldo. 'L'età del traspasso fra storiografia antica e storiografia
medievale (320–550 D.C.).' *La storiografia altomedievale. Settimane* XVII.
Spoleto 1970; pp 89–118

– 'The Lonely Historian Ammianus Marcellinus.' *Annali della Scuola
Superiore di Pisa; Classe di lettere e filosofia*, serie III, iv, 4 (1974) 1393–
1407; rpt in Arnaldo Momigliano. *Essays in Ancient and Modern Historiography*. Middletown, Conn: Wesleyan University Press 1977; pp 127–40

Monod, Gabriel. 'Les aventures de Sichaire. Commentaire des chapitres xlvii
du livre VII et xix du livre IX de l'*Histoire des Francs* de Grégoire de
Tours.' *Revue historique* 31 (1886) 25–90

Mor, Carlo Guido. 'Simbologia e simboli nella vita giuridica.' *Simboli e
simbologia nell'alto medioevo. Settimane* XXIII. Spoleto 1976; pp 17–29

Mordek, Hubert. 'Livius und Einhard. Gedanken uber das Verhältnis der
Karolinger zur antiken Literatur.' *Livius: Werk und Rezeption. Festschrift
für Erich Burck zum 80. Geburtstag*. Ed Eckard Lefèvre and Eckart Olshausen. München: Verlag C.H. Beck 1983; pp 337–46

Mrabet, Mohammed. *Harmless Poisons, Blameless Sins*. Trans Paul Bowles.
Santa Barbara: Black Sparrow Press 1976.

– *Look & Move On*. Trans Paul Bowles. Santa Barbara: Black Sparrow Press
1976

Murray, Alexander. 'Peter Brown and the Shadow of Constantine.' *Journal of
Roman Studies* 73 (1983) 191–203

Needham, Rodney, ed. *Right and Left: Essays on Dual Symbolic Classification*. Chicago: University of Chicago Press 1973

Nelson, Janet L. 'Symbols in Context: Rulers' Inauguration Rituals in
Byzantium and the West in the Early Middle Ages.' *Studies in Church
History* 13 (1976) 97–119

Nicolescu, Corina. See Wessel, Klaus.

Ogilvie, R.M. *A Commentary on Livy Books 1–5*. Oxford: Clarendon Press
1965

Ogris, W. 'Festuca.' *Handwörterbuch zur deutschen Rechtsgeschichte*. Vol
1. Ed A. Erler and E. Kaufmann. Berlin: E. Schmidt Verlag 1971; cols
1111–14

Ourliac, Paul, and J. de Malafosse. *Droit romain et ancien droit. I. Les
Obligations*. Paris: Presses universitaires de France 1957

Patlagean, Evelyne. 'Discours écrit, discours parlé. Niveaux de culture à
Byzance aux VIIIe–XIe siècles (Note critique).' *Annales. Economies-
sociétés-civilisations* 34 (1979) 264–78

Peil, Dietmar. *Die Gebärde bei Chrétien, Hartmann und Wolfram; Erec-*

Iwein-Parzival. Medium Aevum-Philologische Studien 28. München: Wilhelm Fink 1975

Pertusi, Agostino. 'Insigne del potere sovrano e delegato a Bisanzio e nei paesi di influenza bizantina.' *Simboli e simbologia nell'alto medioevo*. *Settimane* XXIII. Spoleto 1976; pp 481–563

Petsch, Robert. 'Die Lehre von den "Einfachen Formen." ' *Deutsche Vierteljahrschrift für Literaturwissenschaft und Geistesgeschichte* 10 (1932) 334–69

Pickering, F.P. *Literatur und darstellende Kunst im Mittelalter*. Grundlagen der Germanistik 4. Berlin: E. Schmidt Verlag 1966

– 'The Western Image of Byzantium in the Middle Ages.' *German Life and Letters* 28 (1975) 326–40; rpt in F.P. Pickering. *Essays on Medieval German Literature and Iconography*. Cambridge: Cambridge University Press 1980; pp 146–63, 221–3

Piltz, Elisabeth. See Wessel, Klaus.

Prati, A. *Vocabolario etimologico italiano*. Torino: Garzanti 1951

Ranke, Kurt. 'Einfache Formen.' *Internationaler Kongress der Volkserzählungsforscher in Kiel und Kopenhagen (1959) – Vorträge und Referate*. Ed Kurt Ranke. Berlin: 1961; pp 1–11. Trans W. Temple and E. Alsen in *Journal of the Folklore Institute* 4 (1967) 17–31

Reynolds. L.D., ed. *Texts and Transmission: A Survey of the Latin Classics*. Oxford: Clarendon Press 1983

Riché, Pierre. *Education et culture dans l'occident barbare, VIe–VIIIe siècles*. Patristica Sorbonensia 4. Paris: Seuil 1962

– *Ecoles et enseignement dans le haut moyen âge, de la fin du Ve siècle au milieu du XIe siècle*. Paris: Aubier Montaigne 1979

Richter, Will. 'Charakterzeichnung und Regie bei Livius.' *Livius: Werk und Rezeption. Festschrift für Erich Burck zum 80. Geburtstag*. Ed Eckard Lefèvre and Eckart Olshausen. München: Verlag C.H. Beck 1983; pp 59–80

Roberts, J.T. 'Gregory of Tours and the Monk of St. Gall: The Paratactic Style of Medieval Latin.' *Latomus* 39 (1980) 173–90

Rodgers, B.S. 'Constantine's Pagan Vision.' *Byzantion* 50 (1980) 259–78

Röhrich, Lutz. 'Gebärdensprache und Sprachgebärde.' In his *Gebärde-Metapher-Parodie. Studien zur Sprache und Volksdichtung*. Düsseldorf: Schwann 1967; pp 7–36

Rosen, Klaus. *Studien zur Darstellungskunst und Glaubwürdigkeit des Ammianus Marcellinus*. Bonn: Habelt 1970

Ryberg, Inez Scott. *Rites of the State Religion in Roman Art*. Memoirs of the American Academy in Rome 22. American Academy in Rome 1955

Rydén, Lennart. *Bemerkungen zum Leben des heiligen Narren Symeon von Leontios von Neapolis*. Uppsala: Almqvist & Wiksell 1970

Saxer, Victor. *Morts martyres reliques en Afrique chrétienne aux premiers siècles. Les témoignages de Tertullien, Cyprien, et Augustin à la lumière de l'archéologie africaine.* Théologie historique 55. Paris: Beauchesne 1980

Scheibelreiter, Georg. 'Justinian und Belisar in fränkischer Sicht. Zur Interpretation von Fredegar, Chronicon II 62.' βυζαντιος. *Festschrift für Herbert Hunger zum 70. Geburtstag.* Ed W. Hörandner, J. Koder, O. Kresten, E. Trapp. Vienna: Ernst Becvar 1984; pp 267–80

Schmidt-Wiegand, R. 'Gebärden.' *Handwörterbuch zur deutschen Rechtsgeschichte.* Vol 1. Ed A. Erler and E. Kaufmann. Berlin: E. Schmidt Verlag 1971; cols 1411–19

– 'Chrenecruda. Rechtswort und Formalakt der Merowingerzeit.' *Arbeiten zur Rechtsgeschichte. Festschrift für Gustaf Clemens Schmelzeisen.* Ed H.-W. Thümmel. Stuttgart: Klett-Cotta 1980; pp 252–73

– 'Gebärdensprache im mittelalterlichen Recht.' *Frühmittelalterliche Studien* 16 (1982) 363–79

Schneider, Johannes. 'Die Geschichte vom gewendeten Fisch. Beobachtungen zur mittellateinischen Tradition eines literarischen Motivs.' *Festschrift Bernhard Bischoff zu seinem 65. Geburtstag dargeboten von Freunden, Kollegen und Schülern.* Ed Johanne Autenrieth and Franz Brunhölzl. Stuttgart: Hiersemann 1971; pp 218–25

Schramm, P.E. *Herrschaftszeichen und Staatssymbolik. Beiträge zu ihrer Geschichte vom dritten bis zum sechzehnten Jahrhundert.* MGH Schriften 13 (3 vols). Stuttgart: Hiersemann 1954–6

See, Klaus von. 'Was ist Heldendichtung?' *Europäische Heldendichtung.* Ed Klaus von See. Darmstadt: Wissenschaftliche Buchhandlung 1978; pp 1–38

– et al. *Europäisches Frühmittelalter. Neues Handbuch der Literaturwissenschaft* 6. Ed Klaus von See. Wiesbaden: Aula 1985

Ševčenko, Ihor. 'Levels of Style in Byzantine Prose.' *Jahrbuch der österreichischen Byzantinistik* 31 (1981) 289–312

Severus, E. von. 'Gebet. I.' *Reallexikon für Antike und Christentum.* Vol 8. Ed Th. Klauser. Stuttgart: Hiersemann 1972; cols 1134–1258

Shepherd, G.T. 'The Emancipation of Story in the Twelfth Century.' *Medieval Narrative: A Symposium.* Ed Hans Bekker-Nielsen, Peter Foote, Andreas Haarder, and Preben Meulengracht-Sørensen. Odense: Odense University Press 1979; pp 44–57

Simson, Otto G. von. *Sacred Fortress: Byzantine Art and Statecraft in Ravenna.* Chicago: University of Chicago Press 1948

Sittl, Carl. *Die Gebärden der Griechen und Römer.* Leipzig: Teubner 1890

Smalley, Beryl. 'Sallust in the Middle Ages.' *Classical Influences in European Culture A.D. 500–1500.* Ed R.R. Bolgar. Cambridge: Cambridge University Press 1969; pp 165–75

Sorrento, Luigi. 'Tito Livio dal Medio Evo al Rinascimento.' Luigi Sorrento. *Medievalia: problemi e studi.* Brescia: Morcelliana 1943; pp 376–475

Sot, Michel. 'Arguments hagiographiques et historiographiques dans les "*Gesta episcoporum.*"' *Hagiographie, cultures et sociétés IVe–XIIe siècles.* Paris: Etudes Augustiniennes 1981; pp 95–104

Stache, U.J. *Flavius Cresconius Corippus. In laudem Iustini Augusti Minoris. Ein Kommentar.* Berlin: Verlag Nikolaus Mielke 1976

Stafford, Pauline. *Queens, Concubines, and Dowagers: The King's Wife in the Early Middle Ages.* Athens, Georgia: University of Georgia Press 1983

Stock, Brian. *The Implications of Literacy: Written Language and Models of Interpretation in the Eleventh and Twelfth Centuries.* Princeton: Princeton University Press 1983

Suntrup, Rudolf. *Die Bedeutung der liturgischen Gebärden und Bewegungen in lateinischen und deutschen Auslegungen des 9. bis 13. Jahrhunderts.* Münstersche Mittelalter-Schriften 37. München: Wilhelm Fink 1978

Tambiah, S.J. 'A Performative Approach to Ritual.' *Proceedings of the British Academy, London* 65 (1979) 113–69

Tessier, Georges. *Le baptême de Clovis.* Paris: Gallimard 1964

– 'La conversion de Clovis et la christianisation des Francs.' *La conversione al cristianesimo nell'Europa dell'alto medioevo.* Settimane xiv. Spoleto 1967; pp 149–89

Thürlemann, Felix. *Der historische Diskurs bei Gregor von Tours. Topoi und Wirklichkeit.* Geist und Werk der Zeiten; Arbeiten aus dem Historischen Seminar der Universität Zürich 39. Bern: Lang 1974

Toelken, Barre. 'The "Pretty Languages" of Yellowman: Genre, Mode, and Texture in Navaho Coyote Narratives.' *Genre* 2:3 (September, 1969) 211–35; rpt in *Folklore Genres.* Ed Dan Ben-Amos. Austin: University of Texas Press 1976; pp 145–70

Toynbee, Arnold. *Constantine Porphyrogenitus and His World.* London: Oxford University Press 1973

van Dam, Raymond. *Leadership and Community in Late Antique Gaul.* Berkeley: University of California Press 1985

van Dijk, S.J.P. 'The Urban and Papal Rites in Seventh- and Eighth-Century Rome.' *Sacris Erudiri* 12 (1961) 411–87

Vinay, Gustavo. *San Gregorio di Tours. Saggio.* Torino: 'Barbaries,' 1940

– 'Epilogo.' *La Bibbia nell'alto medioevo.* Settimane x. Spoleto 1963; pp 753–68

– *Alto medioevo latino. Conversazioni e no.* Napoli: Guida 1978

Vogel, Cyrille. *Introduction aux sources de l'histoire du culte chrétien au moyen âge.* Spoleto: Centro italiano di studi sull'alto medioevo 1965

Vogt, J. 'Constantinus der Große.' *Reallexikon für Antike und Christentum.*
Vol 3. Ed Th. Klauser. Stuttgart: Hiersemann 1957; cols 306–79
– 'Ammianus Marcellinus als erzählender Geschichtsschreiber der Spätzeit.'
*Akademie der Wissenschaften und der Literatur zu Mainz. Abhandlungen
der geistes- und sozialwissenschaftlichen Klasse.* 1963; no 8
Volbach, W.F. *Elfenbeinarbeiten der Spätantike und des frühen Mittelalters.*
3rd revised ed. Mainz am Rhein: Verlag Phillipp von Zabern 1976
Wagner, Norbert. 'Alboin bei Thurisind.' *Zeitschrift für deutsches Altertum*
111 (1982) 243–55
Walde, A. *Lateinisches etymologisches Wörterbuch.* 2nd ed. Heidelberg:
Carl Winter 1910
Waletzky, Joshua. See Labov, William.
Wallace-Hadrill, J.M. 'The Bloodfeud of the Franks.' *Bulletin of the John
Rylands Library, Manchester* 41 (1958–9) 459–87; rpt in J.M. Wallace-Hadrill.
The Long-Haired Kings and Other Studies in Frankish History. London:
Methuen 1962; pp 121–47
– *The Frankish Church.* Oxford: Clarendon Press 1983
Walsh, P.G. *Livy: His Historical Aims and Methods.* Cambridge: Cambridge
University Press 1961
Wartburg, Walter von. *Französisches etymologisches Wörterbuch.* Basel:
Zbinden 1966
Wessel, Klaus. 'Gesten.' *Reallexikon zur byzantinischen Kunst.* Vol 2. Ed K.
Wessel and M. Restle. Stuttgart: Hiersemann 1971; cols 766–83
Wessel, Klaus, Elisabeth Piltz, and Corina Nicolescu. 'Insignien.' *Reallexikon
zur byzantinischen Kunst.* Vol 3. Ed K. Wessel and M. Restle. Stuttgart:
Hiersemann 1975; cols 369–498
Wetherbee, Winthrop. 'Some Implications of Bede's Latin Style.' *Bede and
Anglo-Saxon England.* Papers in honour of the 1300th anniversay of the birth
of Bede, given at Cornell University in 1973 and 1974. Ed Robert T. Farrell.
London: British Archaeological Reports 1978; pp 23–31
White, Hayden. 'The Value of Narrativity in the Representation of Reality.'
Critical Inquiry 7:1 (Autumn 1980) 5–27; rpt in *On Narrative.* Ed W.J.T.
Mitchell. Chicago and London: University of Chicago Press 1981; pp 1–23
Wiseman, T.P. *Clio's Cosmetics: Three Studies in Greco-Roman Literature.*
Leicester: Leicester University Press 1979
Yourcenar, Marguerite. *Mishima ou la vision du vide.* Paris: Gallimard 1980
Zöllner, Erich. *Die politische Stellung der Völker im Frankenreich.* Veröf-
fentlichungen des Instituts für österreichische Geschichtsforschung 13.
Wien: Universum Verlag 1950

Index

Note on Plates

PLATE 1 (page 170)

Panel from an ivory diptych ('Symmachus Diptych')
Late fourth century
London, Victoria and Albert Museum
Photo courtesy of Victoria and Albert Picture Library

PLATE 2 (page 171)

Panel from an ivory diptych ('Barberini Diptych')
Sixth century
Paris, Louvre
Photo courtesy of Réunion des musées nationaux

PLATE 3 (page 172)

Ivory panel, the Ascension
Circa 900
Darmstadt, Hessisches Landesmuseum
Photo courtesy of Hessisches Landesmuseum